Songs to Make the Dust Dance

Songs to Make the Dust Dance

The Ryōjin hishō *of Twelfth-Century Japan*

YUNG-HEE KIM

University of California Press

BERKELEY   LOS ANGELES   LONDON

University of California Press
Berkeley and Los Angeles, California

University of California Press, Ltd.
London, England

© 1994 by
The Regents of the University of California

Library of Congress Cataloging-in-Publication Data

Kim, Yung-Hee
    Songs to make the dust dance: the Ryōjin hishō of twelfth-century
Japan / Yung-Hee Kim.
        p.   cm.
    Includes bibliographical references and index.
    ISBN 0-520-08066-1
    1. Ryōjin hishō.   2. Japanese poetry—Heian period, 794–1185—
History and criticism.   3. Songs, Japanese—History and criticism.
4. Ballads, Japanese—History and criticism.   5. Japanese poetry—
Heian period, 794–1185—Translations into English.
PL787.R943K86   1993
895.6'11409—dc20   93-10237
                                                                  CIP

Printed in the United States of America
9 8 7 6 5 4 3 2 1

To my mother and to the memory of my father

Contents

Acknowledgments

Before this book took its present shape, it went through several stages of incarnation. This long process of birth was due mainly to the complexity of *Ryōjin hishō* itself, for this Heian song compilation contains ideas, subject matters, sentiments, and poetic forms that are multidimensional and heterogeneous in nature. Even selecting songs for analysis proved rather onerous; it was always necessary to keep in mind the character of the anthology as a whole and to select representative samples accordingly. These factors required repeated adjustments in perspective and focus. In the end, this book strives to present the essence of *Ryōjin hishō*—its diversity in both meaning and form.

Along the way, a number of individuals and organizations offered me invaluable help. First of all, I would like to thank Karen Brazell at Cornell University, who first introduced me to the unimaginable riches of *Ryōjin hishō* and inspired me to pursue a study of the anthology. Much appreciation goes to Brett DeBary, also at Cornell, for her ready and generous assistance, which has extended beyond the process of preparing this book. Michael Cooper has always been there to supply ample encouragement and good humor.

At the Ohio State University, awards from the Special Research Assignment Program in the College of Humanities and the University Publication Subvention Fund provided me with time and resources to concentrate on research and writing. One of the most challenging tasks of this project was translating the *Ryōjin hishō* songs. The guiding principle throughout was to stay close to the original in spirit and form but make the songs as authentic-sounding as possible in English. In this I am most grateful to Anthony Libby at Ohio State, whose final poetic touch truly made the songs sing. Early on Gary Ebersole of the University of Chicago, my former colleague at Ohio State, gave an incisive critique after a thorough reading of the entire working draft; to him I am indebted. The following people at Ohio State also have been exceptional sources of assistance: Maureen Donovan at the Main Library, Yoshiko Uchida at the Department of East Asian Languages and Literatures, and Michael Garofano and Joo Hee Yoo at the Humanities Computer Center.

No words can do full justice to the encouragement given by Jeanne Sugiyama at the University of California Press, who recognized the importance of publishing this study. I remain grateful for Anne Canright's insightful comments and meticulous editing, which enhanced this book. Jenny Tomlin at the University of California Press has been invaluable in guiding the manuscript through the various editing and production stages. Most of all, it is thanks to the patience, understanding, and professional expertise of Betsey Scheiner at the Press that the manuscript has finally emerged as a book.

Lastly, to my family, whose continuing moral support has helped me through the high and low points of writing, I owe my deepest gratitude.

Abbreviations

From Nihon Koten Bungaku Taikei and Nihon Koten Bungaku Zenshū

NKBT   Nihon Koten Bungaku Taikei
NKBZ   Nihon Koten Bungaku Zenshū
RH   *Ryōjin hishō* (1179) (NKBT, vol. 73; NKBZ, vol. 25)
WRS   *Wakan rōeishū* (ca. 1013) (NKBT, vol. 73)

From *Shinpen kokka taikan*, vol. 1 (Kadokawa Shoten, 1983)

GSIS   *Goshūishū* (1086)
GSS   *Gosenshū* (commissioned 951)
KKS   *Kokinshū* (ca. 920)
SGSIS   *Shingoshūishū* (1384)
SIS   *Shūishū* (ca. 1005–11)
SKKS   *Shinkokinshū* (1206)
SKS   *Shikashū* (ca. 1151–54)
SZKKS   *Shinzokukokinshū* (1439)
SZS   *Senzaishū* (ca. 1188)

From *Shinpen kokka taikan*, vol. 2 (Kadokawa Shoten, 1984)

KKRJ   *Kokin(waka)rokujō* (ca. 987)

From *Shinpen kokka taikan*, vol. 5 (Kadokawa Shoten, 1987)

KYISU   *Kaya no In shichiban utaawase* (1094)

Introduction

Songs are meant to be sung. When performed, they come alive and serve their purpose to the fullest. In a performative context, the melody is the primary medium for aesthetic stimulation and appreciation, with lyrics tending to play a secondary or complementary role, at most. This fact accounts for the phenomenal success of some songs with lyrics of minor literary merit but with great musical articulation. In extreme cases, even one line of lyric can become a magnificent song, when carried by a melody of superb variation and modulation.

What happens, then, when we find song lyrics written or printed on the pages of books, to be read and appreciated as poems without the benefit of their music? What are we to do with them? Do we treat them as regular poems? If so, by what criteria do we appraise them? What occasioned them and who wrote them? In cases of anonymous poets, how do we know what the lyrics are really about? Who sang them? Who was the audience, and how did the songs function? What are we to do with them, especially, when they are popular songs of anonymous common people—the unofficial voices from an age long past?

Ryōjin hishō (Treasured Selections of Superb Songs) is one such collection of songs, whose meanings can be partially deciphered when some of these questions are answered. Compiled in 1179, *Ryōjin hishō* is the largest extant collection of *imayō* (meaning "modern style"), a popular song genre that flourished for over two centuries, from the mid-Heian to the early Kamakura period. The work's primary distinction is that it was not a commissioned project but was compiled personally by the emperor Go-Shirakawa (1127–92). Go-Shirakawa's involvement in the plebeian *imayō* as a devoted patron, practitioner, and critic, rather than in *waka*, the "proper" literary form of his age, scandalized many in the inner court. Undaunted, the emperor dedicated most of his adult life to promoting *imayō*. This effort culminated in *Ryōjin hishō*, which took him more than two decades to complete—concrete evidence of the emperor's single-minded pursuit of the art he loved.

Presumably the original *Ryōjin hishō* consisted of two distinct parts, each comprising ten books. The first part is thought to have been a collection of *imayō* lyrics (*kashishū*). Customarily, the name *Ryōjin hishō* refers to this *kashishū*. The other part, called *Kudenshū* (Collections of Oral Transmission), is believed to have consisted of assorted information about the origins of *imayō*, musical scores and notations, instructions on *imayō* performance along with appropriate examples, and anecdotes related to these components.[1] Regrettably, only small parts of the original are extant: from the *kashishū*, a fragment of Book 1 (21 songs) and the complete Book 2 (545 songs), making a total of 566 *imayō* songs; and from the *Kudenshū*, a fraction of passages from Book 1 having to do with a mythical exegesis on the origin of *imayō*, as well as the complete Book 10, which is Go-Shirakawa's memoir. The large number of songs in Book 2 of the *kashishū* suggests that the original *Ryōjin hishō* was quite vast in scope and size. Despite its fragmentary condition, *Ryōjin hishō* is still the largest extant collection of *imayō*.[2]

An interesting but brief note on the origin of the name of *Ryōjin hishō* is attached to the end of the fragment of Book 1. It explains that the title derives from ancient Chinese legends about two famous singers named Yü Kung and Han Ê. Tradition has it that their peerless voices moved listeners to tears, and the reverberating sound made the "dust on the rafters" (*ryōjin*) dance for three days before it settled down. Thus, the term *ryōjin* came to refer to beautiful voices.[3] The anecdote also underscores the power of music to move not only human hearts but insentient beings as well.[4] Given these various associations, the title of *Ryōjin hishō* can be translated as "Treasured Selections of Superb Songs."

After its completion, *Ryōjin hishō* was probably circulated among those who were close to the emperor. Sometime during the mid–fourteenth century, however, the anthology completely disappeared. The last known textual reference to it is a brief comment by Yoshida Kenkō (ca. 1283–ca. 1352) in his *Tsurezuregusa* (ca. 1330) that "*imayō* lyrics of *Ryōjin hishō* are deeply moving."[5] In the succeeding centuries, the anthology became an unknown and lost entity. Scattered efforts were made in the seventeenth century by a few scholars of the National Studies Movement (*kokugaku*) to determine the whereabouts of the text, but their attempts were futile.

Then, in the fall of 1911, the historian Wada Hidematsu (1865–1937) happened upon a two-volume text titled *Ryōjin hishō* while browsing in a used book shop in Tokyo. Wada entrusted his find to his friend Sasaki Nobutsuna (1872–1963), the renowned Japanese classics scholar, for a textual verification. Sasaki's scrutiny established that the text was a complete copy of Book 2 of *Ryōjin hishō* dating from the late Edo period. Subsequently Sasaki unearthed the fragments of Book 1 of *kashishū* and Book 1 of *Kudenshū* in the Aya no Kōji family archives, and in August 1912 he published the first modern annotated edition of *Ryōjin hishō*, consisting of these three different parts.[6]

Thus, after six centuries of complete silence, *Ryōjin hishō* sang out once again. Its reception by Japanese scholars was nothing short of ecstatic—an understandable reaction given the dearth of information on popular literature of the Heian period, especially in the poetry genre. Indeed, the early 1910s and 1920s saw something of a *Ryōjin hishō* boom, as the anthology engaged the attention of major literary scholars who repeatedly yielded newer editions of the text. Konishi Jin'ichi, an expert on *Ryōjin hishō*, observed that the work would have been called "the second *Man'yōshū*" had it been preserved in its entirety.[7] The anthology rapidly became a major source of material not only for scholars of Japanese literature, but also for students of folklore, religion, and the performing arts.

The sensational rediscovery of *Ryōjin hishō* and its introduction to the reading public provided powerful inspiration to a number of leading modern poets and writers, such as Saitō Mokichi (1882–1953), Kitahara Hakushū (1885–1942), Satō Haruo (1892–1964), and the novelist Akutagawa Ryūnosuke (1892–1927). Among them, *Ryōjin hishō*'s impact was perhaps most strongly felt by the *tanka* poet Mokichi, as his collection of literary criticism, *Dōbamango* (1919), indicates, for in it he included thirty-six songs from *Ryōjin hishō* as his favorite poems. Mokichi's second poetry collection, *Aratama* (1921), is also considered to have been clearly influenced by *Ryōjin hishō*.[8]

The extant *Ryōjin hishō* displays a wide spectrum of subjects and themes. Its songs lift their voices to praise the boundless mercies of buddhas, then reveal with no qualms the world of gamblers and courtesans. Between these extremes, the topical range of *Ryōjin hishō* explores the lives of the Buddha's disciples, eminent priests, and pilgrims, of shrine-maidens and nuns, of common soldiers, petty officials, and guards at provincial checkpoints, of woodcutters, potters, and menial workers, and even of abject beggars and nameless loafers on the streets of the capital. When we add to the list all the trees, birds, animals, articles of clothing and accessories, foodstuffs, shrines, temples, cities, rivers, and mountains that come crowding in, the anthology achieves kaleidoscopic dimensions.

For all that, the riot of motifs in *Ryōjin hishō* can be simplified and appreciated in terms of contrasting relationships—sacred and profane, high and low, serious and frivolous, men and women, old and young. While many of the songs concern metaphysics and religious pedagogy, they do not shy away from the infirmities, squalor, and cacophony of secular life. A man in search of salvation is flanked by a courtesan beckoning him to a tryst; the mountain ascetic's discipline and hardship are juxtaposed to the wayward wanderings of a young gambler; an old man steeped in carnal desire is contrasted with a mother worrying over a wanton daughter. *Ryōjin hishō* represents, therefore, a curious coalescence of the idealistic and realistic, esoteric and obvious, exotic and indigenous, and other-worldly and this-worldly. This comprehensive coverage of life as it is lived finds no parallel in the stylized poetry of Heian aristocrats; thus the anthology provides a relatively inclusive and multiple perspective from which to view Heian society.

The range of poetic voices also covers a whole gamut of characters: learned, proselytizing priests; villagers and city dwellers, many of whom demonstrate penetrating insight into the world around them; courtesans of sharp wit and engaging savvy; pilgrim-seducing shamans; mountain ascetics; even fishermen on the shore. One should, however, guard against the easy assumption that these songs were in fact created by such people. Evidence from other song traditions, as well as Japanese examples, suggests that the composers of the lyrics, many of whom may well have been the singers also, freely adopted the voices and perspectives of all sorts of people to create their lyric personae. In real life, in other words, courtesans did not necessarily sing *only* about the life of prostitutes, priests about religion, or fishermen about fishing. Rather, the *imayō* poets/singers, in assuming the surrogate voices of many classes of people in Heian society, projected the typical, unique, or problematic situations of these characters in their songs.

Coupled with the thematic diversity of *Ryōjin hishō* are distinctive formal and technical characteristics—the songs' prosody, mode of delivery, and rhetorical devices. Although these songs are products of the "age of *waka*," they represent a poetic orientation totally different from that of *waka*. Most conspicuous is the breakaway from the sacrosanct adherence to the thirty-one-syllable prosodic standard. *Ryōjin hishō* songs exemplify a lyrical discourse that verges on prose narrativity, as well as an expository mode of delivery; this looseness results in the telling of stories and informing the mind, in contrast to *waka*'s predilection to create pure lyric moments within a strict poetic formula. Some of the *shiku no kamiuta* (four-line god songs) in the anthology, for example, are quite lengthy.[9] Furthermore, no rules bind the choice of vocabulary, which in many instances violates aristocratic decorum or lexicon.[10] Unlike *waka, imayō* do not usually utilize such poetic devices as pillow words (*makurakotoba*), pivot words (*kakekotoba*), or verbal associations (*engo*) but instead turn to repetition, onomatopoeia, orchestra words (*hayashikotoba*), honorifics, and exclamatory particles to produce poetic effects and emphasis. For readers accustomed to Heian court poetry, this different, plastic literary form becomes a refreshing treat, leading into an untrodden world of poetic experience and meaning.

Although *Ryōjin hishō* has long been a subject of scholarship in Japan, it is little known in the West. It first came to the attention of Western readers through Arthur Waley's translations of a handful of songs in 1921,[11] but no comprehensive, sustained inquiry resulted from that exposure. This study attempts to appraise *Ryōjin hishō* in the larger context of cultural, social, and political developments of the late Heian period and to define its place in the Japanese literary tradition, while trying to answer some of the questions raised at the beginning of this Introduction. Wherever possible, readers are reminded of the performative context of *imayō* songs for optimal appreciation of the song texts we now have in hand. Although it is tempting to concentrate on the most aesthetically appealing texts, my approach has been to present as fair and balanced a view as possible of the anthology as a whole. Because of the miscellaneous character of the extant *Ryōjin hishō*, one finds little consistent evolution of themes or motifs; rather, the anthology shifts from one topic to another, often in a distracting manner. My choice of songs necessarily reflects this mosaic nature, although I do try to bring a sense of unity to the themes discussed.

Ryōjin hishō deserves attention not only for its intrinsic value as a literary anthology but also for its wealth of information about the Heian period. Given careful probing, *Ryōjin hishō* yields important insights into the lives, both spiritual and worldly, of people in that age and into the tradition of song (*kayō*) in premodern Japanese literature. It supplies rare information on the performing arts and artists, especially regarding female entertainers. It reveals the religious ethos and even the social and political developments of the late Heian period. And, most important, it helps to correct the perception of Heian culture as the monolithic achievement and closed domain of the elite, much as the eleventh-century *Konjaku monogatari* does in the prose genre. *Ryōjin hishō* provides, in short, an alternative way of looking at the Heian society, since most poems are the works of anonymous commoners and are about their most pressing concerns. The reader whose literary sensitivity is attuned to Heian aristocratic poetry—generally known for its ritualized, uniform, and controlled exclusivity—finds in *Ryōjin hishō* a broad and open vista into the popular culture, a culture full of vitality, diversity, and realistic impulses to deal with life in all its guises, negative as well as positive. The plurality of Heian culture and society is the real subject of this anthology, and in that plurality can be found the animate spark of an age long past.

1　Emperor Go-Shirakawa and *Imayō*

Emperor Go-Shirakawa and His Career

Public opinion about Emperor Go-Shirakawa (Prince Masahito, 1127–92) was divided, and the views held by his contemporaries were often unflattering. Before his ascension to the throne, for instance, his own father, Emperor Toba (1103–56),[1] was said to have belittled him, declaring that he was totally unfit for the emperorship owing to his indulgence in frivolous merrymaking.[2] During his reign, even his trusted retainer, Shinzei (Fujiwara Michinori, 1106–59), and Kujō Kanezane (1149–1207), the minister of the right, disparaged him as a dull-witted man who was neither aware of the traitors around him nor heedful of truthful counsel—altogether a hopeless sovereign, without precedent in Japan or China.[3]

Go-Shirakawa's political career, which spanned thirty-seven years as both reigning and retired emperor, was, indeed, rarely free of controversy or strife.[4] From the outset, his brief formal reign (1155–58) was marred by a bloody power struggle within his own court, called the Hōgen Disturbance (1156), plotted by the resentful ex-Emperor Sutoku (r. 1123–41), Go-Shirakawa's elder brother, who had been forced to abdicate by Toba.[5] The insurrection was short-lived, and Go-Shirakawa quickly banished Sutoku to Sanuki, whence he never returned alive, and ordered the swift execution of other participants in the rebellion.[6] Largely because of his harsh handling of the incident, Go-Shirakawa was perceived as a ruthless monarch who would tolerate no threats or challenges to his authority. The tragic family feud hastened the rise of the two rival military clans, the Taira and the Minamoto, whose meddling in court politics ushered in the "age of the warrior."[7]

Soon after Go-Shirakawa's abdication came the Heiji Disturbance (1159),

1

in which he lost his chief advisor, Shinzei, and witnessed the passing of political hegemony to the Taira clan, headed by Kiyomori (1118–81). Thereafter, by pitting factions of the Taira and Minamoto against each other through his singular talent for maneuvering, and often by dint of sheer resilience and a good deal of luck, Go-Shirakawa presided over one of the most turbulent periods in Japanese history. It included the Taira despotism, during which Go-Shirakawa was even put under house arrest by Kiyomori in 1179; the carnage of the Genpei War (1180–85); the final destruction of the Taira clan; and the establishment, in 1185, of the Kamakura regime by Minamoto Yoritomo (1147–99); and it was a time, moreover, when many of the emperor's relatives and close associates perished.

Go-Shirakawa, subjected as he had been to ordeals and humiliation at the hands of many military leaders, retained one burning urge: to preserve his position as the patriarch of the imperial clan and the last, staunch defender of the Heian civil government. This determination was epitomized in his stubborn refusal to confer, despite constant pressure, the coveted title of *shōgun* on Yoritomo. The frustrated Yoritomo, in turn, denounced the emperor as "the biggest goblin in Japan."[8] Only after Go-Shirakawa's death in 1192 was Yoritomo finally able to wrest the title from the incumbent emperor, Go-Toba, an event that marked the official beginning of the Kamakura government. Thus Go-Shirakawa, enthroned amid skepticism and discord, proved to be a resourceful and imaginative politician and a survivor.

When political responsibilities were not consuming his attention, Go-Shirakawa had personal interests that involved him in a variety of cultural and artistic activities, either as a sponsor or as an active participant. The best-known area of his artistic enterprise was the *imayō* genre: he was, in fact, its unsurpassed patron and practitioner. It has even been conjectured that one reason for Go-Shirakawa's abdication after only three years' reign was his desire to devote himself freely to *imayō* without the burden of emperorship.[9] In addition, Go-Shirakawa invested an enormous amount of resources, human energy, and time in commissioning the *waka* anthology *Senzai(waka)shū* (Collection of a Thousand Years, ca. 1188) and numerous picture scrolls (*emakimono*) and in undertaking religious pilgrimages. To be sure, many of these costly activities were possible only because of his imperial privileges; nonetheless, the intensity and grandiose scale with which he pursued his interests puts him in a class by himself.

The *Imayō* Genre

Go-Shirakawa's role in the cultivation and promotion of *imayō* began long before he entered the political arena. As we have seen, his father, Emperor

Toba, expressed serious doubts about Go-Shirakawa's qualifications to be emperor owing to the young man's reputed absorption in "merrymaking" (*asobi*). Go-Shirakawa himself frankly admits in his memoir, *Kudenshū*, that he spent his youth in the carefree pursuit of pleasure: "Quartered at the Toba Palace, I passed as many as fifty nights singing. A group of my companions and I flocked to the Tōsanjō Palace also and for some forty days enjoyed boating and making merry through the night until day-break."[10]

It is understandable that Go-Shirakawa, with no immediate regal prospect in sight, exploited his princely prerogatives to the fullest. Yet his was not a passive appreciation of entertainment provided by others, for he, too, was an artist. From his teens, he had developed into an accomplished musician and singer in his own right. He was an expert flute player and excelled in such varied genres of vocal music as *saibara, rōei, shōmyō*, and *imayō*.[11] His lifelong obsession, however, was with *imayō*, in which genre he was a superb performer.[12] Thanks to Go-Shirakawa's consuming love for and patronage of *imayō*, that song form was elevated from the level of popular entertainment to a refined and sophisticated art.

The compound term *imayō* was originally generic and only later came to be used to designate a specific popular song genre. *Yō* signifies style or mode, while *ima* is presumed to derive from the adjective *ima mekashi*, with meanings that range from contemporary, modern, popular, novel, fresh, and lively to frivolous, vulgar, and lewd.[13] *Imayō*, therefore, came to denote songs in modish style, with vivacious and buoyant melodies—in a sense, the pop music of the Heian age. Most likely, the term *imayō* was adopted to set these newly popularized songs apart from older song forms such as *saibara, fuzoku*, and *rōei*, which long had been the staples of the nobles' music repertoire.[14]

Kudenshū lists at least twenty different categories within *imayō*.[15] Although it is impossible to determine just what musical characteristics distinguished these types from one another, the large number of these subgroups suggests that *imayō* must have reached a high degree of sophistication by the mid to late twelfth century to warrant such minute classifications.

We do not know when or how the *imayō* genre came into being. The earliest known literary mention of the word *imayō* occurs in *Murasaki Shikibu nikki* (Diary of Murasaki Shikibu [ca. 978–ca. 1016], ca. 1010), and further reference is made in *Makura no sōshi* (The Pillow Book, 11th cent.) by Sei Shōnagon (ca. 965–ca. 1024), a contemporary of Murasaki's.[16] During the time of Emperor Ichijō (r. 986–1011), then, *imayō* were apparently already in existence and had begun to enter court circles.

Some source materials suggest that *imayō* were of plebeian origin, sung among common people before they reached the aristocracy. *Kojidan* (Stories About Ancient Matters), a Kamakura-period collection of tales, for example, relates that the abbot Genshin (942–1017), while walking on Mount Kinbu, met a female shaman who entertained him by singing *imayō*.[17] And a passage in *Sagoromo monogatari* (The Tale of Sagoromo, 1069–72) describes a cart puller singing *imayō*.[18] Even the *Kudenshū* substantiates the notion that *imayō* were the legacy of common people, since the majority of Go-Shirakawa's early *imayō* teachers were themselves rural women of the lower classes.[19]

By the time of Emperor Go-Suzaku (r. 1036–45) *imayō* had gained considerable popularity and were often performed at court banquets. Even so, the song form did not receive the approval of all members of the court, many of whom still found the music unfamiliar and odd-sounding. About thirty years later, however, during the reign of Emperor Shirakawa (r. 1072–86), the records of *imayō* performances at court and among the courtiers increased measurably, signifying the flourishing of the genre, as documented in courtiers' diaries such as *Chūyūki* (Record of the Middle-Right) by Fujiwara Munetada (1062–1141) and *Taiki* (Record on a Desk, 1136–55) by Fujiwara Yorinaga (1120–56).[20]

It was the reign of Go-Shirakawa some eighty years later, though, that marked the peak of *imayō* popularity. This state of affairs is humorously described in *Bunkidan* (Literary Table Talk, 1278–88): "In those days, all classes of people, regardless of their status, hummed some tune or other, swinging their heads to and fro [to the beat of the rhythm]."[21] The compiler of the collection also stresses that the people simply followed what their superiors were doing, which suggests that Emperor Go-Shirakawa was their ultimate model.

When *imayō* were performed at court, it was usually on congratulatory occasions or at banquets such as those following the New Year's Day ceremony, the *daijōsai* (enthronement ceremony), the *shinjōsai* (or *niiname matsuri*, a ceremony of the eleventh month in which the year's new grains are dedicated to Shinto gods), and certain Buddhist rites; accordingly, the *imayō* selected consisted principally of celebratory themes, not those related to the darker side of the commoner's life.[22] Such *imayō* were performed as solos or duets, occasionally in conjunction with *kagura* or *saibara* but more usually with *rōei*, a more up-to-date song form. Accompaniment was generally no more than the simple rhythm of a fan or drum, though sometimes an orchestral accompaniment of reed pipes (*shō*), flutes, and flageolet (*hichiriki*), or of *koto*, *biwa*, flutes, and other wind instruments, was featured. The festivities often lasted all through the night until dawn, perhaps ending with a climactic dance performance (*ranbu*), in which courtiers participated.[23]

Thus seen, the flourishing of *imayō* coincided with the *insei* period, when retired emperors exercised political control from behind the scenes. The imperial patronage of *imayō* also meant that the emperors actively contributed to the evolution of the new cultural form, serving as its critical arbiters. In this sense, the *insei* period marked a turning point in Japanese history, and not simply for political reasons: it was also a watershed in the development of new aesthetic tastes and cultural preferences and choices. And *imayō* patronage by Go-Shirakawa was a telling indication that a new era was in the making.[24]

Imayō Singers

Women played a decisive role in promoting and performing *imayō*, particularly such women of lower-class origin as *miko* (shrine-maidens or shamans), *asobi(me)* (courtesans), and *kugutsu(me)* (female puppeteers). These groups are thought to have developed over time from a single caste of shamanic females (*miko*).[25] At one time early in Japanese history these women were at the center of the religious life of both the court and the ordinary folk, performing shamanic functions and ritual services.[26] Over the centuries, however, their roles and status were degraded and desacralized. By the time these women appeared as singers of *imayō* in the Heian period, most of their original religious functions had been severely attenuated.[27] While the *miko* group was still tied to its original shamanic profession, the *asobi* and *kugutsu* had moved into the secular realm of entertainment.

All of these female entertainers cultivated *imayō* as their primary medium of entertainment, but many also practiced prostitution. Female *imayō* singers were in fact marginal figures in the highly stratified Heian society, and were often forced to wander from place to place. Yet their musical talents and accomplishments in *imayō* brought them into close contact with aristocrats and even into the very heart of the aesthetic life of elite society. Had this paradoxical relationship not existed, nothing of the literary content and entertainment value of *imayō* would have been noticed or preserved.

MIKO

Some twenty songs about *miko* are found in *Ryōjin hishō*.[28] Many of them describe *miko* performing shamanic rituals, while others deal with aspects of personal conduct and moments in the women's emotional lives.

Some songs are rendered with a light touch; others, such as the following, convey a mixed sense of fascination and surprise:

RH 560

kono miko wa	This shrine-maiden
yōgaru miko yo	she is an eyeful!
katabira ni	Her robe with slit sides above
shiri o dani	and loosened behind,
kakaide	she's raving.
yuyushū tsukikataru	Look!
kore o mitamae	The gods have got hold of her!

This description of a *miko* in shamanic ecstasy is reminiscent of the mythic portrayal of Ameno uzume no Mikoto, the archetypal shamaness whose similarly disheveled appearance, sexually suggestive dance, and song lured Amaterasu, the Sun Goddess, out of the Heavenly Rock-Grotto.[29]

The involvement of *miko* in *imayō* performance and other popular entertainment is no accident. In fact, the *miko's* professional performances, with their characteristic trancelike dance and utterances, always accompanied by bells and drums, could easily be perceived as erotic; it was a short step from there to secular entertainment. This liminal nature of *miko's* ritual performance, located on the threshold between the sacred and profane, even made it easier for *miko* to fluctuate between their sacerdotal functions and their performative roles as entertainers—an intriguing and paradoxical blend indeed. The following song captures the entertainment value of *miko*:

RH 265

kane no mitake ni aru miko no	On Mount Kinbu's Holy Peak
utsu tsuzumi uchiage uchioroshi	the shrine-maiden beats the drum, up and down,
omoshiro ya	wondrous sound!
warera mo mairaba ya	Let's go see.
teitontō to mo hibikinare	Bong, it echoes,
hibikinare	echoes, bong.
utsu tsuzumi ikani uteba ka	It keeps on, how does she do it?
kono ne no taesezaruramu	Never stops.

The encounter between the priest Genshin and a *miko* on Mount Kinbu cited previously illustrates the *miko's* use of *imayō* for seductive entertainment. With the craze for pilgrimage ever accelerating, the vicinity of shrines where pilgrims and worshipers converged away from home was fertile ground for *miko* to carry on prostitution; in this, the use of popular *imayō* was a good part of their allure. It is quite possible that these *miko* authored some of the *imayō* songs in *Ryōjin hishō*, including the Shinto-Buddhist syncretic songs or *miko* songs in the *shiku no kamiuta* (four-line god songs) section of *Ryōjin hishō*.

In the late Heian period a new type of *miko*, called *arukimiko* (walking *miko*) appeared. Unlike regular *miko*, who kept a fixed abode and were associated with specific local shrines, *arukimiko* wandered around the country combining their religious function with prostitution and entertainment.[30] Their uprooted and precarious livelihood is depicted in the song of an anxious mother whose daughter is an *arukimiko*:

RH 364

waga ko wa jū yo ni narinuran	Almost a woman, my daughter, now—
kōnagi shite koso arikunare	I hear she's a wandering shrine-maiden.
tago no ura ni shio fumu to	When she walks the salty shore at Tago Bay
ikani amabito tsudōran	the fishermen must pester her,
masashi to te toimi towazumi nabururan	squabbling about her prophecies, finding fault with whatever she says.
itōshi ya	Her life, how painful![31]

Much of the regional description found in *Ryōjin hishō* owes its color and piquancy to this on-the-move group of female shaman/entertainers. They, along with *kugutsu*, another *imayō* singer group who took a similar itinerant life-style, are also credited with the propagation and cross-fertilization of the *imayō* repertoire, made possible by their wandering from one region to another.

ASOBI

Asobi were among the first female performing artists to be given a formal group designation. They were also the earliest-known female group specializing in a single artistic genre. Their origin is traced to the ancient professional lineage of *asobi-be*, the court morticians.[32] Females formed the backbone of this group, with assistance coming from male members; the women performed the most crucial rites of the funeral, including dances, songs, and incantations, and their professional, ritual skills were secretly transmitted within the group.[33] Owing to the gravity of their function in the critical rites of death at court, and probably also to their ritual pollution deriving from contact with the dead, *asobi-be* were exempted from conscript labor and taxes. Thus they possessed a certain social distinction and accompanying privileges in early Japanese society.[34]

With the Taihō Reform of 701, however, *asobi-be* lost much of their social status; and within fifty years, the group's ritual functions at court had ceased to exist.[35] As a result, many of the female *asobi*, having neither land nor other skills to maintain a livelihood, became socially uprooted and adopted an itinerant mode of life. Increasingly, for sustenance, they turned to performing arts and to prostitution.

Sometime during the Heian period, *asobi* began to abandon their migratory lives in favor of permanent settlements, chiefly at strategic transportation loci along rivers and at inland seaports, where travelers, merchants, and cargo boat crews sought lodging. *Asobi's* popularity grew in direct proportion to the prosperity of the ports, which saw the amassing of luxury goods from various parts of the country to supply the demanding tastes of aristocrats in the capital. The most fabled *asobi* colonies were in Eguchi, on the Yodo River, and in Kanzaki and Kanishima, on the Kanzaki River, those two rivers being the main passageways to the Heian capital from the Inland Sea. As "Yūjoki" (Record on Courtesans, ca. 1087), a short tract on *asobi* by Ōe no Masafusa (1041–1111), put it, "Kanzaki and Kanishima of Settsu Province are lined with the *asobi* quarters one door after another."[36]

Asobi conducted their business in a distinctive manner, enticing potential customers by singing from their boats and then, once their patrons were on board, entertaining the men by singing *imayō* and bestowing sexual favors while floating on the water. An average *asobi* boat carried three members: a principal *asobi*, who entertained the customers by singing to the beat of her small drum; an apprentice *asobi*, who sheltered her mistress with a large parasol and looked to her needs; and an elderly *asobi*, who was in charge of rowing the boat.[37] "Yūjoki" further describes this exotic trade as follows:

> *Asobi* row their small boats toward the passenger boats and invite the travelers to their beds. Their singing stops the clouds over the valleys and their rhymes are on the wings over the river. All the passengers cannot help but forget their homes while floating along the isles with rushes and breakers. Hordes of fishermen's and merchants' boats throng stern to stern toward *asobi* boats, with almost no empty space left on the water. This must simply be the best pleasure world under heaven. . . . From aristocrats down to commoners, none hesitates to sleep with these women and to lavish their love on them. Some of the [*asobi*] get married to these men and some become concubines to be

cherished until their death. Even men of wisdom and men of character cannot avoid such deeds.[38]

It must be stressed here that the primary distinction of *asobi* from other women who sold their favor was their superb skill in singing *imayō*. Lacking this musical competency, other courtesans at Eguchi or Kanzaki were simply called *yahochi*, meaning mere prostitutes, not *asobi*.[39]

As a group, *asobi* seem to have maintained a loose internal structure headed by a female leader. These headmistresses are believed to have reached their position of authority by virtue of superior skill in singing *imayō*, personal charm as courtesans, and, undoubtedly, excellent business and managerial skills. Presumably, too, they protected group members from undue exploitation by customers, maintained a certain order within the group, and sometimes supervised the distribution of goods.[40]

In addition, *asobi* sought a further safeguard for their business prosperity in the worship of a deity named Hyakudayū. Hyakudayū worship was apparently a phallic cult, its object of veneration being representations of the male sexual organ made of wood, paper, or stone.[41] The cultic practice stems from the fetishistic belief that by praying to and honoring Hyakudayū, the courtesans could ensure continued success in attracting male customers. The powerful appeal of the Hyakudayū worship to *asobi* is evidenced in "Yūjoki," which notes that *asobi* kept hundreds and even thousands of these objects.[42]

Hyakudayū worship was not, however, confined to private observances by *asobi*. Besides keeping a large stock of phallic-shaped objects for their personal devotion, *asobi* made it a point to go on pilgrimages to shrines famous for their Hyakudayū practice, most notably the Hirota and Sumiyoshi shrines.[43] Coincidentally, the Sumiyoshi Shrine was also a favorite pilgrimage destination for aristocrats from the capital. Thus, sacred sites such as these became mingling grounds for *asobi* and aristocrats, each group following separate paths and harboring different sets of aspirations. Here a series of interactions was played out, resulting in an utterly secular form of carnal and material satisfaction. The benefits of visiting these shrines reinforced and successfully promoted the Hyakudayū cult among *asobi*, and the shrines also benefited, since more visits by the affluent aristocrats drawn by *asobi* meant increased income in the form of offerings. This triangular symbiotic relationship among *asobi*, the shrines, and the aristocrats undergirded the Hyakudayū worship practiced at the shrines, producing a singular coalescence of diverse interests in a most unlikely setting.

Songs in *Ryōjin hishō* reveal the importance of the Hyakudayū cult among *asobi*:

RH 375

miyako yori kudarishi
   tokenohoru

That girl Tokenohoru came

shimae ni ya tatete sumishikado

away from the capital and built
herself a house in Shimae.

somo shirazu uchisutete

After all that he left her!

ikani matsureba hyakudayū

What good her prayers to
Hyakudayū,

gen nakute hana no miyako e
   kaesuran

except to send her back to the
capital?[44]

RH 380

asobi no konomu mono

A courtesan's favorite things:

zōgei tsuzumi kohashibune

her many arts, the drum, the
little boats,

ōgasakazashi tomotorime

the woman who holds her large
parasol, and the woman who
rows her skiff,

otoko no ai inoru hyakudayū

and Hyakudayū, the one she
prays to for a man's love.

Some Heian nobles such as Ōe no Koretoki (or Yukitoki, 955–1010) wrote poems on the topic of *asobi*, declaring that the pleasure derived from a tryst with *asobi* cruising along the river was as exciting as their wedding-night experience:

WRS 720

suichō kōkei

Though the crimson wedding
chamber,

banji no reihō kotonari to
   iedomo

curtained in green, is held
supreme,

fune no uchi nami no ue

no less is the tryst of a lifetime,

isshō no kankai kore onaji

in a small boat, on the waves.

Even the female author of *Sarashina nikki* (Sarashina Diary, mid–11th cent.) was not immune from their charms; she had this to say about an *asobi* she encountered one night on the water:

> In the Autumn I had occasion to go down to Izumi. After Yodo the country became more beautiful and impressive than I can say. We spent the night on our boat in Takahama. Late at night, when it was

extremely dark, I detected the sound of oars. Someone asked who was there and I was told that it was a woman singer [*asobi*]. My people became very interested and called for her boat to be rowed alongside ours. By the distant light of the flares I could see the woman standing there in an unlined dress with long sleeves, hiding her face with a fan as she sang for us. It was a very moving sight.[45]

In fact, it has been observed that high court nobles and even imperial family members, after completing pilgrimages to shrines and temples, frequently made excursions to *asobi* quarters in Eguchi and Kanzaki in pursuit of pleasure. The list of these highborn visitors contains such illustrious figures as Emperors Ichijō and Go-Sanjō (r. 1068–72), Fujiwara Michinaga (966–1027), the most powerful regent in Japanese history, and his son, Yorimichi (992–1074). In the year 1000, on his return from a pilgrimage to the Sumiyoshi Shrine, Michinaga, in the company of the Empress Dowager Tōsanjō-in (962–1001), his sister and the mother of Emperor Ichijō, dropped by Eguchi, where he is reported to have shown favor to an *asobi* named Kokannon. Although the relationship was a brief, one-time affair, Kokannon presented herself to Michinaga again when he later revisited Eguchi as a lay priest, embarrassing him to no small measure. In the year 1031, Yorimichi followed his father's suit, falling in love with an *asobi* named Nakanogimi in Eguchi.[46]

Diaries and letters of Heian court nobles often contain references to *asobi*, further suggesting the attraction these women exerted. Particularly informative are *Kaya no in suikaku utaawase* (Poetry Match Held at a Pond Pavilion in Kaya no In), a record of the *waka* competition held at Kaya no In, Fujiwara Yorimichi's residence, on the sixteenth day of the fifth month of 1035, which contains a description of the winning party's pleasure trip to the Yodo River with *asobi*; *Chōshūki* (Record of Long Autumn), a diary by Minamoto Morotoki (1077–1136), especially the entry for the third day of the ninth month of 1119, which provides detailed information on the relationship between nobles and *asobi*; and Fujiwara Yorinaga's *Taiki*, which mentions his tryst with an *asobi* in the entry for the twenty-first day of the third month of 1148.[47] The *asobi* coveted these visits because they were often accompanied by lavish material donations, at times up to hundreds of bushels of rice and hundreds of skeins of silk. Such gifts far surpassed the fees paid by ordinary customers. In some cases at least, material donations of this sort were given because the nobles took pity on the women.[48]

In rare cases, a relationship between a nobleman and an *asobi* went beyond temporary infatuation and developed into a lasting commitment. One *asobi* by the name of Tanba no Tsubone captured the attention of

Emperor Go-Shirakawa, went on to become one of his consorts, and bore him a prince. This honor was made possible in part by her talents as an *imayō* singer. She is even mentioned in *Kudenshū*, the emperor's personal memoir, unlike his numerous other consorts from noble families.[49]

According to tradition, even religious figures were fascinated by *asobi*. Perhaps the most famous case involves the legendary encounter, which supposedly took place in 1178, between the priest Saigyō (1118–90) and an *asobi* at Eguchi. Their meeting is included in *Shinkokinshū* (New Collection of Ancient and Modern Times, 1206), where it is rendered as a poetic dialogue between Saigyō and an *asobi* named Tae:

SKKS 978   Saigyō. Composed upon Saigyō's being refused a room for the night in Eguchi, where he was detained by rain on his way to Tennōji Temple.[50]

yo no naka o	Here in the world
itou made koso	it's hard to renounce
katakarame	everything;
kari no yado o mo	how can you deny me
oshimu kimi kana	a night's borrowed lodging?

SKKS 979   *Asobi* Tae

yo o itou	From what I hear
hito to shi kikeba	you've left this world;
kari no yado ni	I wouldn't want
kokoro tomu na to	your heart to be dragged back
omou bakari zo	by a night's borrowed lodging!

At least two poems by *asobi* are included in the imperial anthologies:

GSS 1197   *Asobi* Miyagi. Composed when the priest Shōkū would not receive her offerings on the occasion of his sutra lectures, when many others dedicated offerings.[51]

tsu no kuni no	In Settsu Province
nani wa no koto ka	anything at all
nori naranu	becomes Dharma,
asobi tawabure	even flirting, even love play—
made to koso kike	yes, so I hear.

SZS 819   *Asobi* Koko. Thinking of a past love affair with Fujiwara Nakazane, then governor of Bitchū Province.[52]

kazu naranu	I don't count.
mi ni mo kokoro no	But in this body
ari gao ni	there's a heart—

hitori mo tsuki o   also alone,
nagametsuru kana   how I stare at the moon.

The rise of *asobi* and their acceptance into the court circle testify that there existed a positive artistic dialogue between the high and low cultures in Heian society, largely through the powerful medium of *imayō*.

KUGUTSU

Of the major female *imayō* performance groups, the *kugutsu* were most seriously involved in cultivating *imayō* as an art form. Unlike both the *miko* and *asobi*, they had a long-established tradition of oral transmission of *imayō*.[53] The *Kudenshū* reports that they took pride in this tradition and guarded it jealously.[54] The fact that Emperor Go-Shirakawa, after a long association with other groups of *imayō* singers, chose as his teacher Otomae (1086?–1169), a performer of *kugutsu* background, strongly suggests these women's artistic accomplishments.

Ōe no Masafusa, in his essay "Kairaishiki" (Record on Puppeteers, ca. 1087), an excellent source of information on *kugutsu* and a companion tract to "Yūjoki," sees *kugutsu* primarily as artists of foreign ethnic origin. This is seen in his description of the group's exotic mode of life:

> *Kugutsu* have neither fixed abodes nor houses to live in. They put up woolen tents and lead a nomadic life, a custom similar to that of the northern barbarians. The males make use of bows and horses when hunting. They juggle a pair of swords or daggers and balls; they manipulate wooden dolls in such a way as to make them look alive or make them fight each other. Their performances are similar to magic shows. They also change sand and pebbles into gold coins and transform trees into birds and beasts. They can dazzle people's eyes.
>
> As for the females of the group, they let out coquettish cries and swagger around swinging their hips and smiling bewitchingly. They make up their faces with rouge and white powder. These women lure people with their lewd songs and music. Neither their parents nor husbands nor sons-in-law reprove them. Without hesitation, the women entice wayfarers and travelers for a night's tryst. For such services, they are paid well. These women own clothes embroidered with golden threads, brocade robes, golden hair ornaments, and beautiful cosmetic boxes with mother-of-pearl inlay.
>
> *Kugutsu* neither till a single furrow of rice paddy nor gather the leaves from a single branch of mulberry. Since they are under no official provincial control, none of them are settled peasants, but instead they are transients. They do not know who the sovereign is or who the nobles are, and they do not fear the local magistrates.

Since they are exempt from taxes and conscript labor, they spend their lives in pleasure. At night, they worship Hyakudayū and pray for good fortune by making a racket with their dances and drum.[55]

It is evident from this depiction that, like *asobi*, *kugutsu* females cultivated the Hyakudayū cult and engaged in prostitution; and also like *asobi*, *kugutsu* followed a migratory life-style. In this same tract, however, Masafusa underscores the fact that a number of *kugutsu(me)* were well known for their superb skill in singing *imayō*; indeed, in his view they equal the famed Chinese female singer Han Ê.[56]

Even in their migratory life, the *kugutsu* apparently kept their musical skills refined, as reported in the lengthy and vivid account by the author of *Sarashina nikki* on her meeting with a group of female singers in the wilds of Mount Ashigara in Sagami Province:

> From somewhere in the dark three women singers [*asobi mitari*] emerged, the eldest being about fifty, the others about twenty and fourteen. . . . The oldest woman told us that she was the granddaughter of the famous singer, Kohata. Their hair, which was extremely long, hung beautifully over their foreheads; they all had fair complexions and looked attractive enough to serve as waiting-women.
>
> Our party was charmed by their appearance and even more impressed when they started singing, for they had fine, clear voices that rose to the heavens. The women were invited to join us. One member of our group remarked that the singers in the western provinces were no match for these performers, whereupon they burst out into the splendid song, "Should you compare us with those of Naniwa . . ." Yes, they were really pretty to look at, and their beautiful singing ended far too soon. We were all so sad to see them disappear into those fearful mountains that we wept as they walked away.[57]

Because of their vagrant mode of life, similar to that of *arukimiko*, *kugutsu* are considered to have also been effective agents in the transmission and circulation of *imayō*.[58]

By the late Heian period some *kugutsu* had given up their wandering existence and had begun to settle in fixed locations, having gained renown for their accomplishments in the genre of *imayō*. In contrast to *asobi*, who sought their livelihood along the waterways, *kugutsu* settled near inland way stations, most prominently around Aohaka (Otomae's birthplace), Sunomata, Nogami, and Akasaka in Mino Province, all of which were frequented by travelers making their way along the Tōsandō Highway.[59] The aforementioned author of *Sarashina nikki* and her retinue were obviously entertained by female singers of this region, as she records in her diary: "At the border of Mino province we took the ferry at Sunomata and reached a place called Nogami. Here again we were joined by a band of entertainers [*asobi domo*], who sang for us all night long, bringing back fond memories of Mount Ashigara."[60]

Female *imayō* singers of *kugutsu* background underwent strenuous musical training. *Kudenshū* reports an account Go-Shirakawa's teacher, Otomae, told him of the great self-discipline and concentration required of *imayō* aspirants: "Kiyotsune gave intensive, rigorous musical training to Tōri and Hatsukoe. To ward off sleep at night, Tōri would rush outside and splash her eyes with water and even pluck her eyelashes to wake herself up. Still she would feel sleepy. She stayed up every night, and even when the dawn came she would keep on singing without opening the shutters."[61] A similar seriousness is reflected in Otomae's insistence that she would not waste her efforts on a student who lacked determination or an earnest desire to learn *imayō*, even if her pupil were already under the patronage of influential court nobles:

> The Middle Councillor Ienari sent Sasanami to my house with the request that I instruct her; and so I taught her *ashigara, kurotoriko, ichiko, furukawa, furukoyanagi, tauta,* and other songs. She made a great to-do of having her palanquin wait for her in front of my house while she studied a number of different kinds of songs. This may well have led to some errors in her singing. As I did not intend to force my teaching upon her, I did not make any special effort to correct her, either. Since I did not really teach her anything, I do not consider her to have received a complete transmission from me.[62]

Even Go-Shirakawa had to discard his previous *imayō* training once he came under Otomae's guidance, for she required him to relearn the entire repertoire according to her style. Through strict adherence to these principles of music training, then, singers of the Mino *imayō* tradition succeeded in establishing themselves as an uncontested artistic lineage; for generations the transmission of *imayō* through female lines continued unchanged, until during Go-Shirakawa's time when male aristocrats were finally admitted as members of the lineage.

Like some poetically talented *asobi*, a few *kugutsu* left *waka* poems. At least three are included in two separate imperial anthologies, all occasioned by partings that took place in Mino or Owari Province:

SKS 186   *Kugutsu* Nabiki (or Nabiku).[63] Composed at dawn upon her lover's departure for Azuma.

hakanakumo   So sad
kesa no wakare no   parting this morning,
oshiki kana   so little time—

itsuka wa hito o	when can I gaze at him again?
nagaraete mishi	Long, so long there's no end.

SZKKS 900 *Kugutsu* Ako. Composed when the man, who came down to Owari from the capital and with whom she pledged a lovers' vow, said that he would be returning to the capital the next day.

shinubakari	If it is the path
makoto ni nageku	of real sorrow,
michi naraba	like death,
inochi to tomo ni	let me stretch it out
nobi yo to zo omou	as long as my life.

SZKKS 980 *Kugutsu* Jijū. Composed in response to a poem written by the priest Kankaku, who stopped over in Aohaka on his way from Azuma.

azumaji ni	So the road to Azuma
kimi ga kokoro wa	has caught your heart?
tomaredomo	For me it's the capital.
ware mo miyako no	Someone there
kata o nagamemu	has caught my eye.

The inclusion of these poems in the imperial anthologies may be considered a recognition of the literary achievements of the *kugutsu* as a whole. This also supports the opinion that *kugutsu*, together with *asobi*, had a large share in composing *imayō* lyrics.

DECLINE OF *IMAYŌ* PERFORMERS

We do not know why the *asobi* and *kugutsu imayō* singers vanished so completely. Perhaps all we can say at this point is that when the governmental seat was transferred to Kamakura in 1186, a concomitant shift of emphasis in national life occurred. The warrior class, consciously seeking to distance itself from many of the ways of court, offered a set of values that differed sharply from those of Heian courtiers. The courtiers who had once been the lavish patrons of *imayō* now found themselves stripped of political and economic power and the prerogatives to sustain their aesthetic pursuits. With the relocation of the capital, the pulse of the nation shifted geographically as well, to the east. Major routes now led to Kamakura along the Tōkaidō Highway. The prosperity of Eguchi and Kanzaki declined and the busy crossroads connecting Aohaka and Sunomata with the Tōsandō Highway were deserted. Those *asobi* and *kugutsu* whose livelihood depended on the travelers on these thoroughfares faded away.

Another factor may be found in the appearance of a newly rising group of female entertainers, known as *shirabyōshi* (women performers in white costume), toward the end of the Heian period.[64] The *shirabyōshi*, with their combination of song and dance, added momentum to the decline of the more one-dimensional vocal entertainment of *imayō* singers, vying with them for aristocratic patronage. Two celebrated cases of late Heian nobles' patronage of *shirabyōshi* are Taira Kiyomori's bestowal of favor on Giō and Hotoke, and Minamoto Yoshitsune's (1159–89) romantic involvement with Shizuka.[65] Finally, it is said that Emperor Go-Toba's infatuation with Kamegiku, another woman of *shirabyōshi* background, was partial cause for the Jōkyū Revolt in 1221.[66] Other types of entertainers, as diverse as *jushi* (acrobatic performers) and *sarugaku* ("monkey music") musicians and dancers, likely posed serious competition as well. The increasing popularity of these newer forms of performing arts may also have contributed to the disappearance of *imayō* singers and their art.[67]

Thus the vicissitudes of *imayō* and its transmitters seem to be closely related to social and political developments during the latter part of the Heian period. Ironically, the very success of *imayō* singers was what spelled their downfall, for if the singers "succeeded" in attracting noble and even imperial patronage, they thereby rendered themselves highly vulnerable to shifts in political fortune.

Go-Shirakawa and *Imayō*

Emperor Go-Shirakawa played a crucial mediatory role in the history of *imayō*. Under his aegis, a number of *imayō* concerts in which *asobi* or *kugutsu* participated were held in his palace. In addition to performing, these singers actively participated in informal critical discussions on *imayō* as an art form, demonstrating their mastery and esoteric knowledge of the medium.[68] What emerges from these occasions is a picture of an unusual artistic moment, in which upper and lower classes interacted in a special and creative milieu.

As his memoir indicates, when it came to *imayō* Go-Shirakawa did not hesitate to associate with members of the lower classes; in fact, he sought them out as his musical instructors and companions: "I associated not only with courtiers of all ranks, but also with commoners of the capital, including women servants of various places, menial workers, the *asobi* from Eguchi and Kanzaki, and the *kugutsu* from different provinces. Nor was this company limited to those who were skillful. Whenever I heard of any *imayō* singers I would have them sing together, and the number of these people grew quite large."[69]

In the *Kudenshū*, Go-Shirakawa records the different phases of his involvement with *imayō* and reiterates its central position in his artistic life. The memoir chronicles his growth as a practitioner, patron, connoisseur, and authority as the head of his own school of *imayō* singing. He opens the memoir by detailing his long and arduous training. It was not unusual for him to forgo sleep for days or to endure physical discomfort in his efforts to master the art. His interest was not transitory, as some around him may have assumed. It seems clear that the aesthetic satisfaction he derived from *imayō* was in no way inferior to that which other courtiers found in *waka*. He wrote:

> I have been fond of *imayō* ever since my youth and have never neglected it. On balmy spring days when cherry blossoms open on the branches and then fall to the ground, and in the cries of the bush warbler and the song of the cuckoo, I have perceived the spirit of *imayō*. On lonely autumn nights as I gazed at the moon, *imayō* added poignancy to the cries of the insects. Ignoring both summer's heat and winter's cold, and favoring no season over another, I spent my waking hours in singing; no day dawned without my having spent the whole night singing. Even at dawn, with the shutters still closed, I continued singing, oblivious to both sunrise and noon. Rarely distinguishing day from night, I spent my days and months in this manner.[70]

He was clearly not pushed to study *imayō*, but rather found it to be the most congenial medium of self-expression. In writing about the art form, Go-Shirakawa employs the same poetic idiom and images usually associated with *waka* aesthetics: the spring and cherry blossoms, bush warblers and cuckoos, and the autumnal moon and the cries of insects. For him, *waka*'s refined sentiment of *aware* could be evoked equally well by *imayō*; if *waka* helped to heighten one's aesthetic sensibility, so did *imayō*. Indeed, in power, utility, and effect *imayō* is just as potent as *waka*, if not superior.

Go-Shirakawa devoted himself to *imayō* with a fervor verging on fanaticism. In its intensity, this severe self-discipline suggests that for the emperor *imayō* was a religio-aesthetic way (*michi*), not inferior to other forms of religious discipline:

> On occasion I gathered together some people to dance and enjoy the singing. At times we gathered in groups of four or five, or seven or eight, simply to sing *imayō*. Sometimes I set up a schedule for my close retainers to take turns as my singing partners as I practiced *imayō* day and night. On other occasions, when I was by myself, I opened *Zōgeishū* and, beginning with the *imayō* on the four seasons, *hōmon*, and *hayauta*, I exhausted the repertoire. Three times I lost

my voice. Twice I sang to the point where, even as I tried to follow the set rules as closely as possible, I could no longer produce a sound. Straining my voice in this way gave me a sore throat and made it painful even to swallow water. In spite of this affliction, I still managed to keep on singing.

Sometimes, after first practicing for seven, eight, fifty, or one hundred days, I continued singing for even a thousand days on end. Although there were times when I did not sing during the day, no dawn broke without my singing.[71]

The lengths to which Go-Shirakawa went to train himself in the art of *imayō* recall the ascetic's grueling regimen pursued in hopes of attaining ever higher levels of religious consciousness. In this sense, the emperor's self-discipline reflected a cultural trend of his time. A similar attitude is observable in certain of his contemporaries, such as in Fujiwara Shunzei (1114–1204) and his son, Teika (1162–1241), who increasingly combined aesthetic and meditative practice.[72] Yet *imayō*, a popular rather than courtly form, seemed an inappropriate focus of devotion to many and elicited some censorious remarks, notably from Go-Shirakawa's own father, Emperor Toba.

Undeterred by such criticism, Go-Shirakawa pursued his desire to perfect his skills in *imayō*. To gain expertise in singing he sought out tutors, who invariably came from the lower classes. Among those summoned to Go-Shirakawa's imperial residence to instruct him were female *asobi*, including a woman from the Kanzaki area named Kane who was employed as a servant to his mother.[73] His free association with commoners sharply contrasts with the attitude of some court attendants of earlier periods, such as Sei Shōnagon, who found even the snow on the houses of common people disagreeable.[74]

Go-Shirakawa's training in *imayō* prior to his accession to the throne was uneven and lacking clear direction. He continued in this manner for some fifteen years, becoming in time a rather accomplished *imayō* singer. He even boasts in the *Kudenshū*: "I could not find anyone who far surpassed me in knowledge of *imayō*."[75] The Hōgen Disturbance in 1156 brought his *imayō* practice to a sudden halt, though only temporarily; for as soon as order was restored, Go-Shirakawa resumed his training. Now, however, he began systematic professional training, inviting the undisputed authority in *imayō*, Otomae, a woman in her mid-seventies, to court.[76]

Otomae radically transformed Go-Shirakawa's involvement in *imayō*. She had him relearn his entire repertoire in her singing style, the only one she considered authentic. The training continued for almost ten years, from 1159 until Otomae's death in 1169. By then, Go-Shirakawa had become the uncontested successor to her school of *imayō*. Their relationship was indeed an extraordinary one. Otomae, apparently seeing in Go-Shirakawa a worthy disciple, spared no effort to make him a virtuoso in the art. The deep mutual esteem and affection that developed between them is evident in his moving description of his visit to her sickbed near the end of her life:

> Otomae fell ill in the spring of her eighty-fourth year [1169]. Since she had been in good health and did not appear to be suffering from any specific illness, it did not seem likely that her health would take a serious turn. But shortly afterward the news reached me that her condition was critical. As I had her living close by in a house built for her, I hurriedly slipped out of my residence to visit her. She was sitting up, leaning against her daughter and facing me. As she looked feeble, I recited a chapter from the Lotus Sutra for the sake of her well-being in this as well as the next life. I then asked her, "Would you like to hear a song?" She was extremely pleased and nodded her head.

> > In the time of Imitation Dharma,
> > the vows of Yakushi are trustworthy!
> > Hear his sacred name once only,
> > they say, and escape even a million ills.[77]

> I repeated the song two or three times over for her, and she enjoyed it even more than my sutra chanting. Rubbing her hands and weeping with happiness, she exclaimed, "Now that I have heard the song, my strength seems to have returned." A deep emotion filled my heart and I returned home.[78]

This poignant rendering of the last meeting of master and disciple is followed by Go-Shirakawa's account of Otomae's death and his reverent words of homage:

> Later, when I was performing the ascetic ritual of reciting the Rishu Sutra at Ninnaji, a report reached me saying that Otomae had passed away early on the nineteenth day of the second month [in 1169]. Although death at her age was not something to be mourned, my grief was boundless because I had known her for so many years. It was not the first time that I grieved for those who had gone ahead of me, but my memories of her kept surging up. She was my teacher from whom I had learned so much, and so at the news of her death I started reading the sutra in the mornings to purify the six roots of evil, and in the evenings for fifty days I read the Amida Sutra continuously to pray for her rebirth in the Western Pure Land.[79]

On the first anniversary of Otomae's death, Go-Shirakawa sponsored a special memorial service in which he sang *imayō* he had learned from her and dedicated an eloquent memorial prayer in tribute to her. Thereafter, he offered annual memorial services on her behalf. Close to one-third of the *Kudenshū* is devoted to describing people associated with Otomae and anecdotes concerning her, revealing the special place she had in his life. Moreover, Go-Shirakawa affirms in *Kudenshū* his status as an authentic transmitter of Otomae's *imayō* tradition, by relating a dream by his secondary consort Tanba no Tsubone in which Otomae appeared and joyfully communicated her approval of and pride in Go-Shirakawa's *imayō* singing.[80] It is generally believed that *Ryōjin hishō*, which presumably was undertaken soon after Go-Shirakawa initiated his lessons with Otomae, was inspired by his teacher as an effort to commit to writing the oral instruction he received.

Summing up his master-disciple relationship with Otomae, Go-Shirakawa states in the *Kudenshū*: "For ten years I had received training from Otomae. In order to give unity to my songs in accordance with her style, I even corrected and relearned all the songs that I had sung and collected by listening to different people in the past. I received a complete transmission from Otomae, with absolutely no omission."[81] Later, after searching in vain for a disciple to whom he could transmit all he had learned from Otomae, Go-Shirakawa laments:

> I have been contemplating transmitting to someone this tradition to which I have dedicated myself for years, so that it may continue in the future. Although I have a number of people who practice singing with me, it is to be regretted that I have no disciple who can succeed me in this endeavor. Even though a number of people ranging from courtiers to commoners gather for the purpose of singing, not one of them sings with my zeal.[82]

Finally, however, around 1179 Go-Shirakawa settled on two disciples, Minamoto Suketoki (b. 1159) and Fujiwara Moronaga (1137–92): "These two are my disciples who have received an authentic transmission of melodies and style from me. Anyone who sings in the same way as these two men can be said to have correctly received the training, but any method of singing that deviates from that of Suketoki or Moronaga should be considered unauthentic."[83] Go-Shirakawa's act of faithfully transmitting the *imayō* tradition to worthy disciples was both an ultimate tribute to his own master, Otomae, and insurance for the survival of the vocal *imayō* art.

As a patron of *imayō*, Go-Shirakawa held a number of informal *imayō* gatherings to which he invited his retainers as well as singers of the *asobi* and *kugutsu* backgrounds. But one formal *imayō awase* (*imayō* competition) held under his sponsorship from the first to the fifteenth day of the ninth month of 1174 at his Hōjūji Palace caught the attention of various historical and musical commentators for its rare magnitude and splendor, as recorded, for instance, in *Kikki* (Felicitous Record), a diary by Fujiwara Tsunefusa (b. 1143).[84] Presumably modeled after the *utaawase* (*waka* competition) popular among the aristocrats, this *awase* featured two teams and fifteen rounds of competition. The participants were courtiers, with Fujiwara Moronaga and Minamoto Sukekata serving as judges. Unfortunately, no details survive indicating what kinds of *imayō* were chosen and sung for the occasion. But *Kikki* makes a special note that on the thirteenth day, after the competition when the participants held a musical recital accompanied by string and wind instruments, Emperor Go-Shirakawa joined in the singing of *imayō* himself and that his performance was absolutely sublime.[85]

As a practitioner of *imayō*, Go-Shirakawa helped to create a new cultural milieu in which commoners and aristocrats could enjoy and learn from each other's artistry. His patronage added an aura of prestige to the popular song genre, transforming it to a higher form of entertainment to be cultivated by all.

2 Emperor Go-Shirakawa as a Patron of Heian Culture

Go-Shirakawa's patronage was not by any means limited to *imayō*. The emperor made important contributions in many other cultural areas as well, allowing them to thrive under his sponsorship. These areas suggest the cultural diversity and riches created and enjoyed by Heian society, and also hint at the emperor's wide-ranging cultural entrepreneurship.

Senzaishū (Collection of a Thousand Years, ca. 1188)

Go-Shirakawa's commissioning of the twenty-volume *Senzaishū*, the seventh imperial *waka* anthology, was based in large part on his concerns for his kingly position and its mandates. Although not himself an expert in *waka*, Go-Shirakawa skillfully used the talents and aspirations of Fujiwara Shunzei to restore the prestige of the courtly poetic tradition, which had been diminished by *Senzaishū*'s two immediate predecessors, *Kin'yōshū* (Collection of Golden Leaves, ca. 1124–27) and *Shikashū* (Collection of Verbal Flowers, 1151–54), both comprising only ten books and without prefaces. Owing to the reinstatement of the preface and the restoration of the twenty-book format, *Senzaishū* is considered an attempt to return to *Kokinshū* (ca. 905) in terms of organization, structure, and content, and is considered to have been a veritable forerunner of *Shinkokinshū*, which immediately followed it.[1] In fact, the very names of these three imperial anthologies—*Kokinshū* (Collection of Ancient and Modern Times), *Senzaishū* (Collection of a Thousand Years), and *Shinkokinshū* (New Collection of Ancient and Modern Times)—indicate a single, shared aspiration: to disseminate the best poems of their times, which will transcend the passage of time itself.

Go-Shirakawa commissioned Fujiwara Shunzei to undertake the compilation of *Senzaishū* around 1183. The emperor had never been known as a *waka* enthusiast. He openly preferred *imayō*, and unlike other royal family members, such as Emperor Sutoku, he had never cultivated a *waka* circle around him. Even at the regular flower dedication ceremonies at his court, *imayō* remained the center of the ritual.[2] Why, then, would he support the compiling of an anthology devoted to *waka*, a form he apparently had little interest in, and why during the Genpei War at that? Moreover, why did he select Shunzei, who, although a poetic icon of his day, was a protégé and confidant of Sutoku, to oversee the compilation? Scholars have shown that the anthology was conceived and executed according to calculated, political motives.[3] For Go-Shirakawa, it was one way of countering the rancor and hostilities that were rending the fabric of his society and making havoc of everyday life.

Historical sources indicate that Shunzei received the official imperial order to begin the *Senzaishū* project in the second month of 1183. According to *Meigetsuki* (The Record of the Clear Moon, 1235), a diary by Shunzei's son Teika, the first meeting between Go-Shirakawa and the seventy-year-old poet took place at the emperor's Hōjūji Palace on the tenth day of the eleventh month of 1181, to be followed by a second within four days and a third about a month later. Taniyama Shigeru suggests that these conferences were not ordinary social calls; rather, they were planning sessions in which both parties sounded out the other's intentions and confided their respective aspirations and needs.[4] It is believed that the emperor communicated his plans for the imperial anthology, while Shunzei promoted himself as the man best suited to become the compiler.

The years 1180 and 1181 had been particularly trying for Go-Shirakawa, both as far as family matters were concerned and in terms of the national welfare. To begin with his third son, Prince Mochihito (1151–80), spurred on by Minamoto Yorimasa (1104–80), issued a secret edict urging the Minamoto clan warriors to rise against the Taira; his plans were prematurely discovered, however, and he was killed at Uji by the Taira army in the fifth month of 1180. This incident prompted Minamoto Yoritomo to rise in arms and eventually plunged the country into the full-scale Genpei War. Then, in the sixth month of the same year, Go-Shirakawa, together with ex-Emperor Takakura and Emperor Antoku, had to move to Fukuhara, a new capital established the preceding year. In the latter part of the eleventh month of 1180, however, the capital was moved back to the Heian city and the court again was obliged to move; this caused further strain on an imperial family already coping with traumatic adjustments. Shortly thereafter, toward the end of the twelfth month, the rebellious monks in Nara, who opposed the Taira hegemony, provoked the Taira army to take action against them; Kōfukuji, Tōdaiji, and numerous other temples were burnt to the ground, and there was massive loss of life. The next month the ex-Emperor Takakura, who had been trying to mediate the ever-intensifying animosity between Go-Shirakawa and Kiyomori, died at the age of twenty-one. As if these political events were not enough, the entire nation was suffering from a serious famine.

Beleaguered by this series of calamities, Go-Shirakawa turned to his courtiers for advice but received little support. Especially critical was Kujō Kanezane, the minister of the right, who questioned Go-Shirakawa's wisdom in ordering the reconstruction of Kōfukuji and Tōdaiji during a famine. When Go-Shirakawa requested counsel about his proposed pilgrimage to the Grand Ise Shrine to offer a special prayer, the court officials rebuffed him, saying that since there was no precedent for such an act, it was difficult for them to advise him. Despite Go-Shirakawa's wish to promote unity within the court, he was met only with increasing hostility.

As a last-ditch effort, Go-Shirakawa even delivered a conciliatory message from Minamoto Yoritomo to the Taira, but the leader and heir of that clan, Munemori (1147–85), rejected the proposal outright.[5] It was against this backdrop of continuously unfolding political crisis during the Genpei War, then, that the meetings of Go-Shirakawa and Shunzei took place.

The proposed *Senzaishū* was to serve at least three purposes for Go-Shirakawa, all intended to prevent an imminent national catastrophe. A primary concern was to appease the soul of the late Emperor Sutoku. One such attempt had been made in 1177, when the posthumous title of "Sutoku-in" was conferred on the late emperor, who until then had been known as "Sanuki-in" after the place of his banishment. Now, however, faced with impending attack by the Minamoto forces, residents of the capital began to speculate that a grudge borne by Sutoku against Go-Shirakawa for his political ruin was the true cause of the troubles. In fact, *Hōgen monogatari* reports Sutoku's allegedly intense bitterness by saying that he vowed to become a great devil in Japan and thereby make the emperors commoners and the commoners, emperors.[6] Considering Sutoku's poetic talent and love for *waka*, Go-Shirakawa seems to have decided that an appropriate memorial to him would be an imperial *waka* anthology.

Shunzei had enjoyed a special relationship with Sutoku; in some ways he owed his career to the late emperor, who first recognized his poetic gifts and became his patron. In fact, it was Sutoku who in 1143 appointed Shunzei, then a little-known poet of thirty, as compiler of *Kyūan hyakushu* (Collection of One Hundred Poems of the Kyūan Era, 1150).[7] Under Sutoku's patronage, Shunzei became the central figure of court *waka* circles. Sutoku's banishment to Sanuki in 1156, therefore, must have been a severe blow to Shunzei. From Sanuki, Sutoku wrote poems to Shunzei, wistfully recalling their old days as *waka* companions while giving vent to his grievances.[8] After Sutoku's death, Shunzei reportedly composed a poem in his memory and secretly took it to his tomb, where he vowed to seek a reunion in the next world.[9]

As any *waka* poet would, Shunzei had long cherished the dream of being appointed compiler of the imperial anthology, a dream apparently dashed by Sutoku's banishment. He suffered another setback when Emperor Nijō bestowed the honor of compiling *Shokushikashū* (Later Collection of Verbal Flowers, 1165) on Fujiwara Kiyosuke (1104–77), Shunzei's rival.[10] Shunzei then started his own collection of *waka*, realizing that Kiyosuke's personal *waka* collection had served as the basis of *Shokushikashū*. Shunzei's anthology, which took more than ten years to complete, was called *Sangodaishū* (Collection of Fifteen Eras, ca. 1177–79). Although he tried to promote this collection, then in its final stages of completion, as an imperial anthology, the death of Emperor Takakura in 1180 shattered his hopes once again.

In the end, however, Shunzei's faithful cultivation of his art paid off. With the death of Kiyosuke in 1177 Sunzei's poetic accomplishment began to be publicly recognized, culminating in Kujō Kanezane's praise of him as the "Elder of the *waka*."[11] At the time of his audiences with Go-Shirakawa in 1181, his dream of compiling the imperial anthology must have been uppermost in his mind, a sort of crowning point for his growing poetic stature. He already had the manuscript of *Sangodaishū* in hand; all he needed to do was rework it as Kiyosuke had. On Go-Shirakawa's part, he was well aware that Shunzei had been a devoted retainer of Sutoku and was a recognized authority on *waka*. The selection of Shunzei as compiler of *Senzaishū* was thus not only expedient, but also entirely fitting.

Senzaishū was also intended to mitigate the Taira's growing aggressiveness. Although the Taira were a military clan, they had produced a number of poets of worth, including Tsunemori (1124–85), Tadanori (1144–84), and Shigehira (1157–85), to name but a few. Perhaps, if matters so dictated, Go-Shirakawa could weaken Taira solidarity by luring some defectors from their camp with a tactful inducement—inclusion in the anthology. At the same time, the compilation of an imperial anthology at such a critical moment was a symbolic statement that the emperor was still in charge and not shaken by immediate goings-on. Given this background, Shunzei's selection can be seen as politically astute as well, for he counted a number of Taira clan members in his *waka* circle. For instance, *Heike monogatari* (The Tale of the Heike, 13th cent.) highlighted the fact that Tadanori, confident of Shunzei's appreciation for his artistic work, risked his life to entrust his poems to Shunzei during the hurried flight of the Taira from the capital in 1183.[12] Thus, in the second month of 1183, Go-Shirakawa selected Taira Sukemori, the newly appointed imperial secretary, rather than a court noble, to deliver the imperial order commissioning Shunzei to compile *Senzaishū*.[13]

A third purpose of the *Senzaishū* anthology was to give the aristocrats a much-needed moral uplift. They had the most to lose in the civil war and precisely for this reason were apprehensive about the current state of affairs. Many realized that their golden days were over, no matter how the war ended. Go-Shirakawa had to offer these dispirited courtiers something to cling to. The most hallowed of traditional court literary practices, the imperial anthology, could demonstrate, he hoped, that the court still transcended political crisis.[14]

Senzaishū was finally completed in 1188, after the Genpei War had ended. Shunzei is known to have based the work on his *Sangodaishū*, with certain alterations made to accommodate the changed sociopolitical situation.

Worthy of note in *Senzaishū* is the number of poems by Emperor Sutoku—twenty-three altogether. No previous imperial anthology ever included so many poems by a single emperor, an indication perhaps that Sutoku was one of the superior poet-emperors in Japanese history. Another interpretation is that with this edition both Emperor Go-Shirakawa and the compiler Shunzei were paying a special tribute to Sutoku. This possibility becomes even stronger when we consider that Go-Shirakawa must have approved the use of so many of Sutoku's poems; then too, it is noteworthy that the anthology includes only seven poems by Go-Shirakawa himself. All in all, thirty-six of Shunzei's poems are included; in addition, we find at least eight poems by members of the Taira clan, some identified by name, some anonymous.[15] Both Go-Shirakawa and Shunzei seem to have been united in their willingness to brave possible criticism from the Kamakura military government for using these poems in an imperial anthology, although they did discreetly withhold some of the poets' names. The following are a few selected poems by the figures closely linked to *Senzaishū*:

SZS 41 Emperor Sutoku. On spring.

asa yū ni	In the morning, in the evening,
hana matsu koro wa	when I yearn for cherry blossoms,
omoi ne no	they come in dreams.

yume no uchi ni zo   In the thoughts of sleep
sakihajimekeru   they start to bloom![16]

SZS 259   Fujiwara Shunzei. On autumn.

yū sareba   As evening darkens,
nobe no akikaze   the autumn wind in the fields
mi ni shimite   pierces the body;
uzura nakunari   quails cry in the deep grass
fukakusa no sato   of Fukakusa village.[17]

SZS 66   Anonymous [Taira Tadanori]. Thinking of cherry blossoms
   at home.

saza nami ya   Oh, Shiga, once capital
shiga no miyako wa   of the rippling waves:
areni shi o   in ruins.
mukashi nagara no   On Nagara, the mountain
                                        cherry,
yamazakura kana   as always, blooms.[18]

SZS 360   Emperor Go-Shirakawa. Composed when a group of men
   wrote about the moon shining on the autumn maple leaves.

momijiba ni   Let the moon
tsuki no hikari   fix its beam
sashi soete   on the fall leaves:
kore ya akaji no   red
nishiki naruran   brocade!

The overall mood of *Senzaishū* is reflective, of nostalgia for a past
irrevocably lost, desolate loneliness, and sadness over the transiency of
this world. This atmosphere pervades even poems on the seasons and love,
but it is strongest in the Miscellaneous section. In fact, among the Miscellaneous sections of the first eight imperial anthologies, that in *Senzaishū* has the largest number of songs that express such sentiments.[19] The
link between the dismal political and social situation of the times and the
dark, rueful tone of the anthology is quite clear.

Picture Scrolls (*Emakimono*)

Go-Shirakawa was deeply interested in other arts and crafts besides poetry
as well. Some contemporary nobles' diaries report the unconventional
manner in which he indulged his interests. Kujō Kanezane, for instance,
in *Gyokuyō* (Leaves of Jewel), relates an incident he heard about from
Fujiwara Mitsunaga, a contemporary picture scroll illustrator. Emperor
Go-Shirakawa was passing a certain alley and, through an open gate,

chanced to see an old lacquer worker bent intently over his work. The emperor had his carriage stopped and without ceremony stepped into the artisan's drab house and sat on a stool in front of him to watch him work. After a while, when he was leaving, the emperor asked the old man, probably in jest, whether he would give him some souvenir. The craftsman, having nothing to offer, was at a loss. Yet he evidently took the emperor's request seriously, for a few days later he appeared at the palace with a beautifully wrought lacquer box in hand. A courtier had a quiet talk with the artisan and sent him on his way.[20]

This episode illustrates a certain eccentricity on the part of the emperor, but at the same time it underscores his love and admiration for the arts. While he seems to have been attracted to all types of arts, scroll painting apparently held a special allure. According to one unofficial record, he kept ten *emaki* chests in the treasure house of his Rengeōin Palace, and Komatsu Shigemi, a scholar of scroll painting, goes so far as to call Go-Shirakawa an *emaki* "maniac" (*mania*).[21] At least eight scroll paintings are known to have resulted from his official commissions: *Hōgen sumōzu emaki* (Picture Scroll of the Sumo Wrestling Matches in the Hōgen Era), *Hōgen jōnanji keiba emaki* (Picture Scroll of the Horse Races at the Jōnanji Palace in the Hōgen Era), *Genshū kōtei emaki* (Picture Scroll of Emperor Hsüan Tsung), *Nin'an gokei gyōkō emaki* (Picture Scroll of the First Imperial Attendance at the Festival of Thanksgiving in the Year of Nin'an), *Gosannen kassen emaki* (Picture Scroll of the Later Three Years' Battle), *Shōan gosechi emaki* (Picture Scroll of *Gosechi* Dancing in the Year of Shōan), *Nenjūgyōji emaki* (Picture Scroll of Annual Rites and Ceremonies), and *Sueba no tsuyu taishō emaki* (Picture Scroll of the Tale of General Sueba no Tsuyu).[22] Unfortunately, the originals of these *emaki* are now lost; all that remain are a seventeenth-century copy of part of the *Nenjūgyōji emaki* and an Edo-period reproduction of the *Shōan gosechi emaki*.[23]

Nenjūgyōji emaki offers concrete representations of the manners and customs of both aristocrats and commoners in late-Heian Japan. The original scroll is believed to have been a massive sixty-volume set that was kept in the Rengeōin Palace treasure house.[24] Komatsu Shigemi, though working from admittedly incomplete data, suggests that the work was ordered around 1157–58 and completed no later than 1171; its illustrator was Tokiwa no Genji Mitsunaga, and the headnotes were written by Fujiwara Norinaga (1109–80), a renowned calligrapher of the day (these two are known to have collaborated as well in the creation of *Ban Dainagon ekotoba* [Picture-Narrative Scroll of Ban Dainagon]); Fujiwara Motofusa (1144–1230), the regent at the time, provided editorial supervision.[25] What remained of the original was lost during the great Kyoto fire of 1661; only sixteen scrolls, which the father-and-son team of Sumiyoshi Jokei (1599–1670) and Gukei (1631–1705) had copied from the original, then in the possession of ex-Emperor Gomizuno-o (1596–1680), remained following this disaster.[26] Indeed, various sources suggest that even the original was by this time missing large portions, with only sixteen scrolls left.[27] Of the copies, only the first seven are painted in color; the other nine are in monochrome sketch.

Nenjūgyōji emaki is devoted chiefly to the depiction of important annual ceremonies and religious observances conducted at court. Mixed in are occasional sketches of the festivals of commoners, a rare juxtaposition of upper- and lower-class cultures that is nevertheless almost to be expected with Go-Shirakawa.

In the scenes that feature court activities, the backdrop is always the imperial palace. By Go-Shirakawa's reign, the old palace had fallen into severe disrepair, and the emperors usually took up residence in mansions specially prepared and offered by the Fujiwara regents outside the palace compounds. After the Hōgen Disturbance in 1156, however, Shinzei, who became a far closer advisor to Go-Shirakawa in the wake of the incident, suggested a plan for reconstruction of the imperial palace, in part to help restore dignity to the imperial household. This proposal was approved in the second month of 1157, the third year of Go-Shirakawa's reign, and construction started immediately, with funds raised from taxes on the temples, shrine landholdings, and nobles' estates.[28] By the tenth month of the same year the palace was completed. In celebration, an imperial banquet was held on the twenty-second day of the first month of 1158, the first time in 123 years such an event had been staged at the palace. In many senses, the event was a symbolic declaration of the power and autonomy of imperial rule. At the musical party that followed the feast, Go-Shirakawa himself sang songs to instrumental accompaniment provided by his courtiers.[29] The purpose of *Nenjūgyōji emaki*, in short, was to provide a visual documentary of the revival of court ceremonies and activities, thus preserving the record of the dignity and prestige of the imperial institution. In this regard, *Nenjūgyōji emaki* is quite different from other *emaki* based on literary works, which were intended mainly for artistic appreciation.[30]

The portions of the extant scroll that relate to court activities include scenes of the emperor's visit to his parents in the new year, cockfights in the imperial courtyard, football games, archery contests on horseback, imperial poetry contests and banquets, the regent's banquets for the courtiers, Buddhist ceremonies to ensure the welfare of the country, the purification rite of the sixth month, and the regent's visit to the Kamo Shrine. In side-by-side format, the scroll also depicts events from the lives of commoners, such as the Inari and Gion festivals, Kamo festival parades, cockfights, a ball game that resembles modern hockey, and processions of prisoners through the city streets.

As a record of urban life generally, *Nenjūgyōji emaki* is very revealing. The scroll is filled with scenes showing commoners rushing and milling about or crowding onto the site where an event is taking place. The wide range of people represented—men, women, and children, the old and the young, laypeople and religious personages, peddlers and sightseers—the liveliness of their expressions, and the endless variety of their movements, postures, and gestures dramatically convey the mood of festivity and the excitement that these occasions generated. The focus on popular culture in *Nenjūgyōji emaki* can be taken as another manifestation of Go-Shirakawa's acceptance of the diversity of his own society, in a manner consistent with his interest in *imayō*.

Go-Shirakawa's decision to store so many scrolls and other artifacts in his palace may well have stemmed from his ambition to compete with the Shōsōin at Nara, the Shōkōmyōin treasure house at the Toba Palace built by Emperor Toba, and the Byōdōin at Uji, a residence of Fujiwara Yorimichi.[31] It is known that he housed one thousand statues of Thousand-armed Kannon in his Rengeōin Palace. With this diverse collection of costly art objects it seems that Go-Shirakawa hoped to demonstrate the range of his influence and to assert the prestige and authority of the imperial house, not to mention his political ambition to outdo his predecessors.[32]

It is noteworthy that Go-Shirakawa's era saw a proliferation of picture scrolls. Although their precise dates are unknown, the four *emaki* masterpieces *Genji monogatari emaki* (Picture Scroll of the Tale of Genji), *Ban Dainagon ekotoba*, *Shigisan engi* (Legends of the Shigisan Temple), and *Chōjū jinbutsu giga* (Scroll of Frolicking Animals and People) are believed to be products of Go-Shirakawa's time. To them might be added *Nezame monogatari emaki* (Scroll of the Tale of Nezame), *Kibi Daijin nittō ekotoba* (Picture Narrative of the Minister Kibi's Visit to China), *Kokawadera engi* (Legends of the Kokawa Temple), *Jigoku zōshi* (Scroll of Hell), *Gaki zōshi* (Scroll of Hungry Ghosts), and *Yamai no sōshi* (Scroll of Diseases and Deformities).[33] The following song in *Ryōjin hishō* suggests a poetic transcription of a part of the picture scroll *Chōjū jinbutsu giga*:

RH 392

ubara kogi no shita ni koso	Under the small brambles
itachi ga fue fuki saru kanade	the weasel plays the flute,
kai kanade	the monkey dances a scratchy dance,
inago maro mede hyōshi tsuku	while the grasshopper beats the time.
sate kirigirisu wa shōgo no	Cricket strokes the drums and cymbals,
shōgo no yoki jōzu	his sound is very fine.

It is not clear why the graphic arts flourished during Go-Shirakawa's time. But we may speculate that without court sponsorship in terms of interest and finance, such costly and time-consuming undertakings would have been impossible. Hence, the ample artistic harvest of picture scrolls at the end of the Heian period may owe much to the emperor's fascination with the visual arts.

Pilgrimages

Go-Shirakawa's enthusiasm also manifested itself in his religious activities, especially the making of pilgrimages. It is generally agreed that the religious pilgrimage tradition in Japan was instituted in the mid-Heian period (ninth century) by high priests who themselves had once made long pilgrimages to China.[34] Most representative of these leaders are Saichō (Dengyō Daishi, 767–822), founder of the Tendai sect of Buddhism; Kūkai (Kōbō Daishi, 774–835), founder of the Shingon sect; Ennin (Jikaku Daishi, 794–864); and Enchin (Chishō Daishi, 814–91).[35] Once implemented, pilgrimage became a lasting mass practice in Japan.

One region that particularly captured the popular imagination as a pilgrimage destination was Kumano in the south. The Kumano area has been important in Japanese history from mythical times, beginning with the story of Izanami, who reportedly was buried in the village of Arima. The people there are said to have commemorated her death by playing flutes, beating drums, and dedicating flowers and flags to her memory.[36] Although clearly this account describes funeral processions in general, it also conveys a particular association of Kumano with the mysterious, dark region of the dead.[37] The mythological significance of the Kumano region was heightened by its connection with Emperor Jinmu (r. 660–585 B.C.), who is said to have been guided through its terrain by a three-legged crow until he safely reached the Yamato plain.[38]

The first pilgrimage to Kumano by a sovereign was made by ex-Emperor Uda (r. 887–97) in the tenth month of 907. His journey did not, however, inspire an immediate following among the royal family, for a full eighty years passed before the next imperial pilgrimage was made, by ex-Emperor Kazan (r. 984–86) around 987. In fact, it was not until the *insei* period that the Kumano pilgrimage gained a real prominence at court. Emperor Shirakawa visited Kumano nine times after his abdication in 1086, Toba undertook the trip twenty-one times, and Go-Toba, twenty-eight. But it was Go-Shirakawa who set the record, making thirty-two pilgrimages to Kumano.[39]

Go-Shirakawa's first pilgrimage to Kumano took place in the year 1160, two years after his abdication. Thereafter, he repeated the journey almost annually for more than thirty years, making his last trip in 1191, a year before his death.[40] In some years he even went on the Kumano pilgrimage twice.[41] One round-trip to Kumano usually took about a month; considering the distance, preparations, retinues, accommodations, and, most of all, expense, it was an enormous undertaking.

The Kumano pilgrimage, which involved the endurance of significant austerities en route, was said to bring one longevity in this world and rebirth in paradise.[42] Its popularity and powerful appeal arose from a complex interplay of religious trends toward the end of the Heian period, including a syncretic fusion of indigenous mountain cults and the esoteric Shingon cosmology, which envisioned the region as the "matrix realm." The mountains of Kumano, reached only by a dangerous and arduous climb up forbidding precipices and through thick vegetation and forests, aroused a sense of otherworldliness in the pilgrims, as if they were nearing the presence of the divine. The Nachi Falls area and the nearby breathtaking shoreline were associated with the southern seashore at the foot of Mount Potalaka (Fudaraku in Japanese), the Pure Land of Kannon, and drew a large number of ascetics and pilgrims. Occasionally people drowned themselves there, in hopes of thereby attaining the Pure Land.[43]

Court diaries, such as Fujiwara Tamefusa's *Tamefusakyō ki* (Record of the Lord Tamefusa), Minamoto Morotoki's *Chōshūki*, Fujiwara Munetada's *Chūyūki*, Fujiwara Teika's *Meigetsuki*, and Go-Shirakawa's *Kudenshū*, all include personal accounts of the Kumano pilgrimage.[44] The devotional journey was preceded by an exacting preparatory regimen, involving strict abstinence from certain taboo foods and purification by bathing in the morning and evening prior to departure. Such discipline was required along the way as well, putting the pilgrims' will and perseverance to an extreme test. Sometimes they were pressed to pour cold river or well water over their bodies, and at other times to bathe in the sea, regardless of the time of year.[45] Accompanying the imperial retinue were priests, who performed the appropriate religious rites. Since Emperor Shirakawa's first Kumano pilgrimage had given this honor to priests of the Onjōji (Miidera) Temple, it became the rule to select the leader of the Kumano pilgrimage from that temple; thus a powerful alliance was forged between the court, Onjōji, and the Kumano region.[46]

A large number of subsidiary shrines sprang up along the Kumano pilgrimage route from Kyoto to the main Hongū Shrine, reportedly as many as ninety-nine; these served as resting places for pilgrims, offering a respite from physical strain and supplying material goods for the next leg of the difficult journey.[47] Nor was the pilgrimage utterly lacking in diversions. On at least three different occasions recorded in *Kudenshū*, Go-Shirakawa and his company, after completing basic religious observances, enjoyed some music on their way to Kumano, including the emperor's singing of *imayō* before an admiring audience.[48] Sometimes these performances were accompanied by dancing and acrobatics or by *koto* and *biwa* recitals as well.

Go-Shirakawa's frequent journeys to Kumano no doubt fueled the popularity of sacred pilgrimages in general and of pilgrimages to Kumano in particular.[49] Such expressions as "ari no kumano mōde" (the pilgrimage of ants to Kumano—a reference to the endless lines of people climbing the steep Kumano mountains)[50] convey vividly the fervor of this and probably similar trips of devotion.

Besides the long journeys to Kumano, Go-Shirakawa made a number of shorter trips to shrines and temples nearer the capital. *Kudenshū*, for example, lists pilgrimages to the Kamo (1169) and Iwashimizu Hachiman shrines (1178) and, farther to the west, the Itsukushima Shrine (1174).[51] During the Genpei War, when Go-Shirakawa could not travel as far as Kumano, he frequently visited the much closer Hie Shrine. During his last few years he often called at the Tennōji Temple, where, in the eighth month of 1187, at the age of sixty, he was consecrated in an esoteric rite of anointment.[52]

Each of the six pilgrimage accounts in *Kudenshū* records mystical revelations encountered on Go-Shirakawa's journeys. Sometimes these epiphanies were experienced directly by Go-Shirakawa himself, though more often they involved supernatural manifestations that appeared to members of his entourage or to a local shaman, who then delivered the divine message to the emperor. One such event occurred in the first month of 1162:

> Late that night [on the twelfth day] I went up to the main shrine [at the Kumano Shingū] again and, after circumambulating it, I stayed up all night in the ceremonial hall chanting the Sutra on the Thou-

sand-armed Kannon. Other people were there, but they dropped off to sleep in the corner of the hall, and nobody was sitting in front of me. Even Michiie, who was supposed to assist me in rolling the sutra scroll, was dozing off.

The noise of the offerings gradually subsided just past midnight. As I gazed toward the sanctuary, the sacred mirror was glittering faintly in the dim light. I was deeply moved; tears began to flow, and my heart became clean. About dawn, as I continued weeping and reciting the sutra, Sukekata, his own nightlong religious service over, came into the ceremonial hall. I said to him: "How about singing *imayō*? Now is the perfect time!" But he sat motionless out of respect for me. Since there was nothing else for me to do, I started out myself:

> Far above the vows of ten thousand buddhas
> trustworthy the vows of Thousand-armed Kannon;
> even withered grass and trees, so it is said,
> blossom and bear fruit in a moment. [RH 39]

I sang the song over and over again, and both Sukekata and Michiie joined in. Perhaps because of the serenity of my heart, the song seemed better and more enjoyable than usual. The priest Kakusan had completed his circumambulation and was performing an all-night ceremony under a pine tree in front of the shrine when he heard a voice from the top of the tree say, "Now is the time for our hearts to melt." It sounded so eerie that he was startled. He came rushing into the ceremonial hall and hurriedly reported to us what had happened. When a person concentrates single-mindedly on cleansing his heart, such things do happen.[53]

Regardless of the channels through which such extraordinary communications came, they served for Go-Shirakawa as public acknowledgment of divine favor. It must be noted that Go-Shirakawa promoted the idea that these miraculous events were rewards for his cumulative merit gained from daily, private religious observance. Even as they legitimized the difficulties, personal sacrifices, and expenses he bore on his pilgrimages, they confirmed his position as the sacred king. This point is borne out by a remark he cites in *Kudenshū*, uttered by his retainers on a trip he made to the Kamo Shrine in 1169: "Every time His Majesty comes in person, it seems that strange sounds are heard."[54] Thus Go-Shirakawa's many pilgrimages, culminating as they often did in mystical revelations, both fulfilled his desire to be in contact with the divine and augmented his worldly political status.

Go-Shirakawa's promotion of pilgrimage was demonstrated not only by his own visits to sacred sites around the country, but also by his construction in the capital of proxy shrines. For instance, the Ima-Hie Shrine, built in 1160 in the Higashiyama area in the eastern part of the Heian capital, invoked the divinities of the Hie Shrine to protect his Hōjūji Palace. Go-Shirakawa is known to have made thirty-six pilgrimages to the shrine over the years.[55] In similar manner, the nearby Ima-Kumano Shrine, erected in 1161, summoned the Kumano triad as overseers; this shrine is noted for its elaborate and imposing rituals and celebrations.[56] The basic idea was that a shortened and simplified form of pilgrimage was as effective and valid as one made to the distant shrines themselves. Apparently these shrines also served religious purposes for common people, who had neither the financial nor the physical means to undertake long pilgrimages to distant regions like Kumano.[57]

In his sponsorship of religious and cultural activities, Go-Shirakawa was to a great extent motivated by political considerations, including the desire to restore imperial prestige and power. Yet in his view, artistic performances—particularly of *imayō*—could also serve as vehicles of spiritual salvation. By anthologizing *imayō* in *Ryōjin hishō*, he implied a correspondence between art and religion: rather than being the handmaiden of religion, art was worthy of the same degree of devotion as religion.

3 Go-Shirakawa and *Ryōjin hishō*

Compilation of *Ryōjin hishō*

The compilation of *Ryōjin hishō* and *Kudenshū* was an ambitious undertaking. What primarily compelled Go-Shirakawa was the lack of any critical appraisal of *imayō* up to his time, as he states in the preamble of *Kudenshū*: "Many treatises and commentaries have been written on *waka* poems, but as no such precedent exists for *imayō*, I have put together this collection using Toshiyori's *Zuinō* as a model."[1] Go-Shirakawa's choice of *Zuinō* (Poetic Essentials, ca. 1115) by Minamoto Toshiyori (or Shunrai, 1055–1129?) as his exemplar is significant.[2] This work stands in the tradition of Japanese *waka* poetic treatises, beginning with the preface of *Kokinshū* (ca. 905) and continued by Mibu no Tadamine's (fl. 898–920) *Wakatei jusshu* (Ten *Waka* Styles, 945; also known as *Tadamine juttei*, Tadamine's Ten Styles) and Fujiwara Kintō's (966–1041) *Shinsen zuinō* (Essentials of Poetry, Newly Compiled) and *Waka kuhon* (Nine Styles of *Waka*), both supposedly completed between 1004 and 1012. An innovative poet in his own right, Toshiyori in *Zuinō* lamented the sterility of *waka* in his time and advocated the revitalization of *waka* practice through a new, freer, more unconventional use of language, diction, and poetic ideas.[3] The most outstanding aspect of *Zuinō* was the inclusion of a group of *setsuwa uta* (poems with historical anecdotes), for which Toshiyori provided critical interpretations that uncovered the stories surrounding the poems.[4] This anecdotal approach and his methods of explication represented the most innovative changes in the history of Japanese poetic criticism and were to be emulated by later poetic tracts.[5] Given this background, Go-Shirakawa's undertaking can be seen as an attempt to canonize the *imayō* genre and accord it its rightful place vis-à-vis *waka*. Indeed, a number of *imayō* in *Ryōjin hishō* have a similar anecdotal or *setsuwa* flavor, as does the very narrative flow of *Kudenshū* itself.

Go-Shirakawa feared that *imayō*, as a purely vocal art, was in danger of dying out: "Those who write Chinese poems, compose *waka*, and practice calligraphy can preserve their works in writing and leave them for posterity, thus saving them from destruction. In the case of vocal music the sad fact is that once I am gone, nothing will be left behind. For this reason, I have committed to writing the oral transmission of *imayō*, hitherto never undertaken, for the sake of future generations."[6] This statement equates *imayō* with the other principal aesthetic pursuits cultivated by the late-Heian elites. Yet one feature distinguishes *imayō* from the other genres mentioned, and that is its orality. While *waka*, Chinese poems, and calligraphy are all written arts, *imayō* is essentially an oral performative art: it disappears the instant a song is completed. *Imayō* can never be recaptured or repeated exactly as it was uttered. Go-Shirakawa's recognition of the irretrievable, temporal nature of *imayō* music and its perishability provided him with the incentive to compile *Ryōjin hishō*. In essence, *Ryōjin hishō* represents Go-Shirakawa's attempt to overcome the limitations inherent in *imayō* as oral art by giving it a chirographic dimension.

An additional impetus could be the fact that Go-Shirakawa had not yet found a disciple to whom he could convey his art. Awareness that his own death would mean the end of the authentic transmission of *imayō* must have stimulated him to commit the oral tradition of *imayō* to writing. At the very end of *Kudenshū*, in fact, Go-Shirakawa laments the fate of *imayō* once he was gone, even though by then he had secured two successors.[7]

Ryōjin hishō represents the most comprehensive attempt since *Man'yōshū* (Collection for Ten Thousand Generations, ca. 759) to collect an oral tradition and put it in writing. By Go-Shirakawa's time, the Japanese aristocracy had passed from the age of orality into that of literacy.[8] The folk tradition, however, was still primarily oral. The transmission of oral material depended entirely on the power of memory through direct master-disciple contact, as is seen in Go-Shirakawa's own training under Otomae and, later, his training of his two disciples. In compiling *Ryōjin hishō*, Go-Shirakawa effectively transformed that oral legacy into a literate medium, for now the songs were available to the entire reading public, not to mention succeeding generations.

Go-Shirakawa apparently realized that his project to collect *imayō* was done in a larger context, that of the entire Japanese song tradition begin-

ning with *kagura*. His sense of this history is recorded clearly in Book 1
of *Kudenshū*:

> There are several song forms that have been transmitted from long
> ago to the present. They are called *kagura, saibara,* and *fuzoku*.
> *Kagura* originated in the age when the Goddess Amaterasu pushed
> open the gate of the rock cave, whereas *saibara* has its origin in the
> songs of people from various provinces who dedicated their tributes
> to the Ministry of the Treasury. These songs are not something to be
> taken lightly, because they convey the people's praise of good govern-
> ment, as well as their censure of the evils of misgovernment. *Saibara*
> is a musical arrangement made possible by adding elegance to Japa-
> nese melodies and accompaniment of *koto, biwa,* and flute. It is
> used for official and private entertainment. All of these song forms
> have the power to move heaven and earth, to pacify the angry gods,
> and are an effective means of governing the country and benefit-
> ing its people. *Fuzoku* is used at palace music rehearsals or on pilgrim-
> ages to the Kamo Shrine. In the olden days, it used to be performed
> at the banquets of aristocrats, but recently it has ceased to be used
> on these occasions. Besides these forms, another oral song tradition
> exists—*imayō*. The number of songs is large and its repertoire
> is wide, with songs in such categories as *kamiuta, mononoyō,* and
> *tauta*.[9]

Here, Go-Shirakawa seeks to establish *imayō* as part of an unbroken
classical song tradition. The earlier song forms, moreover, provided Go-
Shirakawa with models, for they had been collected and put into writing
before Go-Shirakawa's time. The oldest extant *kagurauta* text, for instance, is believed to have been written down during the late tenth or early
eleventh century, some hundred years before Go-Shirakawa began to
compile *Ryōjin hishō*.[10] The same was true of *saibara*, texts of which from
different musical lineages were being committed to writing toward the
end of the Heian period, when Go-Shirakawa was making his collection
of *imayō*.[11] Thus, Go-Shirakawa's cultivation of *imayō* and his compilation
of *Ryōjin hishō* served two functions: to continue the Japanese song
tradition and to anthologize song texts for posterity.

Several features, however, set *Ryōjin hishō* apart from other song
collections. The most conspicuous is the size of the original collection. No
known *kagurauta* or *saibara* collections of the period come close to matching the number of songs included in *Ryōjin hishō*. Furthermore, *Ryōjin
hishō* represents a collection of popular songs that were still being generated and circulated among the people, whereas both *kagurauta* and *saibara*

had already lost their popular appeal, in part because of their longer usage in court and their consequent conservative, ritualized nature.[12]

Go-Shirakawa's interest in *imayō* may be seen in part as an expression of his unconventionality, as he sought to distinguish himself in his pursuit of the new and unorthodox. More significantly, however, Go-Shirakawa probably discerned in *imayō* a possible means of revitalizing court music. As an accomplished singer of both *kagurauta* and *saibara*, Go-Shirakawa surely recognized the enervated status of those traditions and may have wanted to infuse some regenerative elements into existing popular song.

Imayō Poetics

Go-Shirakawa's view of *imayō* is imbued with a mystical sense that allowed him to see the songs as more than a medium of artistic communication. His devotion to *imayō* eventually developed into an esoteric belief concerning the power of song. For Go-Shirakawa, *imayō* possessed a magico-religious potency that could produce a desired result, whether involving immediate, pragmatic benefits in this world or rebirth in the next. Here we must recognize that in his *imayō* poetics Go-Shirakawa saw no distinction between the secular and the profane. This passage in *Kudenshū* is representative: "The *imayō* that are popular these days are not intended simply for entertainment. When they are sung with sincerity at shrines or temples, they bring about divine revelations and fulfill our wishes. They obtain for people their desire for official positions, prolong human life, and immediately cure illnesses."[13] Go-Shirakawa substantiates his claim of the religious efficacy of *imayō* by citing in *Kudenshū* seven publicly known or legendary cases in which either a miraculous healing (four cases) or rebirth in the next world (three cases) was effected through the whole-hearted singing of *imayō*[14]:

> [Fujiwara] Atsuie, who had a superb voice, was detained on Mount Kinbu by the deities as their kin.[15] When Inspector Kiyotsune fell critically ill, Mei sang, "In the age of the Imitation Dharma, what can we do but rely on Yakushi's vow?" and he was instantly cured. More recently, when Michisue, the chief of the left gate guards, was suffering from a dangerous fever, he twice sang the *imayō* "Don't ever slander the Lotus Sutra followers" and, after sweating, was cured.[16] A person suffering from a tumor on his neck was gravely ill and had even been given up on by the doctors, so he secluded himself in Kōryūji Temple and sang *imayō* with the utmost concentration.[17] Immediately the tumor shrank and disappeared. A blind person se-

cluded himself within a shrine for more than a hundred days and sang *imayō*, and he left with his sight restored. The list does not stop here. Tonekuro, an *asobi*, was caught up in some fighting, and before breathing her last she sang "Now is the time for the Western Pure Land," whereby she attained rebirth.[18] Shirōgimi of Takasago attained her lifelong wish for rebirth in the Pure Land by singing "Prince Shōtoku."[19]

Go-Shirakawa's advocacy of the supernatural *mantric* potency of *imayō* is reminiscent of many related practices—in his age, particularly prominent in Pure Land Buddhism—based on the power of words to produce supramundane and religious results (*kotodama*). The incidents he cites illustrate the belief that *imayō* art, when pursued with the utmost dedication, can coerce supernatural intervention in the temporal order and can even substitute for institutionalized religion. Go-Shirakawa's identification of *imayō*'s pragmatic power with such miraculous phenomena thus represents an ultimate sanctification of *imayō*.

As if to underscore this point, Go-Shirakawa also recounts his own six epiphanic moments that occurred as a direct consequence of *imayō* performances. Invariably, such incidents occurred during his pilgrimages to shrines and temples, and mostly at night.[20] All of these visionary experiences are recorded as also having been witnessed by bystanders, usually members of his retinue. One of the most memorable incidents took place at the Kumano Shrine in 1169. After singing *imayō* all night, Go-Shirakawa, who was soon to take the tonsure, realized that this would be his last sacred journey as a layperson. He thus expended extra effort to make the occasion special by covering most of the categories of *imayō*.[21] He recalls:

> When everything became quiet around dawn, I sang this *ichiko* with an especially serene heart. Thereupon, from the western side of the main shrine, an indescribable fragrance wafted in. Narichika asked Chikanobu, "What's happening? Do you notice a fragrance?" While all the people there were puzzling over it, a roaring sound broke out as if the sanctuary were rumbling. Shaken anew, Narichika asked, "What is it all about?" I replied, "It may be the flapping sound of the chickens in their sleep after they have taken temporary shelter elsewhere." After a while, the fragrance completely enveloped the hall. Then the sanctuary curtain rose and swayed as if someone were passing through. The sacred hanging mirror also swayed, and everything else rocked for a while. By then, as though startled, the phantom vanished. It was then between two and four o'clock in the morning.[22]

The reason for the inclusion of this incident in Go-Shirakawa's memoir may have been related to his mystical conception of *imayō* art as able to move the spirits.

But Go-Shirakawa found a significance in *imayō* that ventured far beyond the confines of the temporal order. Ultimately, in his view, *imayō* could be a vehicle of religious salvation:

> Why shouldn't singing *imayō* contribute to my securing a seat on the lotus pedestal in paradise? . . . *Hōmon uta* is no different from the words in the sutra. Each of the eight scrolls of the Lotus Sutra radiates light, and each character in the twenty-eight chapters is a golden buddha. Why shouldn't secular words, too, transform themselves into praises of buddha and become a wheel for propagating the Dharma?[23]

The lyrics of most *hōmon uta* are derived from a number of sutras, most often the Lotus Sutra; some amount to direct quotes from these sacred texts. The *imayō* genre, however, also encompassed openly erotic themes and other profane subjects seemingly opposed to the concerns of the predominantly religious *hōmon uta*. What is noteworthy is Go-Shirakawa's advocacy of *imayō* of different persuasion and content than *hōmon uta* as nevertheless fulfilling the same function as *hōmon uta*. To understand this all-encompassing view of art and its relationship to religion, one must comprehend the concept of *kyōgen kigyo* (or *kyōgen kigo*), "delusive words and decorative language."

During the mid-Heian period, the notion of *kyōgen kigyo* was popular among men of letters, especially those well versed in Chinese poetry and classics. They formed a literary circle called Kangaku-e (Learning Encouragement Meeting) under the leadership of Yoshishige Yasutane (ca. 931–1002). Its main members over the decades included such leading scholars of the day as Minamoto Shitagō (911–83), Fujiwara Arikuni (943–1011), Tachibana Yorihira (dates unknown), Takashina no Moriyoshi (dates unknown), Ki no Tadana (957–99), Minamoto Toshikata (960–1027), Ōe no Masahira (952–1012), Minamoto Tamenori (b. 1011), Fujiwara Koreshige (953–89), and Ōe no Koretoki (or Yukitoki).[24] The chief goal of this group was to achieve a harmonious relationship between their literary activity and Buddhist religious concepts and practices. What helped these literati in their search for such a synthesis and also for a justification of their engagement in secular literature was the Buddhist dialectic embodied in the dictum *kyōgen kigyo*, a phrase coined by the T'ang poet Po Chü-i (772–846): "My aspiration is that the karma wrought by my secular literary work in the present life, with its delusive words and decorative language, becomes for future worlds a medium of praising the Dharma and a cause for propagating the Buddha's teaching."[25]

Traditionally, Buddhism took a negative stance toward human language, warning of its fallibility and inability to transmit ultimate truth. In this conceptual framework, words, especially literature, are the epitome of delusion, absolutely lacking in substance and truth and depicting a phantom world with no reference to reality.[26] Ultimately, literature as a class of human activity is held to exert an insidiously corrupting influence over its readers, luring them from the truth. Under such stringent doctrinal proscription, the conflict faced by the writers of secular literature based on fiction was inevitably acute.

Others, however, argued that like the celebrated parables in the Lotus Sutra, fiction could serve as a superb vehicle—or expedient means (Skt., *upāya*; *hōben*)—of enlightenment.[27] In these critics' view, the conceptual dualism of secular literature and religious truth was itself a form of delusion, focusing only on the superficial differences while missing the essential unity that informs the world of phenomena. Pushed to its logical conclusion, this radical Buddhist dialectic identified transmigration with nirvana and delusion with enlightenment.[28] When these seeming polarities are balanced so that they cancel each other out, a new concept of secular literature and its profane languages emerges, guided by a single ideological purpose: to propagate the Buddhist ultimate truths.

This acknowledgment of the coexistence in a single continuum of the secular and the religious in literature, based on *kyōgen kigyo*, helped to set the poetic ideal for generations of *waka* poets after the Kangaku-e. It gained an ever-widening following throughout the Heian period and eventually provided one foundation for Heian poetics. *Kyōgen kigyo* also figures prominently in the poetics of Go-Shirakawa's contemporaries and the *waka* luminaries Fujiwara Shunzei and Saigyō, where it received further elaboration.[29] The complete passage by Po Chü-i quoted above was even adopted into the *rōei* genre and included in *Wakan rōeishū* (Collection of Japanese and Chinese Poems, ca. 1013), compiled by Fujiwara Kintō.[30]

The application of the *kyōgen kigyo* concept to *imayō* is not limited to an abstract enunciation in Go-Shirakawa's memoir. The same idea is reiterated and embodied in one of the *Ryōjin hishō* songs, which reads:

RH 222

kyōgen kigyo no ayamachi wa hotoke o homuru tane to shite	Crazy words and fancy talk, even these errors hold the seeds of Buddha-praise.
araki kotoba mo ikanaru mo	Reckless speech, or any such thing,
daichigi to ka ni zo kaerunaru	returns to the ultimate truth of the Dharma.

In this salvational scheme, art is a superb vehicle or expedient means. Here we discern an echo of the religious ethos of the late Heian period, which increasingly identified art with religion itself and thereby heightened the status of secular cultural activities by bringing them on par with the sacred.

Imayō Politics

In addition to these literary and religious concerns for *imayō*, there was another important reason for Go-Shirakawa to turn to that song form. The following statement, cited above, in retrospect is full of implications: "All of these song forms have the power to move heaven and earth, to pacify angry gods, and are *an effective means of governing the country and benefitting its people.*"[31] The first half of the passage is almost a verbatim recitation of a passage by Ki no Tsurayuki (ca. 872–945) in the Japanese preface to *Kokinshū*, itself based on Chinese precedents. It is the second half, with its largely Confucian emphasis on the political use of the arts, that interests us here. The implication is that these songs, by virtue of their origin with the people, reflect the popular will and can serve as an index of the affairs of the nation at large. When listened to carefully, therefore, these songs could provide valuable cues for proper and judicious rule.[32]

Go-Shirakawa's statement also represents a certain nostalgia for the golden past when the sovereign, as a living god, ruled over a happy and prosperous land. In Go-Shirakawa's own day, the unsettled political situation and the decline of real imperial power would have made the Confucian ideal, presented in the Confucian classics, all the more attractive.

Go-Shirakawa was of course not the first to recognize the political dimension of popular song. In fact, the prototypes for *kagurauta, saibara,* and *fuzoku* were songs dedicated to the central government on special ritual occasions such as the enthronement ceremony (*daijōsai*) and the new grain dedication ceremony. These songs, all from the nonimperial powerful lineages in the outlying regions, were offered as symbolic tokens of submission to imperial rule and as pledges of loyalty. The importance of the *kagurauta* performed during the *daijōsai* has long been recognized,[33] but attention must be extended to the whole range of performance arts staged during these ritual times. Their delivery signified a yielding of the collective tribal identity, even the very soul of the lineage itself, to the imperial line.[34] More often than not, artistic performances dedicated to the emperor himself were valued as highly as material offerings, signifying as they did ideological surrender to the central government, and frequently became mandatory parts of such rituals at court.[35] Thus Go-Shirakawa, perceiving the unique relationship between politics and popular music, recorded the usefulness of such music in his *Kudenshū* and may have partially exploited the implications of that relationship when he personally involved himself in the collection and preservation of the most widely popular song form of his time, *imayō*.

The imperial anthologies of *waka*, the crème de la crème of elitist poetic endeavors, were all commissioned works, not compilations by emperors. In choosing to compile *imayō* songs himself, Go-Shirakawa stands out as a unique figure. He alone seemed to have possessed a keen awareness of the need to preserve *imayō*, not to mention the perseverance and commitment to complete the task.

4 Poetic Forms and Techniques

Ryōjin hishō contains three major types of songs: *hōmon uta* (literally, songs of Buddhist scriptures; 220 songs), *shiku no kamiuta* (four-line god songs; 204 songs), and *niku no kamiuta* (two-line god songs; 121 songs). These divisions seem to be based on differences in musical mode rather than in subject matter, for a large number of songs related to Buddhism appear not only in *hōmon uta* but frequently in *shiku no kamiuta* and even occasionally in *niku no kamiuta* as well. In addition, song texts are often duplicated in the anthology, either within a single section or in different subsections.[1] The *hōmon uta* probably bore traces of melodic solemnity, as their origins are traced to the Buddhist ceremonial music used in temples. In contrast, both *shiku no kamiuta* and *niku no kamiuta* shared the musical characteristics of *kaguraūta* performed at Shinto shrines, which derived from folk songs and so bear a closer affinity to secular music than do *hōmon uta*.[2]

All three song types take distinctly different poetic forms. *Hōmon uta* usually consist of a four-line stanza, each line with a 7-5 or 8-5 syllable count.[3] *Shiku no kamiuta* are characterized by much looser prosodic structure than *hōmon uta*; although many have a four-line stanza, with each line displaying a 7-5 or 8-5 syllable count (like *hōmon uta*), some deviate from this formula, being irregular in meter and line length. *Niku no kamiuta* are also distinguished by a variety of formal arrangements: a majority exhibit *waka* prosody with the 5-7-5-7-7 syllable count, but a considerable number have far more lines and an irregular meter.

Hōmon uta

The name *hōmon uta* is believed to have been used for the first time in *Ryōjin hishō*; it does not appear in any other contemporary sources. The term may have been coined by the compiler of the anthology, Go-

Shirakawa, to distinguish this subgroup of *imayō* of dominantly Buddhist content from others of secular theme.[4]

The *hōmon uta* section is the largest in the extant *Ryōjin hishō*, making up about 40 percent of the total. It shows the highest degree of uniformity, homogeneity, and stability in terms of themes, prosodic structure, and formal arrangement. The entire section is devoted to the single topic of Buddhism, its elaborate organizational design reflecting Go-Shirakawa's careful attention to his material as well as his knowledge of Buddhist thought and doctrines. This concern may have resulted from Go-Shirakawa's assertion in *Kudenshū* that these songs reflected the sacred scripture itself and for that reason alone deserved meticulous handling.[5]

The *hōmon uta* are divided into carefully defined categories based on the conceptual framework of the "three baskets" or "Three Treasures" of Buddhism—the Buddha, the Dharma (or the Law), and the Sangha (community of Buddhist priests). This tripartite division serves not only as a formal classificatory scheme but also as a reminder of the basic articles of belief in Buddhism. An additional and final division in the section, called *zō* (miscellaneous), represents an amalgam of the elements found in the preceding sections plus a few strains of personal lyricism.

The sutra section of the *hōmon uta* is the largest, comprising 125 songs (56.8 percent of the entire section). The songs are further arranged according to the "Five Periods" of the Buddha's teachings following his enlightenment, a chronology devised by Chih-i (538–97), the founder of the Chinese T'ien-t'ai school of Buddhism (the Tendai sect in Japan). The corresponding five categories of sutras are known as Hua yen (Kegon in Japanese), Lu yüan (Rokuen or Agon), Fang teng (Hōdō), Po-jo (Hannya), and Fa hua Nieh-p'an (Hokke-nehan). A majority (114, or 91.2 percent) of the sutra songs in the *hōmon uta* section are related to the Lotus Sutra, which the Tendai sect especially emphasizes; this fact clearly reflects Emperor Go-Shirakawa's own religious leaning toward Tendai.

The order of arrangement of *hōmon uta* in *Ryōjin hishō* is closely parallel to that of the twenty-eight chapters of the Lotus Sutra, rendering the *hōmon uta* section almost a Lotus Sutra in miniature. The following three songs, which appropriate some of the best-known parables of the Lotus Sutra, illustrate this feature:

RH 73

osanaki kodomo o okotsuru to	To coax the tiny children out
mitsu no kuruma o kamaetsutsu	three carts were built;
kado no hoka ni shi idenureba	but after they passed the gate,
hitotsu guruma ni noritamau	they all rode together in one.[6]

RH 77

chōja wa waga ko no kanashisa ni	In pity for his son, the rich man
yōraku koromo o nugisutete	took off his glorious robe.
ayashiki sugata ni narite koso	Taking on the look of poverty,
yōyaku chikazukitamai shi ka	slowly, he drew the son near.[7]

RH 93

shitashiki tomo no ie ni yuki	Wine-drunk at his friend's house
sake ni ei fushi fuseru hodo	flat out on the floor,
koromo no ura ni kaku tama o	how pathetic, he doesn't know of
shiranu hito koso awarenare	the gem sewn inside his own robe![8]

Hōmon uta versification is considered to have grown out of the Buddhist hymns, especially from *wasan* (Buddhist hymns written in Japanese), which were used in temple services or lecture meetings.[9] *Wasan* were based on *kansan* (Buddhist hymns written in Chinese), which in turn derived from *bonsan* (hymns written in Sanskrit).[10] These were songs praising the Buddha, his major disciples, bodhisattvas, and illustrious priests, as well as interpretations of doctrinal points.

Kansan came to Japan along with Buddhism and were soon being imitated by Japanese Buddhists. Later, a Japanese genre of *kansan* emerged, including a work, "Shihō gokuraku san" (Praise of the Western Paradise), written by Prince Tomohira (964–1009), the seventh son of Emperor Murakami (r. 946–76).[11] Others who composed in this genre included such members of the Kangaku-e as Yoshishige Yasutane, Ōe no Yukitoki, Ōe no Masahira, and Ki no Tadana. In the long run, however, the *kansan* form was felt to be too rigid and abstruse to be understood clearly by the general public; as a foreign linguistic medium, it was simply inadequate to express indigenous thoughts and emotions.[12] The *wasan* form likely arose as an attempt to overcome such drawbacks.

The development of *wasan* coincided with the emergence of a national literature, represented by the *waka* revival in the mid-Heian period. At first, *wasan* creation was centered among mid-Heian Buddhist leaders, especially those scholarly monks of the Tendai school on Mount Hiei.[13] *Wasan* were on the themes of the Buddha, Dharma, and Sangha, the "Three Treasures of Buddhism," and were sung in front of the Buddhas.[14] The earliest known *wasan*, "Honkakusan" (Praise of the Original Awakening of the Buddha), is attributed to the priest Ryōgen (Jie Daishi, 912–

85).[15] This work was followed by such *wasan* classics as "Gokurakukoku mida wasan" (Praise of the Amida in Paradise), by Senkan (918–83), and "Tendai Daishi wasan" (Praise of the Great Tendai Priest [i.e., Chih-i]), "Raigō wasan" (Praise of the Amida's Welcome of His Believers into His Paradise), and "Gokuraku rokuji san" (Praise of the Sixth Hour in Paradise), all written by the abbot Genshin.[16]

Basically, a *wasan* consists of lines with a syllable count of 7-5, and some of the early *wasan* are rather lengthy. "Tendai Daishi wasan," for example, is 230 lines long, while "Gokuraku rokuji san" is epic in scale, having 878 lines.[17] Certain parts of a *wasan*, however, consisted of semantically complete units of four lines, inherently allowing independent four-line stanzas to be formed. It is believed that such fragmentation gave rise to the four-line *hōmon uta* form, especially when the units were suitable for chanting.[18]

Some *hōmon uta* in *Ryōjin hishō*, in fact, are direct extracts from longer *wasan* works. For instance, no. 224, on the priest Chih-i, is taken from Genshin's "Tendai Daishi wasan," while nos. 43 and 227 are based on his "Gokuraku rokuji san."[19] Similarly, nos. 172 and 174, each consisting of four lines, are extracted from "Shari wasan" (Praise of Buddha's Relics) by Yōkan (Eikan, 1032–1111);[20] no. 18 derives from "Kūya wasan" (Kūya's Praise) attributed to Kūya Shōnin (903–72), an early Pure Land proselytizer among the common people; and no. 30 has its origin in "Gokurakukoku mida wasan."[21] The following song is a specimen of such direct quotes:

RH 43

mayu no aida no byakugō wa	The white tuft between Amida's brows
itsutsu no sumi o zo atsumetaru	are five Mount Sumerus put together.
manako no aida no shōren wa	And the lotus-blue of his eyes
shidaikai o zo tataetaru	holds the water of four great seas.[22]

Compared with *wasan*, *hōmon uta* have greater flexibility in lexical choice, syntactic arrangement, and mode of delivery. Despite efforts to make *wasan* a more tractable mode than *kansan*, it still bore the imprint of its predecessor, especially in a rigidity that came from forcing Chinese verses to fit into the native 7-5 or 8-5 prosody.[23] With *hōmon uta*, Japanese poets overcame many of the barriers between the two languages by more skillfully mingling Buddhist terms (couched in Chinese loan-words) with indigenous diction, phrasing, rhetorical devices, and syntactic structuring.

Although not completely free of the constraints inherited from *wasan*, the *hōmon uta* form was thus better able to reduce cumbersome generic constraints, thereby achieving a softer tone. With *hōmon uta*, in other words, a closer approximation to the vernacular could be effected, and the foreign linguistic medium thus achieved a sort of naturalization. In the end, it represents an intermediate poetic form between formalistic temple ritual songs (*kungata, kyōke,* or *wasan*) and subjective or lyrical *waka* on Buddhist themes (*shakkyōka*), which is for personal use, not to be sung in front of the Buddha in the temple.[24] Herein rest the characteristics of the *hōmon uta* as a poetic form.

Shiku no kamiuta

The *shiku no kamiuta* section of *Ryōjin hishō* differs markedly from the *hōmon uta* in terms of organization, formal characteristics, and poetic technique. In place of the exacting categorical divisions of *hōmon uta*, only six general nominal groupings differentiate the *shiku no kamiuta*: *jinbun* (Shinto-Buddhist syncretic ceremony, 35 songs); *butsu* (the Buddhas, 11), *kyō* (the sutras, 7), *sō* (the Sangha, 12), *reigensho uta* (songs on miraculous sites, 9), and *zō* (miscellaneous, 130). Each verse, moreover, has much looser and freer prosody than is the case with *hōmon uta*. As regards subject matter, in contrast to the preoccupation with Buddhist metaphysics in the *hōmon uta* and the accompanying foreign exoticism, the *shiku no kamiuta* focus largely on aspects of mundane Japanese life.

In general, but by no means invariably, *shiku no kamiuta* consist of a four-line stanza (as their name suggests) with a syllable count of 8-5 or 7-5. Thirty-two of the total 204 *shiku no kamiuta* (15.7 percent), however, depart from the four-line format, usually with an increase in line number. For instance, no. 314, the longest song of this genre in *Ryōjin hishō*, has fourteen lines, while no. 257 is a mere three lines long. In addition, almost half the total *shiku no kamiuta* lines deviate from the 7-5 or 8-5 syllabic scheme; this subgenre, in other words, is somewhat loose in terms of prosody. These facts led to speculation that *shiku no kamiuta* were born of the contact between the relatively regulated four-line *hōmon uta* form and the much looser form of folk songs.[25]

Shiku no kamiuta frequently include exclamatory particles such as *ya, yo,* or *na*, orchestra words (*hayashikotoba*) such as *ya*, and repeated words or phrases; occasionally onomatopoeia make an appearance as well. The following song about the mystic power of shamans is one instance in which most of these elements are present, resulting in a striking rhythmic quality:

RH 324

suzu wa saya furu tōta miko	What a way to shake bells, girl!
me yori kami ni zo suzu wa furu	Now shake them above your eyes,
yurayura to furi agete	jingle them high, Tōta, jingle!
me yori shimo ni te suzu fureba	If you shake them low, shrine-maiden,
ketai nari to te	below your eyes, the angry gods
yuyushi kami haradachitamau	will call you lazy.

The most noted technique in *shiku no kamiuta* is known as *mono zukushi* (cataloging device). More than eighty *Ryōjin hishō* songs can be counted in this category, some seventy of which are *shiku no kamiuta*. Four basic syntactic forms characterize the cataloging songs: (1) a line with adjectival + *mono* + *wa*; (2) the same structure, but without *wa*; (3) a line with an adjectival (or *no*) or adverbial + nominal excluding *mono* (it could also be *rentai kei*, attributive form of verbs or adjectives) + *wa*; and (4) the same structure, but without *wa*.

Regardless of differences in the syntactic arrangement, the first line is critical because it sets the topic and mood for each verse. It specifies what the song is about, raising curiosity and expectations. Subsequent lines are usually a straight inventory of objects related to that topic. Although no specific rules govern the number of lines in a song, on the whole *mono-zukushi* songs take a four-line stanza form.

The following are examples for each of the four categories:

RH 332

kokoro no sumu mono wa	Things that cool the heart:
aki wa yamada no io goto ni	clappers to frighten the deer in autumn,
shika odorokasuchō hita no koe	sounding from every mountain watchman's hut;
koromo shide utsu tsuchi no oto	the sound of fulling blocks beating cloth.[26]

RH 429

kokoro sugoki mono	Things that chill the heart:
yomichi funamichi	travel by night, travel by boat,
tabi no sora tabi no yado	the sky above the traveler, the lodging on his way

koguraki yamadera no kyō no
  koe
omou ya nakarai no akade noku

sutras chanted from a mountain
  temple in the dark forest,
lovers parting, ah!, too soon.

RH 334

tsune ni koisuru wa
sora ni wa tanabata yobaiboshi

nobe ni wa yamadori aki wa
  shika
nagare no kyūdachi fuyu wa
  oshi

Always in love:
in the sky, the Weaver Maiden
  and the shooting stars;
pheasants in the fields, the
  autumn deer;
courtesans of the floating world;
  in wintertime, mandarin
  ducks.

RH 432

haru no hajime no utamakura

kasumi uguisu kaeru kari

ne no bi aoyagi mume sakura

michitose ni naru momo no
  hana

The poetic imagery of early
  spring:
mist, bush warblers, geese
  coming home,
the Day of the Rat, green
  willows, plum blossoms,
  cherry blossoms;
the peach blossom bearing fruit
  once in three thousand
  years.[27]

Within the cataloging songs, the *michiyuki* (road travel) type, signaled by the phrase *e mairu michi* ("the road to pilgrimage") or *jūsho wa doko doko zo* ("where, oh where, is the residence") and usually used for listing sacred pilgrimage sites, forms a subgroup with formulaic overtones. For instance, the following song on the major leaders of Heian Buddhism makes use of this list-making technique:

RH 295

daishi no jūsho wa doko doko zo

dengyō jikaku wa hie no yama

yokawa no mimyō to ka

chishō daishi wa miidera ni na

Where do the great masters
  live? Where?
Dengyō and Jikaku on Mount
  Hiei,
they say, in Yokawa's
  mausoleum;
Master Chishō in Miidera
  Temple, yes,

kōbō daishi wa kōya no oyama	and Master Kōbō on holy
ni	Mount Kōya,
mada owashimasu	there still he lives.[28]

In one sweeping stroke, the song names the Buddhist giants of the age and their institutional affiliations, showing respect by honoring them with their posthumous official titles. A who's who of the pillars of Japanese Buddhism, this list would have provided an effective mnemonic device for learning these important facts.

The technique of making poetic lists is by no means a novel invention. A prototype already appeared in two *Kojiki* poems, one in *michiyuki* form (no. 58), the other as a simple enumeration (no. 100).[29] *Nihonshoki* (Chronicle of Japan, 720) contains one *michiyuki*-type poem (no. 94),[30] while four *michiyuki* in *chōka* (long poems) can be found in book 13 of *Man'yōshū* (nos. 3230, 3236, 3237, and 3240). The tradition was continued by Heian-period *saibara*,[31] and by the prose monument in catalog making, the *Makura no sōshi* of Sei Shōnagon. The large number of catalog songs in *Ryōjin hishō* and the variety of techniques that they display may qualify the anthology as the veritable poetic counterpart of *Makura no sōshi*.

Niku no kamiuta

The *niku no kamiuta* section contains the smallest number of songs in *Ryōjin hishō*—only 121—and yet it represents a fascinating study in contrasts in terms of structure and form.

First, we find an elaborately broken-down subsection of *jinja uta* (shrine songs), with sixteen subheadings for only sixty-one songs, sandwiched between two untitled subsections comprising sixty songs in all. Second, while the *jinja uta* are adopted largely from *waka* poems with verified authorship, the songs in the two untitled subsections are entirely anonymous. Third, the name *niku no kamiuta*, generally translated as "two-line god songs," is itself open to interpretation. *Niku* may refer to a poem of two lines; more likely, though, the reference is to songs constructed like a *waka* poem, in which a third line (of five) serves as a caesura, breaking the whole into two "parts."[32] In fact, the majority of *niku no kamiuta*, mostly in the *jinja uta* section, fit this latter formal category. The following song demonstrates this feature well, with *uchitataki* serving as a caesura:

RH 517

| inariyama | Answer, oh god, |
| mitsu no tamagaki | my plea, please, |

uchitataki	I am pounding
waga negi goto zo	on the three jeweled fences
kami mo kotae yo	at Inari Shrine![33]

The *niku no kamiuta*, in fact, include too many exceptions to be called simply "two-line" songs. The following untitled song is an extreme case, comprising seven lines of irregular prosodic scheme:

RH 461

tsuwari na ni kaki mogana	Morning sickness or not, I want oysters!
tada hitotsu kaki mo kaki	Even one: an oyster's an oyster—
nagato no iriumi no sono ura naru ya	one from the rocky crag at the little inlet in Nagato Bay;
iwa no soba ni tsukitaru kaki koso ya	then I'll bear a son,
yomu fumi kaku te mo	a fine reader and writer,
hachijū shugō shima konjiki	with the eighty marks of the Buddha
tarōtaru onokogo wa ume	and golden-colored skin.[34]

The diversity of forms in *niku no kamiuta* led to a theory that *niku* referred neither to the prosody nor to the length of the verse, but to the songs' musical style.[35] This hypothesis further promoted the idea that *niku no kamiuta* were products of the interaction between folk songs, unbound by formal restrictions, and court *kagurauta*, with their prescribed prosody.[36] This would parallel the development of *shiku no kamiuta*, which apparently arose from the interaction of folk songs and the prosodically regulated Buddhist ritual repertoire.[37]

JINJA UTA

The *jinja uta* section, as we have mentioned, is divided into sixteen parts, each of which is named for a specific shrine. Generally speaking, the Shinto shrines are grouped according to an official classification called *nijūni sha*, or "Twenty-two Shrines," which extends from the Ise Imperial Shrine at the top to the Kibune Shrine at the bottom. These were the most prestigious shrines in Japan, and from the mid-Heian period they had gained considerable power and influence as recipients of court support and patronage.[38] Out of these twenty-two, twelve are selected as headings for the *jinja uta*: Iwashimizu, Kamo, Matsuno-o, Hirano, Inari, Kasuga, Ōharano, Sumiyoshi, Hiyoshi, Yoshida, Kibune, and Hirota. The four non–

nijūni sha are Kumano, Itsukushima, Amatsuyuwake, and Konoshima.[39] The number of songs about each of these shrines varies widely, and does not necessarily reflect the official importance of the shrines. For instance, only six songs are devoted to the prestigious Iwashimizu Shrine, second in rank only to Ise, while the lower-ranking Inari and Kasuga shrines are granted ten songs each. Furthermore, eleven songs—the largest number devoted to any one shrine—concern the middle-ranking Sumiyoshi Shrine.[40]

The most important sources for the *jinja uta* lyrics in *Ryōjin hishō* are two imperial anthologies, *Shūishū* (Collection of Gleanings, ca. 1005–11) and *Goshūishū* (Later Collection of Gleanings, 1086; the third and fourth imperial *waka* anthologies, respectively), with eleven poems adopted from each. In addition, two poems come from *Kokinshū* (the first imperial anthology), along with one each from *Gosenshū* (Later Collection, 951; the second) and *Shikashū* (the sixth). The sections in these anthologies that proved most fruitful for the provision of *jinja uta* lyrics were those entitled "Praise" or "Shinto." Privately compiled *waka* anthologies were mined for material as well: *Kyūan hyakushu* provided seven poems; *Kokin(waka)rokujō* (Six Quires of Ancient and Modern Japanese Poetry, ca. 987) and *Kaya no in shichiban utaawase* (Seventy Rounds of Poetry Matches at Kaya no In) supplied five each; and *Horikawa-in hyakushu-waka* (One Hundred Poems for Emperor Horikawa, 1105) and *Tsurayuki-shū* (Collection of Tsurayuki's Poems, date unknown) contributed one each.[41] The fact that *Kyūan hyakushu*, a work personally commissioned by Emperor Sutoku, occupies a conspicuous place in the *jinja uta* section may reflect the same kind of concern as was shown in the compilation of *Senzaishū* (see chapter 2). In any case, it is evident that the *jinja uta* lyrics are rooted firmly in the elite *waka* poetic tradition. The following song, taken from *Goshūishū*, poem no. 1062, composed by Emperor Go-Sanjō (1034–73), speaks clearly for such aristocratic origin:

RH 537

sumiyoshi no	Perhaps the gods
kami wa aware to	of Sumiyoshi
omouramu	will pity me:
munashiki fune o	I have come
sashite kitsureba	rowing an empty boat.[42]

One distinctive feature of *jinja uta* is that every poem mentions either the name of the shrine under which it is grouped or some clearly associated landmark. This lack of ambiguity ensures for the *jinja uta* section a certain exactness and uniformity. For instance:

RH 522

kasugayama	Mount Kasuga
kumoi haruka ni	is far,
tōkeredo	remote as clouds in the sky;
kachi yori zo iku	but I would go there on foot
kimi o omoeba	for love of you.[43]

Many songs in the *jinja uta* section originated as written *waka* poems but were later put to music for *imayō* vocal performance. Most of the other songs in *Ryōjin hishō*, by contrast, were intended for oral performance from the very start. Thus we come full circle as these poems, which originally existed in written form, were now set on paper again but in a very different context: that of *imayō* textual transmission.

UNTITLED *NIKU NO KAMIUTA*

The untitled *niku no kamiuta*, which appear before and after the *jinja uta* in two parts, consist of forty-nine songs and eleven songs, respectively, with the latter section bringing *Ryōjin hishō* to a close. This second group of untitled *niku no kamiuta* is in fact believed to be a later addition.[44] For the sake of convenience, we will call the songs in the untitled parts simply *niku no kamiuta*, in contradistinction to the *jinja uta*.

In terms of form and prosody, the *niku no kamiuta* are a mixture of regular *tanka* and irregular syllabic schemes and line lengths. As in *shiku no kamiuta*, orchestra words, onomatopoeia, and repetition, the trademarks of folk songs, are frequently found in *niku no kamiuta*. For example:

RH 454

fuyu ku to mo	Winter may be coming, but
hahaso no momiji	red oak leaves,
na chiri so yo	don't you fall!
chiri so yo	Don't ever fall!
na chiri so	Never fall!
iro kaede mimu	I'd gaze at your colors unchanging.

The technique of repetition is fully exploited here: the negative imperative, "*na . . . so,*" is used twice, while *chiri* (from *chiru*, to fall) is repeated three times, producing a strong rhythmic resonance. Such a device renders the message of the song compelling—whether it is a wish for long life for an aging mother (*haha*, couched in *hahasoba*, oak leaves) or a plea for changeless love.[45]

The use of onomatopoeia is exemplified by the following song, dramatizing the pain of lost love, where *chō to* and *tei to* aptly convey cracking and jarring noises:

RH 468

yamabushi no	The mountain ascetic's conch shell—
koshi ni tsuketaru	as it falls from the waist
horagai no	where it dangled,
chō to ochi	breaking, crash!
tei to ware	shattered—
kudakete mono o	that's my heart, broken,
omou koro kana	brooding.[46]

Niku no kamiuta also often employ *kakekotoba, engo,* or *joshi* (preface) to give multiple levels of meaning, a fact that sets this particular subsection apart from the other sections of *Ryōjin hishō*. As the following song on jilted love illustrates, the use of these classical *waka* techniques expands and enriches the content of the poem beyond its literal signification:

RH 464

azumaya no	In the end
tsuma to mo tsui ni	no rose-covered eastern bower for me,
narazarikeru	never to be a wife.
mono yue ni	So why did I start this,
nani to te mune o	breast pressed to naked breast,
awasesomekemu	love in vain.

This song consists of a series of puns or plays on homonyms involving the words *azumaya* (a bower, or a house in the east), *tsuma* (eaves, or a wife), and *mune* (a ridge, or breast). First there is a wordplay between *azumaya* and its *engo, tsuma,* which also functions as a *kakekotoba,* producing two layers of meaning: "bower with eaves" and "a wife in the eastern house." Next enters another wordplay between *tsuma* and *mune,* which is another *engo* for *azumaya* and also a *kakekotoba,* to further stretch the meaning of the poem to something like "the breast of a wife in a ridged eastern house."[47] This kind of complex wordplay in *niku no kamiuta,* though infrequent, provides the *imayō* genre with rare but close poetic parallels with *waka.*

As we have seen, the motley nature of *Ryōjin hishō* as an anthology stems in part from the prosodic, rhetorical, and formal diversity displayed in the song lyrics. Even the arrangement and organization of the subsections contribute to the multifariousness of the collection as a whole. It is important to observe, however, that these devices accommodate the content and themes they embody and are governed by certain philosophical, religious, and poetic principles; they are not, in short, haphazardly assembled. The songs with religious orientation, such as the Buddhist *hōmon uta* and the Shinto *jinja uta*, tend to be carefully regulated, while some of the folk song–like *shiku no kamiuta* and *niku no kamiuta* are largely allowed to deviate from tight formal control. This concord of the techniques and formal characteristics of the *Ryōjin hishō* songs will become more apparent in the following chapters, where we will explore the songs from a thematic point of view.

5 The World of Religion in *Ryōjin hishō*

Religion is at the heart of the extant *Ryōjin hishō*. In all, songs on overtly religious themes constitute close to two-thirds of the anthology; and when related songs are factored in, the collection easily qualifies as a religion-oriented work. These songs can be roughly broken into three categories: those of Buddhist inspiration, those expressing Shinto-Buddhist syncretism, and those of Shinto origin.

Most of the songs having to do with Buddhism are concentrated in the *hōmon uta* section, though some are also scattered among the *shiku no kamiuta*, and a few examples are *niku no kamiuta*.[1] Songs of a Shinto-Buddhist syncretic vein, by contrast, are predominantly *shiku no kamiuta*, with a smattering among the *niku no kamiuta*. Finally, Shinto songs are localized among the *niku no kamiuta*, especially in the *jinja uta* subsection. Given not only this distribution of religious thematic concerns, but also the physical organization of the anthology proper, we can say that *shiku no kamiuta* provides a transition from *hōmon uta* to *niku no kamiuta*.

In these songs various poetic responses elicited by religious concerns are articulated, sometimes in a sophisticated manner but often with child-like simplicity. The outcome of such a confrontation with the transcendental sometimes emerges as a happy affirmation of Amida's grace, though sometimes a deep inner turmoil at the realization of spiritual impairment counterbalances the mood. In the case of Shinto shrine songs, spiritual contact with the sacred is understood to be the source of a rich life here and now. In short, the religious songs in *Ryōjin hishō* create a space in which the question of human spirituality is raised, its conditions are revealed, and certain messages are communicated, whether to resolve conflicts or to provide assurance and comfort.

Buddhism

The predominance of Buddhist themes in *Ryōjin hishō* gave the anthology a reputation as "a miniature encyclopedia of Heian Buddhism seen through the form of songs."[2] Indeed, because the songs were created to inform listeners about the fundamentals of Buddhism—the Buddhist canon, creeds, and precepts, as well as legends and stories about the pioneers in the history of the faith—most present these facts in expository rather than lyrical, and prescriptive rather than expressive, modes: a public rather than a private voice prevails.

In some cases, the songs are extremely elementary in their content. This does not necessarily mean simple; certain songs, particularly among the *hōmon uta* on the Lotus Sutra, are merely poetic quotations or paraphrases from Buddhist scripture devoid of emotional or subjective interpretation. This tendency is somewhat relaxed in the "Miscellaneous" subsection of *hōmon uta*, which contains a few songs (but only a few) that present personal religious sentiments, musings, or reflections. The exclusive bent toward the theoretical and ideational aspects of Buddhism, which is reinforced by the proselytizing spirit of the poems—especially those included in the *hōmon uta* section—makes the verses rather strained and unwieldy. This quality becomes understandable when we recall that *hōmon uta* derived mainly from *wasan*, various sutras, and other Buddhist oral traditions, all of which share in didacticism, and that some of their predecessors were performed in a religious ritual context where personal elements were eschewed.

Such requirements placed inevitable limits on the thematic range of the Buddhist songs in *Ryōjin hishō*. Therefore, the uniqueness of any given song rests on the choice of the source text, the way it was appropriated, and the elements that were emphasized, rather than on any boldness or originality in exploring new thematic ground. Even so, it is important to remember that these songs, which may sound like platitude or naiveté when judged according to modern poetic standards or sensibilities, were accompanied by *imayō* music, which may have been as appealing and satisfying to late-Heian listeners as modern gospel music is to its audience.

PAEANS OF BUDDHAS

The Buddhist songs in *Ryōjin hishō* present major luminaries in the colorful Buddhist pantheon, describing the divinities' abilities, powers, and spheres of activity. Indeed, these figures appear in bewildering number. Included are the Buddha and his two attendants, Monju (Skt., Mañjuśrí, representing perfect wisdom) and Fugen (Samantabhadra, standing for truth and practice); Amida (Amitābha, the Buddha of Infinite Light, the Buddha of the Pure Land), also with his two attendants, Kannon (Avalokiteśvara, Bodhisattva of Compassion) and Seishi (Mahāsthāma-prāpta, Bodhisattva of Wisdom); Miroku (Maitreya, the Future Buddha), Yakushi (Bhaiṣajya-guru-vaidūrya-prapbhāṣa, the Buddha of Medicine and Healing), and Jizō (Kṣitigarbha, a bodhisattva who saves the souls suffering in hell); the Dainichi Nyorai (Mahāvairocana, the Cosmic Buddha of the Shingon sect); and other divinities of the Shingon sect, such as Fudō(myōō) (Acala, the Immovable One), a messenger of Dainichi, and Kongōsatta (Vajrasattva, Diamond-Being). Even more obscure deities such as Myōken (Sudṛṣṭi, Wondrous Seeing, Bodhisattva of the Pole Star) make an appearance.[3] Strictly speaking, however, only the historical Buddha and Amida play a large role in the divine world of *Ryōjin hishō*. These songs also provide a survey of the principal schools and cultic practices that developed in Japanese Buddhism over the centuries until the end of the Heian period, including both the Tendai, Shingon, and Amidist sects and the Kannon, Yakushi, and Jizō cults.

The Saga of Śākyamuni. The historical Buddha is a dominant presence in the *Ryōjin hishō* Buddhist songs. This ubiquity may indicate the pedagogical purpose of the songs, that is, to direct the audience's attention to the basics of Buddhism, beginning with its founder. But a more likely explanation is that most of the songs are extracted from the Lotus Sutra, in which the Buddha is the central figure presiding over the divine assembly gathered on Eagle Peak to hear his ultimate teaching of the sutra. Inevitably, many songs operate on the assumption that the audience knows this background. The following song, which describes the very beginning of the Buddha's teaching of the Lotus Sutra on the mountaintop, is a case in point:

RH 60

shaka no hokekyō toku hajime	As the Buddha's Lotus Sutra began
byakugō hikari wa tsuki no goto	his tuft of white hair shone like the moon,
mandara manju no hana furite	Heavenly Mandārava and Mañjuṣaka flowers fluttered down,[4]
daichi mo mukusa ni ugokikeri	and the great earth quaked six ways.

The immensity of the assembly on Eagle Peak and the vast power of the Buddha as a supernatural being are conveyed indirectly in the next song, taken from the "Hōtōhon" (Apparition of the Jeweled Stūpa), chapter 11 of the Lotus Sutra:

RH 105

ryōzenkaie no ōzora ni	On Eagle Peak the multitudes
hōtō toboso o oshihiraki	saw the sky open doors of jeweled stūpa,
futari no hotoke o hitotabi ni	and then there were two buddhas
yorokobi ogamitatematsuru	to worship together in one joy.[5]

The rare, blissful state of mind attained by revelation of the transcendent Buddha is conveyed in two unusual examples of personal lyricism in *Ryōjin hishō* Buddhist songs:

RH 26

hotoke wa tsune ni imasedomo	The Buddha is always everywhere,
utsutsunaranu zo awarenaru	but it's sad he remains hidden;
hito no oto senu akatsuki ni	at dawn, when human noise is still,
honoka ni yume ni mietamau	in dreams I see his shadow.

RH 102

shizuka ni otosenu dōjō ni	In silence, in the temple,
hotoke ni hana kō tatematsuri	I offer Lord Buddha flowers, incense;
kokoro o shizumete shibaraku mo	if I can calm my heart for a moment
yomeba zo hotoke wa mietamau	as I chant the sutra, he appears.

With the omnipresent cosmic Buddha as a backdrop, ever darkly making his presence known, it is nevertheless the Buddha as a historical being on which the Buddhist songs in *Ryōjin hishō* focus. More than thirty songs, scattered irregularly among the *hōmon uta* and *shiku no kamiuta*, deal with the earthly life of the Buddha from his birth to his nirvanic entrance, including his genealogy and his relations with close disciples as well as stories drawn from the repertoire of *jātaka*, which exalt his deeds in his previous incarnations. We see the person of the historical Buddha, Śākyamuni, in human time and space; his humanity is what emerges most forcefully, rather than a remote and unapproachable divinity. The storytelling or anecdotal style attempts to hold the attention of the audience by establishing narrative interest, within which framework essential personal facts about the Buddha can be communicated. The following song, which establishes the identity of the Buddha as a human being bound in a secular familial relationship, is one such example:

RH 279

shakamuni hotoke no warawa na wa	In boyhood Śākyamuni
shitta taishi to mōshikeri	was called Prince Siddhārtha,
chichi o ba jōbon ō to ii	his father, King Śuddhodana,
haha kore	his mother, she was
zenkaku chōja no musume maya bunin	Lady Māyā, daughter of wealthy Suprabuddha.[6]

Another song relates the landmark decision by which Prince Siddhārtha renounced the princely life and sought the way to the ultimate truth. Here again, the event is presented as a drama that unfolds within the context of the human network centering on the historical Buddha:

RH 207

taishi no miyuki ni wa	On his pilgrimage
kondei koma ni noritamai	the prince rode the steed Kaṇṭhaka;
shanoku toneri ni kuchi torase	his valet, Chandaka, held the bridle
dandokusen ni zo iritamau	on the way to Mount Dantaloka.[7]

Some *hōmon uta* celebrate the historical Buddha's human origin by highlighting stories from his former existence. These are taken from the *jātaka* story tradition, usually emphasizing the salutary karmic effect of his deeds in the previous life. In this way, the historical Buddha's life acquires additional moral dimension. The following *hōmon uta*, based on the sacrificial story about Prince Satta (Sattva or Makasatta) from the *Konkōmyō saishōō* Sutra (*Suvarṇa-prabhāsa-uttamarāja sūtra*, Sutra of the Most Victorious Kings of the Golden Light),[8] is one such example:

RH 209

taishi no mi nageshi yūgure ni	In the dusk the prince threw himself down,
koromo wa kaketeki take no ha ni	his robes discarded on bamboo leaves;

| ōji no miya o ideshi yori | with the prince gone from the palace, |
| kutsu wa aredomo nushi mo nashi | only the sandals remained, bereft of their master. |

The first couplet comes from the story in the sutra in which Prince Satta, the youngest son of King Makarada, flung his body from a bamboo-covered cliff as food for a famished tigress with seven cubs. When his parents arrived at the forest in search of him, all they found was his robe hanging on the bamboo branches.[9] As a poetic version of the *jātaka* story, the song relates the sacrificial feat performed by the prince for the sake of an animal, not even for a human being, thereby illustrating the profound compassion of the historical Buddha in his previous incarnation. The second couplet, like song no. 207 cited above, derives from the story about Prince Siddhārtha's departure from his father's palace to seek enlightenment. What is remarkable about this song is the parallelism used in presenting two momentous events in the lives of the Buddha. Also, by dwelling solely on the personal belongings left behind, the song plays on the popular Japanese concepts of *katami* (memento) and *ato* (trace). *Katami* are personal objects, places, or even progeny that served to recall the memory of a deceased person; they are found throughout Japanese literature, from *Man'yōshū* to *Genji monogatari*.[10] Indeed, one of the earliest examples of Buddhist poetry in Japan, the so-called "Buddha's Footprints Sequence" of the mid–eighth century, uses this notion of making what is lost present by dwelling on what has been left behind.[11] In the present *hōmon uta*, the simple objects left behind—robes and sandals—become poignant metaphors for the grief of the prince's parents and carry the emotional burden of the song.

Prince Siddhārtha's ascetic practices that followed his renunciation of the world are chronicled in yet another *hōmon uta*:

RH 219

makadakoku no ō no ko ni	Even Prince Siddhārtha,
owaseshi sudachi taishi koso	son of King Magadha,
dandokusen no nakayama ni	endured six years of austerity
rokunen okonai tamaishika	in the depths of Mount Dantaloka.[12]

Śākyamuni's enlightenment and his attainment of buddhahood, the climax of his religious pursuit, are captured in the following song, which brings them into sharp relief through the contrast between the cosmic darkness around him and the implied inner light of his awakening:

RH 228

jakumetsu dōjō oto nakute	Silence in his seat of meditation,
gayasan ni tsuki kakure	and the moon hidden behind Mount Gayā;
chūya no shizukanarishi ni zo	in the still dark of midnight,
hajimete shōgaku naritamau	he for the first time attained enlightenment.[13]

The Buddha's teaching career, which ensued from his awakening, figures in another *hōmon uta* about the fabled site of his retreat, the Jetavana Monastery, popularly known in Japan as the Gion Temple:

RH 215

moto kore gida wa taishi no chi	Once Prince Jeta's land,
sudachi kogane o ji ni shikite	the grove was spread with gold
hotoke no mitame ni kaitorite	by Sudatta for Lord Buddha's sake,
hajimete shōza to nashishinari	bought to become Jetavana Temple.[14]

This poetic synopsis of the legend surrounding the foundation of the monastery is a tribute to the Buddha's persuasive religious influence during his teaching career.

The humanization of the historical Buddha is also evident in the following song, which relates the warm and legendary relationship between him and his cousin Ānanda, who accompanied him as personal attendant throughout his teaching career until the Buddha's death:

RH 94

shaka no mideshi wa ōkaredo	Buddha's disciples were many,
hotoke no itoko wa utokarazu	but his cousin was never distant:
shitashiki koto wa tare yori mo	no one was ever closer
anan sonza zo owashikeru	than Ānanda.

Ānanda's devotion to the Buddha was indeed proverbial.[15] His constant presence near the Buddha and his superb power of memory later helped the Buddhist community commit the Buddha's oral teachings to writing through Ānanda's recitation, thereby contributing invaluably to the formation of Buddhist written canon.[16] By presenting him and the Buddha in terms of their intimate familial ties, however, the song calls attention to the human side of the Buddha.

Songs in the *hōmon uta* section include some details about the circumstances surrounding the Buddha's last days. Like other songs about the life of the Buddha, these contain a *setsuwa* flavor, presenting the event in terms of human interaction and quasi-historical facts. The following song is adopted from the popular story that the Buddha's illness and eventual death were caused by food he took from Cunda, a smith, in Pāvā:[17]

RH 172

kushinajō ni wa seihoku hō	Northwest of Kuśinagara
baddaiga no nishi no kishi	near the western bank of Vatī River
shara ya shōju no aida ni wa	On a seat between twin Śāla trees,
juda ga kuyō o uketamau	Buddha took Cunda's food offering.[18]

Upon eating the food, which was conjectured to be pork, the Buddha was taken violently ill. But, mindful of the blame Cunda might get, he told Ānanda that Cunda should feel no remorse for what had happened.[19]

Mortally ill, the Buddha, in the company of the ever-present Ānanda, now headed toward Kuśinagara, the ultimate destination of his earthly journey, and entered the Śāla Grove. There, after teaching one last time, he passed away. The following song narrates this final moment of the historical Buddha's passing into nirvana, bringing his hagiography to a close in the *hōmon uta* section:

RH 174

nigatsu jūgonichi ashita yori	From morning to midnight
korera no hōmon tokiokite	of the fifteenth day of the second month,
yōyaku chūya ni itaru hodo	Lord Buddha slowly completed his teaching;
kōbe wa kita ni zo fushitamau	and at last he lay down to rest, his head to the north.[20]

After the Buddha's mortal passing, the *hōmon uta* focus briefly on ensuing events, especially those involving his disciples of the first order: Mahākāśyapa (or Kaśyapa) and Ānanda. Mahākāśyapa, one of the Four Great Disciples, is traditionally credited with having convened the "First Council of Elders" and with having played a key role in the establishment of Sangha as a religious institution.[21] From the council presided over by Mahākāśyapa, it is believed, the basic canons of Buddhism evolved, clarifying the Buddhist community's disciplinary guidelines and ideological framework.[22] Mahākāśyapa was, in this sense, the first patriarch of the Buddhist ecclesia. The *hōmon uta*, however, are mute about Mahākāśyapa's heroic achievements in Buddhist officialdom. Rather, a less glorious landmark in his career—the disastrous fact that he was the only important disciple to miss the moment of his master's death—is presented. It seems as if the song found Mahākāśyapa's failure and his hidden personal anguish more appealing:

RH 173

shakamuni hotoke no metsugo ni wa	Even venerable Kāśyapa missed
kashō sonja mo awazariki	the hour of Śākyamuni Buddha's passing;
ayumi o hakobite koshika do mo	though he ran and hurried back,
jūroku rakan ni mo okureniki	he was outstripped even by sixteen *arhats*.[23]

A similarly frustrating incident in the lives of the Buddha's disciples is presented in another song about Ānanda. According to popular anecdote, Ānanda, despite his close association with the Buddha, was not immediately admitted to the First Council of Elders because he had not yet attained the status of *arhat*. Thus rejected by the Sangha and put to task by Mahākāśyapa, Ānanda exerted himself all night long and, at dawn, finally achieved awakening, whereupon he was accepted by the council and proceeded to participate in the formation of the canon.[24] The song, based on this quasi-legend, empathizes with the initial shame and insult Ānanda personally suffered—all too human and understandable:

RH 187

kashō sonja no ishi no muro	How shame-stricken Ānanda was
iru ni tsukete zo hazukashiki	inside venerable Kāśyapa's rock cavern,
enshū tsukizaru mi ni shi areba	when heavenly flowers fell to stick on his sleeves!
tamoto ni hana koso tomarunare	A sign of his heart clinging to desires.

The continuing chronicles of the Buddha and his close associates end with the following song, a poetic adoption of apocryphal stories about Mahākāśyapa. According to these sources, after his official work was completed, Mahākāśyapa, carrying the robe that the Buddha had given him as a token of his mandate to preach Dharma, retired to Mount Kukkuṭapāda (Cock's Foot) in Magadha, where he is said to have entered into a nirvanic state waiting for the coming of the future Buddha, Maitreya.[25] This cultic veneration of the leading disciple of the Buddha is encapsulated thus:

RH 183

kashō sonja no zenjō wa	Up above the cloudy Mount Kukkuṭapāda,
keisokusan no kumo no ue	venerable Kāśyapa entered deep meditation;
haru no kasumishi ryūgee ni	he will deliver the entrusted robe at the assembly to be held
fuzoku no koromo o tsutaunari	under the Dragon-flower tree, wrapped in spring mist.[26]

The narrative impulse behind the *hōmon uta* on the Buddha, some of which are based on popularly known stories, makes the most of the *setsuwa* style.[27] Although dominant in these biographical songs is the desire to inform and educate the audience, it is mediated by a concern to engage the interest of the audience. Consequently, the songs impart knowledge not abstractly, but through concrete and entertaining narratives. Their enumeration of basic facts, moreover, suggests an original catechist setting. They met the needs of their audience for simple, fundamental religious information by putting it in question and answer form, easy to memorize and recall. Most important, they show the Buddha as a temporal being, existing in historical human time, space, and relationships. The final purpose of the *setsuwa* technique as it is used here, in other words, is to collapse the gap between the sacred person of the Buddha and ordinary men by demonstrating his humanity.

The following *hōmon uta* announces this identity of the Buddha with common humanity, thereby giving ordinary men hope for achieving a spiritual status like his:

RH 232

hotoke mo mukashi wa hito nariki	The Buddha, too, was a man in ancient days,
warera mo tsui ni wa hotoke nari	and in the end we, too, become buddhas.
sanshin busshō guseru mi to	How sad, not to feel in our bodies now
shirazarikeru koso awarenare	the triple-bodied buddha nature pure.[28]

The Grace of Amida. Next to the historical Buddha, Amida dominates the religious world in *Ryōjin hishō*, providing another leitmotif and an additional spiritual dimension to the anthology. In fact, some of the most memorable songs in *Ryōjin hishō* are related to Amida pietism, their central concern being the question of salvation. The few religious songs with personal lyricism belong to this category. In some cases, as in the following *hōmon uta*, the religious sentiment reaches a level of profound nobility in its conception and overtone:

RH 238

akatsuki shizuka ni nezameshite	Waking in the quiet at dawn,
omoeba namida zo osaeaenu	I wonder, my tears welling:
hakanaku kono yo o sugushite wa	having lived in this world of dreams,
itsuka wa jōdo e mairubeki	will I ever reach the Pure Land?

Metaphorically, of course, dawn is a time of spiritual awakening. The appeal of the song comes from the speaker's ability to face his or her spiritual infirmity calmly and without illusion.

Another song is more explicit in voicing the same concern about salvation, this time from a pronounced Amidist perspective. These songs stand apart from other *hōmon uta* in that they personalize the issue of salvation, in sharp contrast to the impersonal teaching found in a number of *hōmon uta*.

RH 235

warera wa nani shite oinuran	How blindly have we aged!
omoeba ito koso awarenare	So sad, when I look back.
ima wa saihō gokuraku no	It's time to invoke Amida's promise
mida no chikai o nenzubeshi	of paradise in the west.

The unconditional proposition of Amidism, which offers salvation through the simple verbalization of one's faith in Amida's grace, had a special appeal for the masses. The common people, who lacked the time and means enjoyed by aristocrats to pursue elaborate religious practices, were powerfully drawn by the compassion embodied in Amida's vows. The popularity of Amidism gained further momentum during the latter part of the Heian period as the idea of the *mappō* (the age of the Degenerate Dharma) spread, fanned by political and social upheavals. This influence of Amidism on the popular mind is clear in the songs of *Ryōjin hishō*, as in the following *hōmon uta* on the essence of Amida's soteriological proposition:

RH 29

amida hotoke no seigan zo	Endlessly trustworthy,
kaesugaesu mo tanomoshiki	the vow of Amida Buddha.
hitotabi mina o tonaureba	Whoever invokes his sacred name even once
hotoke ni naru to zo toitamau	will become buddha, so it says!

The "vows" here refer to Amida's original forty-eight vows, especially the eighteenth, in which he pledges to postpone his buddhahood until he receives all living beings into his Western Pure Land—the fundamental basis for Amida pietism.

Echoing the same formulaic phrase of the preceding song, *tanomoshiki* (trustworthy), another song reaffirms the unconditional salvation to be achieved by simple trust in Amida:

RH 30

mida no chikai zo tanomoshiki	Trustworthy is Amida's vow, yes!
jūaku gogyaku no hito naredo	Even those of ten evils and five vices
hitotabi mina o tonaureba	who invoke his sacred name even once
raigō injō utagawazu	are welcomed, taken at death to paradise![29]

This song expresses the epitome of Amidism: the contrast between the potential magnitude of the human infraction and the simplicity of the requirement for salvation. The Amida cult proposes a boundless expansion of the radius of salvation. This formulation radically changes the conventional notion of salvation by one's personal effort (*jiriki*), posing instead reliance on other-power (*tariki*) as the means to salvation.

As a variation on the same theme, the following *niku no kamiuta* describes the result of refusing to put one's trust in Amida:

RH 494

amida butsu to	Those who never
mōsanu hito wa	chant Amida Buddha
fuchi no ishi	are rocks sunk in a pool;
kō wa furedo mo	though ages may pass,
ukabu yo zo naki	they will never rise.

The speaker of this *hōmon uta* pleads for assurance of Amida's salvation at his or her death:

RH 236

warera ga kokoro ni hima mo naku	Oh our hearts hunger without end
mida no jōdo o negau kana	for Amida's Pure Land.
rin'e no tsumi koso omoku to mo	Though the weight of our karma is heavy,
saigo ni kanarazu mukaetamae	he will greet and enfold us in the end.

A wistful longing for salvation purely through Amida occupies the mind of the speaker in another *niku no kamiuta*:

RH 493

namu amida	Oh Amida Buddha,
hotoke no mite ni	in your sacred hands
kakuru ito no	hang the threads of life;
owari midarenu	may my heart find its final grace
kokoro to mogana	without entanglement.[30]

The following song approaches Amida pietism by means of several concrete metaphors drawn from nature in an attempt to naturalize the supernatural and render the sacred in concrete and familiar terms. By equating Amida's physiognomy with what each season offers as its most pleasing features, the song suggests the felicity to be derived from faith in him:

RH 28

mida no mikao wa aki no tsuki	Amida's sacred face, the autumn moon;
shōren no manako wa natsu no ike	the ponds of summer, his blue-lotus eyes;
shijū no haguki wa fuyu no yuki	his forty teeth are winter's snow;
sanjūni sō haru no hana	the thirty-two holy marks, spring blossoms.[31]

The invaluable spiritual riches to be had in the heavenly realm by salvation through Amida's compassion are projected into a sketch of Amida's palace decorated with precious gems in this *hōmon uta*:

RH 178

gokuraku jōdo no kuden wa	The palace in the Pure Land paradise
ruri no kawara o aoku fuki	is sky blue with lapis lazuli tiles,
shinju no taruki o tsukuriname	its rafters lined with pearls,
menō no toboso o oshihiraki	its agate gates thrown open wide.

In a fanciful flight, the speaker in the following *shiku no kamiuta* even discovers the praise of Amida in the chirping of insects:

RH 286

gokuraku jōdo no tōmon ni	On the eastern gate of the Pure Land paradise,
hataoru mushi koso keta ni sume	grasshoppers weave on the crossbeam;
saihōjōdo no tomoshibi ni	in the light of Western Pure Land,
nembutsu no koromo zo isogioru	quickly they spin Amida a robe of prayers.[32]

The song plays on the word *hataoru mushi* (weaving insect), a variant of *hataorimushi*, which is an old form of *kirigirisu* (grasshopper). Since *hataoru* is an *engo* of *koromo* (clothes, robe), grasshoppers are associated with weaving. By equating the urgency of the short-lived insects' chirpings with *nembutsu* chanting by Amida followers, the speaker suggests the prevalence of Amida pietism in his time, which embraces even lowly creatures.

In a radically different mood, the following *niku no kamiuta* invokes Amida's protection from ghosts at night. The repetition of *namu ya* (hail) adds an incantatory urgency to the song. The song displays an amalgam of folk belief and Amidism, and perhaps a sense of humor as well:

RH 491

sayo fukete	Night deepens,
kininra koso	ghosts are
arikunare	walking around!
namo ya kiebutsu	Hail Buddha, protect me,
namo ya kiehō	Hail Dharma, protect me!

Amida songs in *Ryōjin hishō*, which range from fine personal lyricism to childlike chants, serve as an index to the variety of poetic responses to religious issues. In so doing they demonstrate the scope of Amidist influence throughout Heian society and the delight its members take in singing about their faith. The songs as a unit provide a new strain in *Ryōjin hishō*, less abstract and much closer to the heart of their audience than doctrinal or pedagogic *hōmon uta*.

The Cults of Kannon, Yakushi, and Jizō. What pulses through the songs of praise to Kannon, Yakushi, and Jizō in *Ryōjin hishō* is the spirit that is also central to Amidism: the notion of salvation through dependence on other-power rather than on personal merit. Although constituting only a handful, these songs continue the populist interpretation of salvation as something given, not striven after, and therefore all the more to be praised and to be grateful for. Underlying the cultic veneration in these songs is a keen awareness of the infirmity, weakness, and helplessness of human beings, which can be overcome only by divine intervention. In turn, their human limits require of believers absolute surrender to the power that willingly takes up the task of setting them free. This continuing interest in the intercessory role of the divine strengthens the other-power leaning in *Ryōjin hishō*.

The following song about Kannon, one of Amida's two attendants, praises his compassionate readiness to help men gain spiritual emancipation:

RH 37

kan'on daihi wa funeikada	Great compassionate Kannon is a raft,
fudarakukai ni zo ukabetaru	floating on Potalaka's seas;
zengon motomuru hito shi araba	when someone seeks the good,
nosete watasamu gokuraku e	he ferries him to paradise.

Kannon is believed to assist people in distress, especially seafarers, by leading them to safety from his residence on Mount Potalaka.[33] Although here Kannon's saving grace is set against an exotic Indian cosmology, it is made concrete and immediate by the metaphor of the "raft," something commoners can easily identify with.

The following *hōmon uta* conveys the same sentiments:

RH 158

kan'on fukaku tanomubeshi	With our lives we should trust Kannon;
guzei no umi ni fune ukabe	his boat floats on the great sea of his vows.
shizumeru shujō hikinosete	Saving those who are drowning,

bodai no kishi made kogiwataru   he will row them to the shores
of awakening.

Among the various forms of this divinity, the Thousand-armed Kannon is a special object of veneration. In another *hōmon uta*, his revitalizing power is praised through the image of rejuvenated plant life:

RH 39

yorozu no hotoke no gan yori mo	Far above the vows of ten thousand buddhas,
senju no chikai zo tanomoshiki	trustworthy the vows of Thousand-armed Kannon are;
karetaru kusaki mo tachimachi ni	even withered grass and trees, so it is said,
hanasaki minaru to toitamau	blossom and bear fruit in a moment.

In contrast to the other-worldly character of Amida's salvation, which usually occurs after death, that of Yakushi, "Master of Medicine," is this-worldly and corporeal. The following two *hōmon uta* forthrightly extol the healing power of Yakushi:

RH 31

yakushi no jūni no taigan wa	Of Yakushi's twelve great vows,
shubyōshichijo zo tanomoshiki	curing every ill is a vow to trust.
ikkyōgoni wa sate okitsu	Matchless: the good done by hearing the sutra,
kairyōmanzoku suguretari	the promise to meet our every need.[34]

RH 32

jōbō tenjite wa	In the time of Imitation Dharma,
yakushi no chikai zo tanomoshiki	the vows of Yakushi are trustworthy!
hitotabi mina o kiku hito wa	Hear his sacred name once only,
yorozu no yamai mo nashi to zo iu	they say, and escape even a million ills.[35]

The word *tanomoshiki* links these songs to other Amida songs with the same rhetoric and theme—that is, the importance of relying on other-power.

In the following *hōmon uta*, the recognition of one's sinfulness and need for salvation is this time addressed to Jizō, who is powerful enough to set even those in hell free:

RH 283

waga mi wa zaigō omokushite	Heavy with bad karma
tsui ni wa nairi e irinanzu	my body will fall to hell,
irinubeshi	in the end it must fall;
karadasen naru jizō koso	but Jizō of Mount Karavīka
mainichi no akatsuki ni	comes to me
kanarazu kitarite toutamae	each dawn without fail.[36]

The speaker, knowing the gravity of his or her transgressions, understands that salvation can be realized only through Jizō's compassionate help. The persuasiveness of the song comes from the speaker's frank admission of hopelessness and of the necessity that an outside power intercede. All these cultic songs are thus based on the realization of the believer's unregenerated condition and trust in the redemptive power of the divine, which, though often magnanimous, operates on the believer's extremely simple faith in such possibilities.

BUDDHAHOOD FOR ALL

The message of universal salvation is the main thrust of the Lotus Sutra itself. Similarly, the religious songs in *Ryōjin hishō* reaffirm the availability of buddhahood to all who aspire to that ideal. All forms of human effort and activity have validity as means of achieving this goal. The following *hōmon uta*, based on the "Expedient Devices," chapter 2 of the Lotus Sutra, suggests that even frivolous actions like children's play can become a means for achieving buddhahood:

RH 62

byōdōdaie no ji no ue ni	On this ground of wisdom and equality,
dōji no tawabure asobi o mo	even the light-hearted play of the child
yōyaku hotoke no tane to shite	is a buddha seed, becoming in time
bodaidaiju zo oinikeru	the great tree of awakening.

Salvation is open to all. Side by side with the disciples of the Buddha, men of limited knowledge and low status also receive the same promise. In another *hōmon uta*, this one based on the "Jukihon" (Bestowal of Prophecy), chapter 6 of the Lotus Sutra, in which the Buddha prophesied that his Four Great Disciples would attain buddhahood, we find a celebration of this privilege of universal salvation:

RH 85

shidaishōmon ikabakari	The Four Great Disciples—I see
yorokobi mi yori mo	how their bodies must have
amaruramu	overflowed with joy,
warera wa gose no hotoke zo to	now that I hear for certain that we, too,
tashikani kikitsuru kyō nareba	will be buddhas in the next world.[37]

The contrast between the august *shidaishōmon* (Four Great Disciples), imposing and high-sounding in Chinese loan-words, and the humble, anonymous *warera* (we) in Japanese vernacular drives the message home.

The wish of ordinary men to benefit from universal salvation is expressed in the next *hōmon uta*. It draws upon chapter 5 of the Lotus Sutra, "Yakusōyuhon" (Medicinal Herbs), in which the Dharma is likened to a shower of rain, falling equally on all vegetation to bring it to bloom and bear fruit:

RH 82

warera wa hakuji no bonbu nari	We are ordinary men, we are arid soil;
zengon tsutomuru michi shirazu	we know not the way to grow good roots;
ichimi no ame ni uruoite	but, soaked by a gust of Dharma rain,
nadoka hotoke ni narazaran	how could we not become buddha?

The use of the word *bonbu* (common men), unprecedented even in *imayō* and here reinforced by the pronoun *warera*, conveys the collective religious aspiration of the common people. The same word *warera* connects this song to the preceding one conceptually as well as linguistically.

One issue of crucial importance to universal salvation is that of evil. We considered this problem briefly with regard to the intervention of Amida and other divine powers, yet the concern persists throughout *Ryōjin hishō*. The following three songs raise the subject of transgression openly. In particular, they address the quandary faced by common people engaged in occupations such as fishing and hunting, which by their nature require violation of the Buddhist prohibition against taking life. Here, the problem of evil and salvation is not abstract, but part of life's ordinary

reality. The speakers' plights are revealed in these confessions, some of
the most frank and direct in *Ryōjin hishō*:

RH 240

hakanaki kono yo o sugusu to te	Passing through this fleeting world,
umi yama kasegu to seshi hodo ni	as I labor on the sea and the mountains,
yorozu no hotoke ni utomarete	I am shunned by many buddhas—
goshō waga mi o ika ni sen	what will become of me in the next life?

RH 355

ukai wa itōshi ya	Cursed is the fisher with cormorants;
mangō toshi furu kame koroshi	I kill turtles which should live ten thousand years, my birds
mata u no kubi o yui	I tie by the neck. So I live in this world;
genze wa kakute mo arinubeshi	
goshō waga mi o ika ni sen	what will become of me in the next?

RH 440

ukai wa kuyashikaru	Wretched is the fisher with cormorants;
nanishi ni isoide asarikemu	why am I so busily fishing,
mangō toshi furu kame koroshikemu	why kill the turtles which should live ten thousand years?
genze wa kakute mo arinubeshi	That's how I move through this life—
gose waga mi o ika ni senzuramu	what will become of me in the next?

The impact of these songs comes from the intensity of religious self-
awareness, as expressed in the gripping sense of guilt and fear. Cormorant
fishermen use a peculiar method, alluded to in these songs: they tie the
necks of cormorants with strings to keep the birds from swallowing their
catch; once the birds return to the boat, the fish are forced out of the
cormorants' throats and become the fishermen's own catch. The fishermen
in turn kill turtles to feed their birds. Because turtles are associated with
longevity and hence are considered a felicitous symbol, killing them is in

a way breaking a taboo.[38] Given the Buddhist injunction against taking lives, the actions of the fishermen in any event constitute a transgression. Yet only in exchange for other animals' lives can they sustain their own. These *Ryōjin hishō* songs capture that hapless dilemma. Similar songs were no doubt performed at special rites such as *Kumano hakkōe* (eight lectures on the Lotus Sutra in Kumano), held for the expiation of sins for those employed in taboo or polluting occupations associated with animal killing. It is believed that mountain ascetics (*yamabushi*) with some Tendai training played an important role in performing this ritual for the fishermen and hunters in the Kumano region.[39]

The concern with the relationship between evildoing and salvation in *Ryōjin hishō* is evidenced by the large number of songs related to the twelfth chapter of the Lotus Sutra, "Daibahon" (Devadatta or Datta)—eighteen, more than for any other chapter.[40] Devadatta, a cousin of Śākyamuni, represents a diabolical and irredeemable sinner. Estranged in his youth from Śākyamuni, Devadatta became his archenemy, relentlessly seeking to destroy him and disrupt his teaching. Eventually he was found guilty of five cardinal sins and was thrown into hell while still alive.[41] Yet, as illustrated by the following song, he is assured of salvation:

RH 114

datta wa hotoke no ata nare do	Devadatta was his enemy, but
hotoke wa sore o mo shirazu shite	Buddha chose to ignore this.
jihi no manako o hirakitsutsu	Compassionate, open-eyed,
nori no michi ni zo iretamau	yes, he drew him onto the path of Dharma.

Even more paradoxical is the fact that in a previous incarnation Devadatta had been the Buddha's mentor:

RH 110

shaka no minori o ukezushite	Rebuffing Śākyamuni's sacred Dharma,
somuku to hito ni wa miseshikado	Devadatta turned against him, so people thought.
chitose no tsutome o kyō kikeba	Now we know Buddha served him a thousand years;
datta wa hotoke no shi narikeru	Devadatta was his teacher, in another life.

RH 111

datta gogyaku no akunin to	Devadatta the evildoer,
na ni wa oedomo makoto ni wa	his name stained with the five vices:
shaka no hokekyō naraikeru	in truth he was this same seer, Asita,
ashisennin kore zo kashi	who taught Śākyamuni the Lotus Sutra![42]

This claim is given more specificity and humanity in another song, which cites a *jātaka* story describing the various arduous ways the Buddha served Asita:

RH 291

myōhō narau to te	To learn the Lotus Sutra
kata ni kesa kake toshi heniki	he wore a stole through passing years;
mine ni noborite ki mo koriki	he even cut wood on the mountain,
tani no mizu kumi	carried water in the valley,
sawa naru na mo tsumiki	picked greens in the marsh.

The case of Devadatta represents the ultimate in the Mahāyāna interpretation of salvation. It proclaims the absolute certainty of universal salvation, even completely reversing the process of karmic retribution. It cancels the dichotomy of reality versus appearance, virtue versus vice, past versus present, sacred versus profane, and transgression versus salvation. This rejection of the conventional dualism nurtures the philosophy of tolerance that enables even the vilest of evildoers to achieve buddhahood.

The need to recognize nirvana in *samsāra* (the realm of transmigration) and the relative nature of perception is upheld in the following *hōmon uta*:

RH 241

yorozu o uro to shirinureba	When we see the world's a dusty dream,
abi no honō mo kokoro kara	we know the flames of hell come from the heart;
gokurakujōdo no ikemizu mo	once our hearts are lucid and serene,
kokoro sumite wa hedatenashi	we feel the ponds of paradise, not far.

In conjunction with Devadatta, the personification of evil, *Ryōjin hishō* deals with the salvation of women—who in Buddhism were considered no better off than transgressors. The focus is on the Nāga Princess, daughter of the Dragon King Sāgara, whose story occupies the second half of the Devadatta chapter.[43] According to this account, Śāriputra, the most brilliant of the Buddha's disciples, flatly rejected the possibility of women's attaining buddhahood on the basis of the "five obstacles," a concept stipulating the innate inferiority of women.[44] Despite his objections, however, the eight-year-old Nāga Princess succeeded in attaining buddhahood—but only by relinquishing her sexuality and changing her body into male form, as symbolized in her offering of a jewel to the Buddha. This aspect of the story obviously reflects lingering reservations about women's potential to achieve salvation. But the fact that the Lotus Sutra addresses the issue at all, and even provides one successful case, was significant, for it represented a radical change from the centuries of prejudice against women enunciated by Buddhist scriptures and institutional practices.

Women, who were considered a necessary evil, had long posed an irksome problem to the Buddhist institution. An antifemale attitude arose early on, especially with the establishment of the vow of celibacy.[45] Women ultimately came to represent the very entity against which the Buddhist order as a whole had to wage war:

> Woman was portrayed as the purely sensual with uncontrollable desires in a number of early sectarian Buddhist texts. . . . Women represented limitations of human nature in much the same manner as Eve and Pandora, but woman glowed with a more intense sexual vitality and was the primeval force of fecundity, as she was in the Hindu religion. Unlike the Hindu Mother Goddess, however, the sexual energy was unequivocally repugnant in early Buddhist sects such as the Theravādin sect. What was feminine or sensual was samsāra, the world of bondage, suffering, and desire, which led to cycles of rebirths. This world of the feminine had to be vanquished at all costs.[46]

Early Buddhist texts like the Nirvana Sutra condemn women in the following terms: "The sum total of all men's sufferings put together from three thousand universes amounts to one single woman's sin." The same sutra says elsewhere: "Women are the devil's chief devouring all men; while in this world they coil around men, and, thus blocking men's path, they become men's bitterest enemy and foe in the next world."[47]

Some scriptural sources went a step further and categorically denied women any hope of salvation. The *Shinjikankyō*, for example, proclaimed that "although all the myriad buddhas' eyes from the three worlds of past, present, and future fall down onto the ground, there will come no time for women to become buddhas."[48] It was within this conceptual framework that the notion of the "five obstacles" developed to finally obliterate women's chance for salvation altogether.[49] Thus they were condemned to the realm of unenlightened existence, that of the six paths (the realm of gods, humans, devils, animals, hungry ghosts, and hell), caught in the continual process of birth, suffering, and rebirth with no hope of ever escaping these transmigrational cycles.

Seen against this backdrop, the message brought by the Lotus Sutra that women might achieve buddhahood would have been revolutionary. Ordinary women of Heian Japan certainly had little inkling of just how the theoretical arguments against women had evolved. But considering the fact that they were barred even from entering major temples, not to mention subjected to numerous other religious taboos, songs such as these would have had considerable impact on them. The following *hōmon uta* no doubt offered and confirmed such an altered religious vision for women, compressing the drama of the Nāga Princess into four lines:

RH 116

nyonin itsutsu no sawari ari	Women have five obstacles;
muku no jōdo wa utokeredo	far from them the purity of the Pure Land.
renge shi nigori ni hirakureba	But even as the lotus blossoms in black mud,
ryūnyo mo hotoke ni narinikeri	so the daughter of the Dragon King has become buddha.

A *shiku no kamiuta* recaptures the same story, but with a colloquial verve befitting its origin in folk song:

RH 292

ryūnyo ga hotoke ni naru koto wa	Through Mañjuśrí's work, I hear,
monju no koshirae to koso kike	the Dragon King's daughter became buddha,
sa zo mōsu	that's what they say!
shagara ō no miya o idete	Leaving the palace of King Sāgara,
henjō nanshi to shite	she had to change into a man,

| tsui ni wa jōbutsudō | but finally she found the buddha path. |

The same message is repeated in two *hōmon uta*, but here the emphasis is on the power of the Lotus Sutra in helping one to achieve such a goal:

RH 113

shagara ō no musume dani	Even the daughter of King Sāgara,
mumarete yatose to iishi toki	only eight when she first heard
ichijō myōhō kikisomete	the ultimate and wonderful Lotus Sutra,
hotoke no michi ni wa chikazukishi	came near the buddha path.

RH 117

ōyosu nyonin hitotabi mo	Just once, if all women heard
kono hon zusuru koe kikeba	a voice chanting this chapter,
hachisu ni noboru chūya made	they'd climb the lotus by midnight,
nyonin nagaku hanarenamu	long out of their female bodies.[50]

The following song expressly salutes the Nāga Princess as an exemplar who was still relevant to Heian women and was to be emulated. At the same time, it challenges the Buddhist theories and prejudices against women by insisting that women do possess an inborn buddha nature:

RH 208

ryūnyo wa hotoke ni narinikeri	If the Dragon King's daughter became buddha,
nadoka warera mo narazaran	why can't we, too, somehow?
goshō no kumo koso atsuku to mo	A thick cloud, the five obstacles, yes,
nyorai gachirin kakusareji	but buddha nature shines through like the moon.

To the common women of Heian Japan with their low social standing, not to mention the female performers of these *imayō*, who were of decidedly marginal social status, the message embodied in the narrative of the Nāga Princess must have been welcome. Especially those *asobi* who made their living on the water's edge likely found poignant resonance in the story of the princess and her heroic feat.[51] And it is presumably from songs such as these that women of the period learned possibilities for their spiritual salvation.

IN PRAISE OF THE LOTUS SUTRA

The lofty tone in *Ryōjin hishō* owes much to the group of songs that pay tribute to the power and efficacy of the Lotus Sutra. Together these songs exalt the absolute necessity of the scripture to the lives of its believers. Often the sutra provides miraculous benefits, both spiritual and material, a fact that reinforces undivided devotion to the holy text. There is a noticeable cultic streak in this veneration. In the following song, for instance, the lyric voice, knowing the rewards, expresses joy at having the rare privilege of hearing the sutra preached:

RH 294

shaba ni shibashi mo yadoreru wa	A pilrigim briefly in this world,
ichijō kiku koso awarenare	I am grateful to hear the Lotus Sutra,
ureshikere	I am joyful,
ya	yes!
ninjin futatabi ukegatashi	How hard to be born a man again,
hokekyō ni ima ichido	but I might hope to hear once more
ikadeka mairiawamu	the Lotus Sutra.

The following *hōmon uta* eulogizes the indispensable guiding role of the Lotus Sutra for its followers, using the symbolic contrast of the moon (the historical Buddha in nirvanic extinction) and sun (Maitreya, the future Buddha):

RH 194

shaka no tsuki wa kakureniki	The Buddha-moon is hidden,
jishi no asahi wa mada haruka nari	the sun of Maitreya not yet risen;
sono hodo chōya no kuraki o ba	in the long night's darkness in between,
hokekyō nomi koso teraitamae	only the Lotus Sutra sheds its light.

Another *hōmon uta* likewise underscores the centrality of the Lotus Sutra as a guide to its believers:

RH 200

hachisu no hana o ba ita to fumi	Crossing lotus blossom planks,
onajiki kuki o ba tsue to tsuite	for staffs the lotus stalks,

korera ni asobamu hito wa mina   all who climb this way
ryōzenkaie no tomo to sen   would be companions on Eagle
                                      Peak.

This song stands out among *hōmon uta* by virtue of its imagery and lexicon. One innovation is the use of the Japanese vernacular *hachisu no hana* in place of the sinicized *renge* for lotus blossom, a common motif in *hōmon uta*. Also, here we find a unique instance of plain and ordinary images such as *ita* (plank or board), *kuki* (stalk), and *tsue* (stave or staff) in *hōmon uta* songs of this nature. Finally, the lines are relatively free of Buddhist terms with their cacophonous clash; the result is a lightness of tone and an unstilted, smooth flow from one line to the next.

The practice of honoring the sutra is emphatically advised in chapter 19, "Hosshi kudokuhon" (The Merits of the Dharma-Preacher), where the text lists miraculous rewards that come to those who venerate the sutra:

> If any good man or good woman shall accept and keep this scripture of the Dharma Blossom, whether reading it, reciting it, interpreting it, or copying it, that person shall attain eight hundred virtues of the eye, one thousand two hundred virtues of the ear, eight hundred virtues of the nose, one thousand two hundred virtues of the tongue, eight hundred virtues of the body, and one thousand two hundred virtues of the mind, by means of which virtues he shall adorn his six faculties, causing them all to be pure.[52]

In short, the five activities of preserving, reading, chanting, explaining, and copying the sutra are primary forms of expressing veneration for the sutra. All these practices are considered equal in value and effect. Essentially, they stem from the desire to deify the sutra and hence ensure the propagation of the sutra, oral and otherwise. The following *hōmon uta* expresses the same message:

RH 139

myōhōrengekyō   The wonderful Dharma of the
                                   Lotus Sutra:

kaki yomi tamoteru hito wa   whoever copies it, reads it, lives
    mina   it, they say,
goshu hosshi to nazuketsutsu   will be called preacher of the
                                    fivefold Dharma,

tsui ni wa rokkon kiyoshi to ka   with his six roots cleansed in the
                                    end!

Some *Ryōjin hishō* songs further illustrate direct and beneficial consequences of carrying out these counsels; for example:

RH 123

hokekyō dokujusuru hito wa	He who chants the Lotus Sutra
tenshodōji gusokuseri	is guarded by a heavenly host;
asobiariku ni osore nashi	he wanders the world without fear,
shishi ya ō no gotoku nari	like a lion king, oh yes, just like a lion.

RH 199

hokke no minori zo tanomoshiki	Trustworthy the Lotus Sutra's sacred Dharma.
shōji no umi wa fukakeredo	Though the sea of life and death holds us in its depths,
shokyō kuriyomu tatoi nite	if we read its chapters over and over,
tsui ni warera mo ukabinan	we will rise in the end to salvation.

The formulaic expression *tanomoshiki* (trustworthy) harks back to the *hōmon uta* on buddhas. Here, its use elevates the Lotus Sutra on a par with the Buddhist divinities.

In the following *hōmon uta*, a poetic conceit associates the merit of copying the Lotus Sutra with deer, introducing an unusual and pleasant change of pace:

RH 239

mine ni okifusu shika da ni mo	Even the deer bouncing or drowsing on the mountain
hotoke ni naru koto ito yasushi	can become buddhas, believe me,
onore ga uwage o totonoe fude ni yui	if as much as a hair is bound into brushes
ichijōmyōhō kaitan naru kudoku ni	to copy the absolute wonder of Dharma.

Carrying out the fivefold practices, however, required economic means, time, and a certain degree of literacy and learning. In early Japan, therefore, only the upper classes—imperial family, courtiers, priests—could follow the recommended procedures.[53] Copying the sutra was an especially expensive proposition, and explaining the scripture, which presupposes not only scholarship but also supreme dedication, was difficult even for aristocrats to do. Gradually, observance of the five practices began to be known among commoners, but their participation was necessarily limited. The basic option open to them was to attend occasional lecture meetings on the sutra, an activity that became increasingly popular during the Heian period.[54]

In *Ryōjin hishō*, the efficacy of *listening* to the sutra is stressed.[55] Such an emphasis on listening, a passive and rudimentary act that does not even appear in the five prescribed measures, signifies a sharp lowering of the threshold for acquiring merits. Likewise, the playing down of the virtue of copying or explaining the sutra supports the view that the songs were aimed specifically at the unlettered laity, including women and commoners.[56] The virtue of listening as a means of achieving salvation is proclaimed in the following song:

RH 103

hokekyō yamaki wa ichibu nari	The Lotus Sutra has eight scrolls;
nijūhachihon izure o mo	whoever listens, even for the blink of an eye,
shuyu no aida mo kiku hito no	to any of its twenty-eight chapters—
hotoke ni naranu wa nakarikeri	he cannot fail to become buddha.

And this song strikes the same note:

RH 69

hokke wa hotoke no shinnyo nari	Lotus Sutra, heart of the Buddha's teaching:
manbōmuni no mune o nobe	above all other Dharma it explains the all.
ichijōmyōhō kiku hito no	For those who hear this ultimate word—
hotoke ni naranu wa nakarikeri	they cannot fail to become buddha.

The following song also celebrates the merits of listening to the Lotus Sutra, but in a more lyrical manner:

RH 138

shaka no minori o kikishi yori	When I hear the sacred Dharma of Śākyamuni,

mi wa sumi kiyoki kagami nite	my body grows clear as the clearest mirror;
kokoro satori shiru koto wa	my heart that knows awakening
mukashi no hotoke ni kotonarazu	reflects the ancient heart of Buddha.

Unlike the more eulogistic *hōmon uta*, the next song expresses an overt cultic vision of the Lotus Sutra. It proclaims the value of the sutra in terms of its power to grant concrete, physical benefits, even medical help:

RH 154

shaba ni fushigi no kusuri ari	The magic potion of this mundane world,
hokekyō nari to zo toitamau	they say, is the Lotus Sutra;
furōfushi no yakuō wa	the eternal Medicine King who never ages
kiku hito amaneku tabarunari	cures with it all who have ears to hear.[57]

Another song, with its graphic details and bold pitch, proclaims the kind of reverence that the Lotus Sutra commands:

RH 163

hokekyō tamoteru hito soshiru	If there's evil talk against the lovers of the Lotus Sutra,
sore o soshireru mukui ni wa	the slanderers will pay,
kashira nanatsu ni waresakete	their heads split into seven parts,
arizu no eda ni kotonarazu	like branches from the Arjaka tree.[58]

The importance that *Ryōjin hishō* gives to the Lotus Sutra reflects the prevailing religious trend during the Heian period.[59] The *hokke-e* (meetings on the Lotus Sutra) ritual, which revolved around the sutra, began to develop as early as 746 during the Nara period, when the abbot Ryōben (689–773) of Tōdaiji conducted the first such meetings. This was even before the establishment of the Tendai school, which is based on the Lotus Sutra. Not until the mid-Heian period, however, did interest in the Lotus Sutra begin to grow rapidly; sponsored by the nobility, Lotus Sutra–related events proliferated.[60]

The most popular and widespread event was the *hokke hakkō*, centering on the recital of the eight scrolls of the Lotus Sutra, usually in conjunction with memorial services for the dead. Fujiwara Michinaga was one of the most famed promoters of such meetings; the *hokke hakkō* held at his residence, Hōjōji, were clear displays of his political and financial power. He is also believed to have performed the first ritual interment of copies of the Lotus Sutra text, in 1007 on Mount Kinbu, a practice that later became fashionable among the nobility during the *insei* period. Most important, Michinaga is thought to have created an entire subgenre of *waka* praising the Lotus Sutra.[61] Other noble families vied with one another to conduct similar rites in the name of that hallowed sutra. Even Shinto shrines joined in, thereby contributing sizably to the syncretic interaction between Buddhism and Shinto.[62] In this way the Lotus Sutra became an integral part of the upper classes' ritual practices during the Heian period.

Eventually *hokke-e* ritual activities filtered down to the common classes. The earliest such events performed for commoners reportedly took place in the Rokuhara Mitsuji Temple around the time of Kūya Shōnin, in the latter half of the tenth century. These gatherings, which lasted several days and were open to all regardless of gender or social status, drew several hundreds of thousands. During the day priests lectured on the Lotus Sutra, while at night both clergy and the assembled masses engaged in chanting. The objective was not so much to memorialize the dead, as was the case with the aristocratic rites, but to teach the audience how to achieve spiritual salvation. In one gathering that lasted four days, the audience was divided into four groups—priests, men, women, and children—with one day allotted to each. Instead of expensive offerings to the temples, an integral part of the nobles' ceremonies, it was common for flowers to be dedicated. In the early decades of the eleventh century, the priest Gyōen (fl. 1018) is known for carrying out the same popular *hokke hakkō* tradition in the Gyōganji Temple in the Heian capital.[63]

Paralleling these gatherings in the capital, another type of *hokke hakkō* designed for commoners began to be held in the countryside, particularly in the Kumano region. These Kumano *hakkō*, called *kechien hakkō* (eight lectures on the Lotus Sutra to establish ties with buddhas), supplemented chanting of the Lotus Sutra with ablution rites for fishermen and hunters, who made their living by killing animals. It is believed that *yamabushi* with some Tendai training played an important role in popularizing both the Lotus Sutra and *kechien hakkō* among common people.[64]

Thus the prominence of the Lotus Sutra in *Ryōjin hishō* mirrors a broad religious trend of the Heian period. The poetry of the Lotus Sutra cult that appears in the songs is in fact an important cultural expression of the Heian Buddhist religious consciousness, especially designed for the instruction of those who might not otherwise have an opportunity to hear the good news contained in the sutra.

The following *hōmon uta*, filled with visionary calm, is representative of the reverence for the Lotus Sutra that resounds through *Ryōjin hishō*:

RH 124

myōhō tsutomuru shirushi ni wa	As reward for serving the wonderful Dharma
mukashi mada minu yume zo miru	in sleep I see what has never been seen.
sore yori sōji no neburi same	Waking from our daily dream of life and death,
kakugo no tsuki o zo moteasobu	I glory in the moon of enlightenment.

The *Ryōjin hishō* songs that relate to Buddhism endeavor to make the religion easy to understand and to show how to come closer to the divine. Such proselytizing efforts take the form of exhortation, coaxing, persuasion, and exemplification; they remove obstacles, arouse interest, and make listeners learn. In the end, the songs affirm the hope and possibilities of spiritual rebirth, as well as the need to let the message make its way into more hearts and minds. Belief in the oneness of human beings and the Buddha shines forth, as in this song:

RH 137

sanshin busshō tama wa aredo	The triple-bodied buddha nature is our jewel,
shōji no chiri ni zo kegaretaru	all soiled by birth and dusty death;
rokkon shōjō ete nochi zo	but after the purification of the six roots,
honoka ni hikari wa terashikeru	softly, yes, it radiates its light.[65]

Shinto-Buddhist Syncretism

The syncretic blend of Shinto and Buddhism, evolving from the Nara period on, represents an important development in both the religious consciousness and the history of Japan. While aiming at the harmonious coexistence of the two distinctive religious systems, the one indigenous, the other imported, the syncretic approach bred an array of new beliefs and observances based on what each component could offer. In this cross-fertilization, innovative notions about the divinities in both the Shinto and the Buddhist pantheon were spawned, with new dimensions being added to their nature, attributes, and power. New cults emerged focusing on ever more complicated combinations of these supernatural beings. The syncretic interaction caused the *yamabushi* and *hijiri* (holy men) traditions to proliferate, which in turn accelerated the process of amalgamation of the two religions.[66] Pilgrimage was similarly reinforced and also began to thrive, firmly establishing itself as an integral part of Japanese religious practice.

Syncretic advancement, however, was not limited to the religious realm. Its influence spread to other areas of culture, including the arts and literature. The pictorial representation of sacred geography in terms of syncretic mandala is one distinctive by-product in the field of fine arts, for example, while the *engi* (origin myths of temples and shrines) experienced a similar efflorescence in the literary sphere.[67] *Ryōjin hishō* too, especially the *shiku no kamiuta*, reveals how the poetic imagination was inspired by the syncretic movement and how that energy was harnessed in lyrical modes.

Among motifs related to Shinto-Buddhist syncretism in *Ryōjin hishō*, three occur with marked frequency: the concept of *honji suijaku* (original nature/trace manifestation), pilgrimage, and *yamabushi* and *hijiri* cults. Occupying considerable space in *shiku no kamiuta*, these topics convey another layer of religiosity embodied in the anthology.

HONJI SUIJAKU

According to *honji suijaku*, indigenous Japanese deities are manifestations (*suijaku*, the traces left behind) of Buddhist divinities (*honji*, the original nature). Practically speaking, this meant selecting important gods from the Buddhist tradition and matching them with Shinto gods (*kami*), then endowing the latter with the functions and capacities of the former. The deliberate effort to establish a correlation between Shinto and Buddhism resulted in the native *kami* being elevated to a metaphysical status they never had prior to contact with Buddhism. Simultaneously, it naturalized or acculturated Buddhism to the existing Japanese religious framework and outlook.

In what manner does the philosophy of *honji suijaku* find expression in *Ryōjin hishō*? We begin with a *shiku no kamiuta* that is in itself a poetic abstract of the concept:

RH 244

buppō hiromu to te	To teach the Dharma,
tendai fumoto ni ato o	buddhas descended to earth
tareowashimasu	below Mount Tendai;
hikari o yawaragete chiri to	dimming their radiance, they
nashi	became dust like us,
higashi no miya to zo	so we worship them at the
iwawareowashimasu	Eastern Shrine.[68]

This song establishes a correspondence between the powerful Shinto shrine of Hie and Enryakuji Temple, the center of the Tendai Buddhist sect in Japan. To present this syncretic relationship, the song plays on two phrases. The first one, consisting of *ato* (trace, *jaku*) and *tare* (to drop, descend, *sui*), renders *honji suijaku* in the Japanese vernacular. The second one is based on *wakō dōjin* (softening the radiance and becoming one with dust), a phrase used to explain the Buddha's historical appearance as a manifestation of the cosmic principle.[69] In the third line of the song, namely, we find the words *kō* (light, *hikari*), *wa* (to soften, *yawarage*), and *jin* (dust, *chiri*), incorporating the meaning of *wakō dōjin* in one line. Thus the song suggests that the buddhas, having relinquished their transcendental existence (*wakō*), incarnated themselves as Shinto divinities (*dōjin*)—synonymous with *honji suijaku*—and are working to spread the Buddha's teaching.

Of the diverse forms of syncretism found in *Ryōjin hishō*, the Tendai-Hie correspondence, in which both major and subsidiary shrines in the Hie complex were matched with various Buddhist temples, is most conspicuous.[70] Its prominence may in part reflect the strength of the actual alliance between the Tendai establishment and the Hie Shrine.

Traditionally, the Hie Shrine complex has been known as the Sannō (mountain king) system because of its links to the worship of nearby Mount Hiei. It consisted of twenty-one shrines, which were ranked according to primary, secondary, and tertiary status. With the rise of syncretism, all these shrines and their respective *kami* were matched with Buddhist divinities. The primary shrine of Ōmiya (Nishimotomiya), for instance, was linked with the historical Buddha; Ninomiya (Higashimotomiya) was identified with Yakushi; Shōshinji (Usamiya), with Amida; Hachiōji (Ōji or Ushiomiya), with Thousand-armed Kannon; and Ichidō (Hayao), with Fudō.[71] The Hie complex thus came to embody a comprehensive and elaborate systematization of Shinto-Buddhist syncretic interactions. It should come as no surprise, then, that the Sannō system was well represented in the *jinbun* (songs sung to Shinto deities) subsection of the *shiku no kamiuta*.

The following *shiku no kamiuta*, which identifies a number of shrines from the Hie complex as major Buddhist divinities, is a classic example of the Tendai-Sannō syncretism:

RH 417

ōmiya ryōjusen	Ōmiya is Eagle Peak;
hingashi no fumoto wa	its base to the east, they say,
bodaiju ge to ka	is the foot of the Bodhi tree;
ryōshosanjo wa shaka yakushi	the two shrines are Śākyamuni and Yakushi;

sate wa ōji wa kanzeon	and the third one; and Ōji is Kannon.[72]

The song approximates a syncretic mandala in verse. First, the focus is on the top-ranking shrine of Ōmiya, where the most important ritual activities in the Hie complex were conducted. Accordingly, it is matched with Eagle Peak, the fabled site of the Buddha's preaching of the Lotus Sutra. The attention then shifts to the eastern base—that is, Ninomiya—which is identified with the Bodhi tree under which Śākyamuni achieved buddhahood. By specifically naming Śākyamuni and Yakushi (Buddha's attendant on his left), the verse reinforces that the two shrines are Ōmiya and Ninomiya. The third shrine, mentioned but not specified, is thought to be Shōshinji, which is paired with Amida. And the song ends by identifying Hachiōji with the Thousand-armed Kannon, rounding out the Sannō syncretic mandala.[73]

In contrast to that sweeping presentation of the entire Sannō system, the next song dwells at some length on each of a handful of shrines within the Hie complex:

RH 247

ōjō hingashi wa chikatōmi	In the east of the capital is Ōmi Province,
tendai sannō mine no omae	where the Tendai-Sannō shrines are;
gosho no omae wa shōshinji	Shōshinji is sacred among the five,
shujō negai o ichidō ni	the prayers of all the living are offered to Ichidō.

Here, the phrase *shujō* (all living beings), a Buddhist diction, is appropriated to express the importance of the Shinto deity Ichidō in the lives of the people, thereby establishing the Shinto-Buddhist correspondence through lexical borrowing.

The following song explicitly equates the main shrine of the Sannō complex, Ōmiya, with the Buddha, and its precincts with the Eagle Peak:

RH 411

ōmiya gongen wa omoeba	Ōmi's avatar, now that I think of it,
kyōsu no shaka zo kashi	is Śākyamuni, founder of Buddhism;
ichido mo kono chi o fumu hito wa	anyone who sets foot on this land just once

ryōzenkaie no tomo to sen	would be a companion on Eagle Peak.

In some songs, the process of equation is reversed and Buddhist gods become part of the Shinto pantheon. In the next song, although the shrine in question is not specified, we can presume it is the Marōdo Shrine in the Hie complex, which is identified with the Eleven-headed Kannon:

RH 275

hontai kanzeon	Kannon's original body
jōzai fudaraku no sen	remains forever on Mount Potalaka;
ido ya shujō	to save all the living, he has been revealed as a great *kami*
shōjō jigen daimyōjin.	for all the cycles of time.

Syncretic rhetoric operates even in songs that praise the beauty of nature. In the following *shiku no kamiuta*, the scenic beauty of Lake Biwa in Ōmi region is praised from a Tendai-Sannō point of view. Here, the lake is described as a pond in the paradise of Yakushi, who supposedly resides on Mount Hiei (called Mount Tendai). The rich imagery is drawn from the usual Buddhist description of paradise, resulting in the Buddhistic sacralization of the Japanese secular landscape:

RH 253

ōmi no mizuumi wa umi narazu	Not a lake, that lake in Ōmi,
tendai yakushi no ike zo ka shi	but Tendai Yakushi's pond, yes!
na zo no umi	What kind of pond?
jōraku gajō no kaze fukeba	When the wind of eternally pure joy blows,
shichihō renge no nami zo tatsu	waves rise, of seven-jeweled lotus blooms.

Similarly in another *shiku no kamiuta*, Mount Kinbu, the center for mountain asceticism, is perceived as the Tuṣita Heaven, the abode of Maitreya, and becomes a setting for the syncretic interaction of a female shaman (the speaker) and a pair of Buddhist monks:

RH 264

kane no mitake wa shijūkuin no ji nari	The land of Mount Kinbu has forty-nine quarters.
ōna wa hyakunichi sennichi wa mishikado	Well, this old woman tried for a hundred,
eshiritamawazu	a thousand, days,

niwaka ni buppō sōtachi no futari	but the god would not reveal himself.
owashimashite	Suddenly along come two Buddhist monks,
okonai arawakashitatematsuru	and with their ritual, the god appears![74]

The song depicts syncreticism in action. When the female shaman failed in her performance of the Shinto ritual task, the Buddhist priests took over and successfully carried it through. In this cooperation, Shinto and Buddhism are melded—though the song may seem to suggest the shaman's surprise and wonder at the superior power of the monks.

Syncretism marks the Shinto shrines in the Kumano area as well, whose major divinities likewise were matched with those in the Buddhist pantheon. The *Kumano sanzan* (Kumano triad), for example—Hongū (Ketsumiko-gami), Shingū (Hayatamamiya), and Nachi (Yui no Miya)—were paired with Amida, Yakushi, and the Thousand-armed Kannon, respectively. Accordingly, the triad was also called *Kumano sansho gongen* (the three avatars of Kumano).[75] Here, the term *gongen* means the Buddha's incarnation in the borrowed form of *kami* and so is equivalent to *suijaku*. Gradually, the Kumano syncretism absorbed nine additional locally worshiped Shinto divinities, allotting to each of them a Buddhist counterpart; they were called *Kumano jūni gongen* (the twelve avatars of Kumano).[76] Knowledge of this syncretic development in Kumano is reflected in the following *shiku no kamiuta* on Nyakuōji, who corresponds to the Eleven-headed Kannon:

RH 259

kumano no gongen wa	The Kumano avatar
nagusa no hama ni koso oritamae	has surely descended on Nagusa Beach;
waka no ura ni shi mashimaseba	he lives on Waka Bay,
toshi wa yukedomo nyakuōji	the lord Nyakuōji, young though years pass.[77]

The light tone and even the meaning of the song derive from two key words: *waka* (young), in the name of the bay, appears also in its sinicized version, *nyaku*, as part of the name of the shrine. The semantic interplay between the two words lends further depth to the song: we now see "a young lord, residing on the young bay, who will not be affected by the passage of time."

The next *shiku no kamiuta* is based on an implied correspondence between the Shinto deity of the Nyakuōji Shrine and the compassionate Kannon:

RH 413

kumano no gongen wa	The Kumano avatar
nagusa no hama ni zo oritamau	has surely descended on Nagusa Beach;
ama no obune ni noritamai	in the small boats of the fishermen
jihi no sode o zo taretamau	he waves the sleeves of his compassion.

This song is reminiscent of *hōmon uta* no. 37, in which Kannon is compared to a rafter.

Given the dominance of the *honji suijaku* concept in *Ryōjin hishō* songs, especially in *shiku no kamiuta*, we can see that by the late Heian period the syncretic view of Buddhism and Shinto was spreading rapidly among the masses.[78] To their credit, some *shiku no kamiuta* display a firm command of *honji suijaku* and even manage a certain degree of poetic conceit—no small feat, considering the difficulty of establishing correct correspondence between the various divinities, particularly in such a limited space. These *shiku no kamiuta* highlight the double religious world in which their poets lived and sang—their own religious internationalism, so to speak.

POPULAR PILGRIMAGE

Like many religious practices, the pilgrimage is a mechanism created to bring men into close contact with the divine. What makes the pilgrimage unique is its requirement that devotees *physically* separate themselves from their familiar, mundane environment and subject themselves to a ritualistic regimen in specific locations far from home. That is, whereas other religious observances, such as prayer, scripture reading, and fasting, can be carried out at home, a pilgrimage is not legitimate until a believer has left home and stayed in sacred sites.

Devotional journeying has a long history in Buddhism. The earliest significant historical precedent for pilgrimage in the Buddhist tradition is generally attributed to King Aśoka (ca. 268–233 B.C.) of India, who reportedly erected numerous sacred *stūpa* and paid homage to them through periodic visits.[79] Other celebrated Buddhist pilgrims in East Asia include Hsüan-tsang (596–664) of T'ang China, who went to India, and Saichō, Kūkai, Ennin, and Enchin of the early Heian period, all of whom endured difficult journeys to China and then made numerous pilgrimages to sites within that country. By their personal examples, these Japanese priests are believed to have begun the Buddhist pilgrimage tradition in Japan.

The practice of pilgrimage in Japan combined native mountain worship with the Buddhist focus on visiting sacred locales. It was further reinforced by the *honji suijaku* notion, in which the mountain *kami* took on the physical manifestations of Buddhist divinities. Therefore, "pilgrimages to these mountains, accompanied and guided by the experienced mountain ascetics, were believed to bring favours from both the Shinto and Buddhist divinities simultaneously."[80] The making of pilgrimages reached its zenith toward the end of the Heian period, coinciding with the wide spread of Amidism, which, as we have seen, identified the Kumano area with Amida's Pure Land and the southern seashore of that region with Kannon's Mount Potalaka. Even within the sacred compounds, syncretic religious vision regulated the view of the holy ground:

> In these mountains, certain areas around the temple are designated as representing *jigoku* ("hell") and *gokuraku* ("pure land" or "paradise"); worshipers are expected to go through the former before entering the latter. In this manner the historic Buddhist notion of perpendicular cosmology, consisting of the three levels of heaven, earth, and underworld, has been reinterpreted to fit into the indigenous religious view of the Japanese.[81]

As a rule, pilgrimage sites in Japan were tucked away deep in the mountains or perched on nearly inaccessible precipices, as in the mountains of Yoshino and Kumano to the south of the capital. These forbidding locations required of the pilgrims determination, physical strength, firm belief in the undertaking, and sometimes even their lives. The popular expression *mizu no sakazuki* (the farewell cup of water), referring to the last drink shared by a pilgrim with those left behind, emerged from this recognition that the traveler might not return alive.[82]

In *Ryōjin hishō*, various aspects of pilgrimage are revealed. One dominant theme concerns the physical hardship of such journeys; this is exemplified in four clustered songs in the *shiku no kamiuta* section, all of which are related to Kumano pilgrimage. For instance:

RH 260

hana no miyako o furisutete	Why should I feel sad, off on a pilgrimage,
kurekure mairu wa oborokeka	leaving the flowery capital.
katsu wa gongen goranze yo	Avatar, I pray, watch over me
shōren no manako o azayaka ni	with your lotus-blue eyes open wide.

Here the play on the *honji suijaku* relationship between the avatar (Kumano Hongū) and Amida, conjured up by the reference to lotus-blue eyes, makes the pilgrim's plea doubly beseeching, hinting at the difficulties he or she expects to encounter along the way.

Another *shiku no kamiuta* on the pilgrimage to Kumano expresses the pilgrim's hardship but with an imaginative conceit:

RH 258

kumano e mairamu to omoedo mo	I want to go as a pilgrim to Kumano,
kachi yori maireba michi tōshi	but the road is long for walking,
sugurete yama kibishi	and the mountains hard.
muma ni te maireba kugyō narazu	Going on horseback would hardly be austere,
sora yori mairamu	so I'd like to fly through the air.
hane tabe nyakuōji	Lord Nyakuō, grant me wings!

Even a short pilgrimage from the capital to the Yawata Shrine, another name for the Iwashimizu Hachiman Shrine, was not easy, as this song suggests:

RH 261

yawata e mairan to omoedo mo	I want to go as a pilgrim to Yawata,
kamogawa katsuragawa ito hayashi	but the Kamo and the Katsura are too rapid,
ana hayashi na	oh lord, rivers too rapid!
yodo no watari ni fune ukete	Please meet me, Great Bodhisattva Hachiman,
mukaetamae daibosatsu	in a boat at the Yodo ford![83]

Here, too, we find evidence of Shinto-Buddhist syncretism, this time in the speaker's address of Hachiman, the powerful Shinto military god, as "Great Bodhisattva."[84] Furthermore, the speaker's qualms about the pilgrimage expressed in the phrase *mairan to omoe do mo* (though I would like) connects this *shiku no kamiuta* with the preceding song in terms of mood and content.

The best-known pilgrimage sites, besides those on the way to Kumano, were on the long circuit routes of the Saikoku Thirty-three Pilgrimage (*Saikoku sanjū-san reijō*) and the Shikoku Eighty-eight Pilgrimage (*Shikoku hachijū-hachi reijō*).[85] The Saikoku pilgrimage, which comprehended thirty-three temples of Kannon, was especially popular among commoners.[86] As they traveled, the pilgrims sang rhythmic chants, which often included lists of holy sites they had visited or intended to visit.[87] In *Ryōjin hishō*, the *shiku no kamiuta* subsection called *reigensho uta* (songs on miraculous places) is noted for its collection of such songs. For example, the following song lists in catalog fashion some of the stops along the Saikoku pilgrimage route:

RH 313

kan'on shirushi o misuru tera	Temples that bear the marks of Kannon:
kiyomizu ishiyama hase no oyama	Kiyomizu, Ishiyama, sacred Mount Hase,
kogawa ōmi naru hikoneyama	Kogawa, and Mount Hikone in Ōmi;
majikaku miyuru wa rokakudō	closer, they can be seen at Rokkakudō.[88]

The longest song in *Ryōjin hishō*, no. 314, is in fact such a pilgrimage route "guide map." It lists important sites and objects on the way to the Kiyomizu Temple, one of the stops on the Saikoku circuit. Although some names and places are unidentifiable now, the list suggests that the route was something quite memorable:

RH 314

izureka kiyomizu e mairu michi	Which way to Kiyomizu Temple?
kyōgoku kudari ni gojō made	Go down Kyōgoku south to Gojō Street,
ishibashi yo hingashi no hashizume	find Ishibashi at the east end of the bridge;
yotsumune rokuharadō otagidera	pass Yotsumune, Rokuharadō, and Otagi-dera,
ōbotoke fukai to ka	pass the great Buddha, then Fukai,
sore o uchisugite yasakadera	and after them Yasaka Temple.
hitodan noborite mioroseba	Climb the hill to Kiyomizu and look below:
sakandayū ga niōdō	there's Sakandayu's Niōdō,
tō no moto amakudari sueyashiro	Gion Shrine at the end of the Yasaka Pagoda;
minami o uchimireba	to the south, the water basins.
chōzudana chōzu to ka	After the ritual washing,
omae ni mairite kugyōraihai shite	we go to the temple for reverent worship.

miroseba	Then look down
kono taki wa	at this curious waterfall
yōgaru taki no kyōgaru taki no mizu	with its delightful streams.[89]

Occasionally pilgrimage route songs focus on places for sightseeing or secular diversion along the way—including even locales where *asobi*-type female entertainment could be found. Apparently, the boundary between the sacred and profane was rather fluid for the pilgrims. The following song, which details the route to Hōrin Temple, located in Arashiyama in the western outskirts of the Heian capital, a pleasure resort known for its cherry blossoms and autumn leaves, is one example:

RH 307

izureka hōrin e mairu michi	Which way to Hōrin Temple?
uchi no dōri no nishi no kyō	From Uchi no Dōri to Nishi no Kyō:
sore sugite	after passing them,
ya	oh yes,
tokiwabayashi no anatanaru	opposite the Tokiwa forest,
aigyō nagare kuru ōigawa	the Ōi River floats courtesans.[90]

Some pilgrimage songs emphasize the positive by outlining the material rewards resulting from the difficult undertaking:

RH 272

iwagamisanjo wa imakibune	Iwagami-Sanjo is Ima-Kibune,
maireba negai zo mitetamau	one visit will answer prayers;
kaerite jūso o uchimireba	when you come home and look around,
musu no takara zo yutakanaru	the number of your treasures is countless.[91]

By emphasizing this-worldly, concrete benefit, this and similar *shiku no kamiuta* may have sought to encourage the act of pilgrimage by relieving the travelers of worry about both physical and mental hardships. Like the Buddhist songs that stress the historical, human aspect of the Buddha and the cultic power of Kannon, Yakushi, and Jizō, these songs emphasize the secularly or more pragmatically meritorious side of religion.

CULTS OF *HIJIRI* AND *YAMABUSHI*

Those who made pilgrimages and observed asceticism as part of their profession were *hijiri* (holy men), *yamabushi* (mountain ascetics), and *shugyōja* (those who undergo austerities; also known as *shugenja*, exorcists), all practitioners of *shugendō*, mountain asceticism.[92] Historically as a group they shunned the official Buddhist establishment, which was closely allied with the ruling class, choosing instead to serve the common people. Their unorthodox attitude toward their religious calling was expressed in their refusal to receive formal ordination, which only the official Buddhist institutions administered. Many of them, including such charismatic leaders as En no Shōkaku (or En no Gyōja, b. 634) and Gyōgi (668–749), to whom the origin of the *hijiri* tradition is usually traced, concerned themselves exclusively with the welfare of the masses.[93]

The ascetics' practice was to retreat into the rugged mountains and suffer extremely harsh privations to become empowered with supernatural abilities. The term *yamabushi*, meaning "one who lies down on a mountain," alludes to these trials. Underlying this form of asceticism is a fusion of magico-religious mountain worship and Buddhism, as Ichiro Hori enunciates:

> The mountain is . . . believed to be the world of the spirits and of the deities, buddhas, or bodhisattvas, where shamans and ascetics must undergo the austerities of hell to receive the powers and blessings of paradise and where souls of the dead also must undergo initiation in order to enter paradise or Buddha's Pure Land. Shugen-dō . . . was built on just these primitive but fundamental common beliefs in mountains.[94]

Thus, *shugendō* is yet another expression of the Shinto-Buddhist syncretism.

In fact, the mountain ascetics made use of various Buddhist and Shinto practices and worshiped numerous divinities whose interrelationships were established by the *honji suijaku* discourse. For instance, one of the main gods of *shugendō*, Fudō, is appropriated from the Shingon pantheon. And Kongōzaō gongen (the Diamond Zaō Avatar), who is said to have endowed En no Gyōja with magical power on Mount Kinbu, is worshiped as a primary divinity by *yamabushi* in the Mount Kinbu area; moreover, he is supposed to have as his original bodies the Buddha, Kannon, and Maitreya.[95] The syncretic sacred geography also plays a large role in *shugendō*, providing the sites for these ascetics' trials. The whole mountain range from the Yoshino to Kumano, the cradle of *shugendō*, for example, is considered the dual mandala of Kongōkai (the Diamond Realm, representing the wisdom of Dainichi and his efforts to destroy all kinds of illusion) and Taizōkai (the Matrix Realm, symbolizing the teachings of Dainichi), the two diagrammatic schemes of the cosmos central to esoteric

Shingon symbolism and ritual practices.[96] En no Gyōja, ascribed as the founder of mountain asceticism in Japan, is linked to a number of *shugendō* practice sites as well, and *Ryōjin hishō* songs that deal with the subject of *hijiri* or *yamabushi* have him as an almost indispensable presence. The following song, for instance, which mentions important Heian-period centers of asceticism, features this combination of syncretic sacred geography and cultic worship of En no Gyōja:

RH 188

ōmine hijiri o fune ni nose	Put the Ōmine holy man on board,
kogawa no hijiri o he ni tatete	Kogawa's holy man at the bow,
shōkyū hijiri ni kaji torasete	let Shosha's holy man take the helm,
ya	oh yes,
nosete watasan	with them we can make the crossing
jōjūbusshō ya gokuraku e	to Buddha's unchanging paradise.

Ōmine is known as the center of the mountain ascetics, with its highest peak, Mount Kinbu, associated with En no Gyōja. Mount Shosha refers to Enkyōji Temple in Himeji City, Hyōgo Prefecture, founded by Shōkū Shōnin and considered to be the Tendai center in western Japan. The temple is the twenty-seventh stop on the Saikoku pilgrimage route. During the *insei* period its reputation as an ascetic center became widely known; and incidentally, its refectory was built by Emperor Go-Shirakawa in 1174.[97]

A number of songs in *Ryōjin hishō*, especially among the *shiku no kamiuta*, exhibit keen interest in *hijiri* and *yamabushi*, the characteristic attitude being one of curiosity, fascination, and occasionally awe. In a manner quite different from its treatment of Buddhist figures, the anthology considers this group of nameless people as a class rather than as individuals, closely examining their modes of life, favorite haunts, and the nature of their asceticism. A common technique is to list ascetic centers, usually with little subjective comment; frequently the names are obscure or refer to places that no longer exist, though they may have been thriving gathering places for *yamabushi* at the time when these songs were composed. The task of deciphering these songs is therefore often far from straightforward. A pair of companion songs, which present the extensive network of ascetic centers, illustrates this point:

RH 297

hijiri no jūsho wa doko doko zo	Where are the holy men? Where?
minō yo kachio yo	Oh, Minō, oh, Katsuo,
harima naru sosa no yama	at Mount Shosha in Harima,
izumo no wanifuchi ya hi no misaki	oh Wanifuchi, oh Hi no Misaki, in Izumo,
minami wa kumano no nachi to ka ya	in the south, I hear, Nachi of Kumano.

Minō refers to Takianji Temple, located in Minō City, Osaka Prefecture, said to have been founded by En no Gyōja. Katsuo refers to the Katsuo Temple, also located in Minō City; it is the twenty-third stop on the Saikoku pilgrimage route and is known for its scenic beauty. Wanifuchi refers to Gakuenji Temple, located in Hirada City, Shimane Prefecture. Legend has it that the temple was founded by the priest Chishun Shōnin at this location after the water from its valley miraculously cured the eye disease of Empress Suiko (r. 592–628). The name of the temple, which means "Crocodile Pool," originated in a story that when Chishun Shōnin accidentally dropped a Buddhist utensil into the pool, a crocodile emerged from the water and brought it back to him. Hi no Misaki Shrine is also located in Shimane Prefecture, to the northwest of Izumo Shrine. Consisting of two shrines, with Susano o no Mikoto (the upper shrine) and Amaterasu (the lower shrine) as the main deities of worship, it competed for prestige with Gakuenji Temple.[98]

RH 298

hijiri no jūsho wa doko doko zo	Where are the holy men? Where?
ōmine kazuraki ishi no tsuchi	Ōmine, Katsuragi, Ishi no Tsuchi,
minō yo kachio yo	oh, Minō, oh, Katsuo,
harima no sosa no yama	Mount Shosha in Harima,
minami wa kumano no nachi shingū	in the south, Nachi and Shingū of Kumano.

Katsuragi is a rugged mountain range between Osaka and Nara prefectures on which En no Gyōja exercised asceticism. Ishi no Tsuchi, located in the eastern part of Ehime Prefecture, is the highest mountain on Shikoku Island. It, too, is associated with En no Gyōja, and sources relate that Kūkai practiced asceticism here also.[99]

These two songs map out the ascetic centers in the south and west of Japan; they also point to the prominence of Kumano in mountain asceticism. The sites mentioned embrace all three types of pilgrimage classified by Joseph Kitagawa: pilgrimage to a sacred mountain, pilgrimage based on faith in certain divinities, and pilgrimage based on faith in charismatic figures.[100] The juxtaposition of shrines and temples on such a grand scale not only portrays the Japanese landscape as a sacred mandala, in the Shinto-Buddhist syncretic mode, but also conveys the wide spread of mountain asceticism during the Heian period.

A greater consecration of the Japanese national geography occurs in songs that cover far larger areas, extending from remote corners of the eastern regions to the far western provinces. Some of the sacred places are associated with unusual natural features, such as hot springs or volcanoes, or with supernatural events from Japan's mythico-historical past. Thus a pilgrimage was not simply a religious exercise, but a cultural and historical journey into the national heritage. On the level of artistic craft, the following song is distinctive in its consistent listing of provinces, with one ascetic center per province being singled out, as if it were representative of the whole province:

RH 310

yomo no reigensho wa	Sacred places in our world's four quarters:
izu no hashiriyu shinano no togakushi	Hashiriyu in Izu, Togakushi in Shinano,
suruga no fuji no yama hōki no daisen	Mount Fuji in Suruga and Daisen in Hoki,
tango no nariai to ka	Nariai in Tango, and so on,
tosa no muroto	Muroto in Tosa,
sanuki no shido no dōjō to koso kike	the holy place, I hear, is Shido in Sanuki.

Hashiriyu (meaning "hot running water") refers to the Izusan Shrine located on Mount Izu in Shizuoka Prefecture, its name being derived from a hot spring in the mountain. The Togakushi (Hidden Gate) Shrine is located on Mount Togaku in Nagano Prefecture. Mount Togaku is considered to be the rock gate that Ame no tachikara o no Mikoto removed from the rock grotto in which Amaterasu was hiding and hurled down to the lower world. Mount Fuji in Shizuoka Prefecture has long been regarded as a sacred realm because of its sporadic volcanic eruptions. Daisenji Temple, located on the precipitous Mount Daisen in Tottori Prefecture, is said to have been founded by Gyōgi. Nariai Temple, located in Kyoto-Fu, is the twenty-eighth stop on the Saikoku pilgrimage route and is known as one of its most scenic spots. The name of the temple has its origins in a miraculous story related to Kannon. A monk who was living on the mountain was on the brink of starvation owing to a heavy snow, when suddenly a deer appeared before him and died. The monk ate it and was brought back to life; but to his horror, he discovered that the wooden Kannon statue he worshiped had fallen to the ground bleeding. As the monk wept in utter shame, realizing that he had eaten part of the statue, Kannon's wound was healed and the statue was restored to its former state (*nari-au*)—hence the name of the temple. Muroto refers to Hotsumisaki Temple located on the seashore of Muroto City at the southeastern tip of Kōchi Prefecture facing the Pacific Ocean. As the celebrated site of Kūkai's enlightenment, it is the twenty-sixth stop on the Shikoku pilgrimage route. Shido Temple, located in Kagawa Prefecture facing Awaji Island across the straits, is the oldest temple in the eastern Sanuki area and the eighty-sixth stop on the Shikoku pilgrimage route.[101]

With these songs one gains an understanding of the complex religious vision of the late Heian period, which sees the country in terms of syncretic sacred manifestations and epiphanic contact points. At the time they were circulated, they may have helped the audience view their lives in the broader setting of religious and cultural tradition. In addition, they may have spurred curiosity about geographic areas beyond the capital or the listeners' home regions.[102] In the larger context of the Japanese literary tradition, songs about ascetic centers may have been the forerunners of Muromachi-period pilgrimage songs such as "Kumano sankei" (Kumano Pilgrimage), which were presented on a much larger scale than *shiku no kamiuta*.[103]

Songs on *hijiri* and *yamabushi* often take the audience to the hidden side of their austerities. These ascetic exercises included fasting, abstention from drinking water, gathering firewood, hauling water from the mountaintop, standing under a frigid waterfall, and even hanging upside down by a rope over a mountain precipice.[104] Sometimes solitary confinement for extended periods in a cave was prescribed. The underlying goal of all this physical discipline was to gain control over one's own body and spirit, thereby gaining complete freedom from limiting human conditions.

Among the trials thus endured, the severest and most demanding occurred in the mountains in the depths of winter. It was often thought that unless an ascetic spent a winter undergoing self-privation in a mountain cave, he could never be a full-fledged *yamabushi*.[105] The following song offers a glimpse of the extreme hardships of winter asceticism that push human endurance to its limit:

RH 305

fuyu wa yamabushi shugyō seshi	The mountain ascetic suffers the austerity of winter:
iori to tanomeshi ko no ha mo	his house of trees has lost

momijishite chirihatete	its autumn-yellow leaves.
sora sabishi	The sky is empty.
niku to omoishi koke ni mo	Even the moss he took for bedding
hatsushimo yuki furitsumite	now freezes, piled with snow.
iwama ni nagarekoshi mizu mo	Even the water falling through the rocks
kōrishinikeri	has turned to ice.

Here nature, once the ascetic's source of support, has become a most exacting testing ground, demanding utter stoicism. The song depicts the state of complete physical deprivation through which the *yamabushi* acquires supramundane power.

The next song reveals that the ascetics also faced more insidious spiritual temptations initiated by the devil. The power of evil was presumably so overwhelming that the ascetics prevailed over it only with difficulty, whereupon they obtained their supernatural potency:

RH 303

shiba no iori ni hijiri owasu	In many ways the devil tempts
tenma wa samazama ni nayamasedo	the holy man in his brushwood hut;
myōjō yōyaku izuru hodo	when the morning star appears, finally
tsui ni wa shitagai tatematsuru	the devil gives up and worships the holy man.

As this song suggests, the invincibility often associated with holy men came from their successful struggle against powers at odds with their spiritual goals.

The pilgrimages made by *hijiri* and *yamabushi,* another mandatory component of ascetic exercises, is the subject of a number of *shiku no kamiuta.* The degree and circumstances of hardship encountered surpassed those of occasional pilgrims. In the following song, the ordeals ascetics confront in traveling through rough and isolated regions in the Noto Peninsula are conveyed plaintively:

RH 300

warera ga shugyō ni ideshi toki	Our penitential pilgrimage began
suzu no misaki o kaimawari uchimeguri	by circling the Suzu Cape, by going round it;
furisutete	leaving all behind,
hitori koshiji no tabi ni idete	I set out for Koshi Road.

| ashi uchiseshi koso | How painful each bruised |
| awarenarishika | footstep![106] |

Another song includes more specific details about the harsh regimen of asceticism and the ascetics' physical appearance:

RH 301

warera ga shugyōseshi yō wa	How we looked, in our asceticism:
ninniku kesa o ba kata ni kake	stoles of endurance hanging on shoulders,
mata oi o oi	and wicker baskets on our backs;
koromo wa itsu to naku shio tarete	robes always soaked with brine.
shikoku no hechi o zo tsune ni fumu	Endlessly we round the edge of Shikoku Island.[107]

Two points in this song are noteworthy. First, the group is obviously undergoing a form of water asceticism. These austerities, at first conceived as a preparatory cleansing, eventually came to be regarded as an effective means of obtaining ascetic power in itself and so found a regular place in ascetic ritual.[108] Second, "walking," indicated here by the word *fumu* (to walk), was a prerequisite and indeed the very soul of ascetic practice, as it constitutes a symbolic negation of the profane.[109] The song, by presenting the image of a group of ascetics constantly on the go, in robes bleached by the blazing sun and salty seawater, vividly evokes the painful process of self-negation that ascetics routinely underwent.

The interest of *Ryōjin hishō* poems in *hijiri* and *yamabushi* extends into taking detailed stock of their personal belongings and paraphernalia—all eccentric, and sometimes even comical. Characteristically, attention is paid largely to the physical side of the ascetics' existence. Three songs, all sharing the same formula, *konomu mono* (favorite things), reveal the preferences of mountain ascetics in personal gear and foodstuffs; they also show the subsistence level of their existence, for their possessions are crude items taken directly from nature:

RH 306

hijiri no konomu mono	Holy men's favorite things:
ki no fushi wasazuno shika no kawa	knots on trees, the young deer's horn, deerskin,
mino kasa shakujō mokurenji	straw coats, sedge hats, staffs, rosary seeds,

| hiuchike iwaya no koke no koromo | flint boxes, and robes like the moss in caves.[110] |

A *yamabushi* clad in the full apparatus was supposed to symbolize one of *shugendō's* main divinities, Fudō, as well as the Diamond and Matrix Realm mandalas.[111] The peculiar appearance of these mountain men aroused a sense of awe and curiosity in onlookers, and likely played a large part in perpetuating the mystique about their supernatural powers.[112]

The following pair of songs list mountain ascetics' food items, which may have medicinal or magical qualities to give their consumer unearthly powers. Yet the primary message of these songs concerns their grim asceticism based on the bare necessities of life:

RH 425

hijiri no konomu mono	Things favored by holy men, who send
hira no yama o koso tazununare	their disciples to Mount Hira
deshi yarite	to search for them:
matsutake hiratake namesusuki	*matsutake, hiratake, namesusuki* mushrooms;
sate wa ike ni yadoru hasu no hai	then, lotus roots living in pools,
nezeri nenunawa gonbō	parsley, water-shields, burdock,
kawahone udo warabi tsukuzukushi	taro root, asparagus, bracken, and horsetails.[113]

RH 427

sugoki yamabushi no konomu mono wa	Things favored by awesome mountain ascetics
ajikina itetaru yama no umo	are modest: frozen wild potatoes,
wasabi kashiyone mizushizuku	horseradish, washed white rice, drops of water,
sawa ni wa nezeri to ka	and, so it is said, parsley from the marshes.

Most of these items grow in the wild, and items such as the mushrooms are rare delicacies with distinctive aroma. Others, such as taro root, and possibly parsley and burdock, possess medicinal value and must have been eagerly sought after, since many *hijiri* were involved in healing practices.[114] Some items may have been associated with the esoteric magical powers of mountains, the secrets of which were known only to *hijiri*.

The lifestyles of these charismatic *hijiri* and *yamabushi* were bound to create awesome impressions on those who had contact with them. The following two songs succinctly express the uncanny and even eerie sensations they aroused, as if they led a ghostly life:

RH 189

ōmine okonau hijiri koso	The holy men practicing on Mount Ōmine
aware ni tōtoki mono wa are	are truly venerable;
hokekyō zusuru koe wa shite	though their Lotus Sutra chanting can be heard,
tashika no shōtai mada miezu	their real shapes cannot yet be discerned.

RH 470

obotsukana	In the fearful depths of the mountain
tori dani nakanu	where even birds are silent,
okuyama ni	the sound of men!
hito koso otosunare	Ah, venerable
ana tōto	the ascetics
shugyōja no tōrunarikeri	who wander in the wilderness.

The enduring interest in *hijiri* and *yamabushi* in *Ryōjin hishō* may owe much to the singers of the *imayō*. Among them, the *miko* were known to have been intimately linked to the ascetics; some worked with *yamabushi* as their assistants or were married to them,[115] and thus would have had ample opportunity to observe the ascetic life-style and outlook or even take part in it. No doubt they injected their firsthand knowledge into *imayō*, which they then circulated. Therefore, one should not necessarily identify the speaker of a poem with the ascetics themselves; rather, the lyric voices of the songs may well be those of *miko* who stepped into the *yamabushi's* lives and sang in their place. The following song, fraught with amorous innuendo and flirtation, throws light on the intimacy binding *miko* and mountain ascetics:

RH 302

haru no yakeno ni	When I pick spring greens
na o tsumeba	in the burned-over field,
iwaya ni hijiri koso owasunare	I come upon a hermit in his rock cave,
tada hitori	all alone.
nobe ni te tabitabi au yori wa	Instead of meeting like this
na	in the meadows,

iza tamae hijiri koso	oh my holy one, come away with me;
ayashi no yō nari to mo	though it's shabby, oh come
warawara ga shiba no iori e	to my brushwood hut.

Since the time is early spring, the *yamabushi* must be about to emerge from the harsh regimen of winter asceticism to renew a more mundane life—a liminal time when an invitation like this might be especially tempting.

The attraction a woman feels toward a young mountain ascetic is also the subject of this *shiku no kamiuta*:

RH 304

mine no hana oru kodaitoku	He is good-looking, the young monk
tsuradachi yokereba mo gesha yoshi	cutting the mountain flowers, and his trousers and stole are beautiful.
mashite kōza ni noborite wa	But still more glorious is his voice
nori no koe koso tōtokere	chanting Dharma from his seat on high.

The spectacle of the pure mountain ascetic seduced by the *miko* has its whimsical side, but it fits the complex syncretic world of religion in *Ryōjin hishō*, where the line between sacred and profane, physical and spiritual, religion and art, and singers and their subjects is not always clear. Rather, these dualities often form a seamless whole, overlapping, coexisting, and interpenetrating.

Shinto Congratulatory Songs

Some of the songs grouped under the rubric of *jinja uta*, a subsection in *niku no kamiuta*, provide yet another tier of religious sentiment in *Ryōjin hishō*. As previously mentioned, these songs are basically recycled from *waka* of known authorship, composed mostly in the congratulatory Shinto ceremonial context.[116] The rites in question were aimed at ensuring the private and exclusive group interests of the aristocracy, and as a consequence the songs' contents tend to dwell on the felicitous and propitious. Indeed, the unseemly side of life treated in other songs—grief, anxiety, death—is deliberately avoided. It seems as if emphasis on the auspicious is expected to lead to good fortune all of itself.

By far the largest number of *jinja uta* are songs of praise or prayers dedicated to Shinto shrines related to the imperial household or illustrious noble families like the Fujiwara or Minamoto. These eulogies, presumably intended for the limited elite class, are characterized by a this-worldly concern for the welfare and prosperity of aristocratic clans. This upper-class orientation of *jinja uta* forms a sharp contrast with both *hōmon uta* and syncretic *shiku no kamiuta*. *Jinja uta*, unlike *hōmon uta*, do not preach religious messages intended for public edification; they totally lack the pulpit consciousness that often informs *hōmon uta*. Nor are they concerned with commoners' religious practices, as are some of the more pious *shiku no kamiuta*. Rather, largely secular interest in worldly blessings is what dominates *jinja uta*.[117]

Jinja uta are deferential and often obliging in tone. In terms of both content and rhetoric, they are formulaic, repetitious, and predictable. Recurrent rhetorical devices include such stylized phrases as *chihayaburu* (awe-inspiring), *kimi ga (mi)yo* (my lord's august reign or world), and *yorozu yo* (myriad generations), which set the incantatory tone of the songs rather quickly.

In the congratulatory mode of expression, however, the songs can be divided into roughly three categories. The first approach is to praise the beauty of the particular shrine or objects within the sacred precincts; in so doing, the speaker in effect expresses reverence for the shrine itself:

RH 538   [GSIS, no. 1175, Priest Renchū (dates unknown)][118]

sumiyoshi no	Sumiyoshi Shrine
matsu no kozue ni	pine branches green
kamisabite	and sublime
midori ni miyuru	against the shrine fence,
ake no tamagaki	crimson!

Praise is obliquely offered through the eye-catching color contrasts of green pine trees and crimson fences. The aesthetically pleasing aspect of the surroundings is equated with the felicitous sentiment the speaker feels in the shrine sanctuary. The next song takes a similar approach, indirectly attributing the speaker's feeling of well-being to the scenic beauty around the shrine:

RH 539   [GSIS, no. 1063, Minamoto Tsunenobu (1016–97)]

okitsu kaze	The wind from the open sea,
fukinikerashi na	ah, it looks to be surging up.
sumiyoshi no	The whitecaps are splashing
matsu no sizue o	the lower branches
arau shiranami	of the pines of Sumiyoshi.

A song on the Iwashimizu Shrine expresses through images of tranquillity the speaker's deferential attitude toward the shrine's sacred, lifegiving water:

RH 496   [GSIS, no. 1174, Priest Zōgi (dates unknown)]

koko ni shi mo	At this very spot
wakite idekemu	it bursts out,
iwashimizu	the rock-clear water of
	Iwashimizu.
kami no kokoro o	Oh I'd know god's heart
kumite shiraba ya	by scooping up the water![119]

This song plays on the word *iwashimizu* on two levels, using it both as the shrine's name and in its literal meaning, "rock-clear water," thus skillfully economizing the poetic space. The water gushing out of the spring in the shrine compound is perceived as a sacred locus; in the ritual gesture of making contact with it, the speaker venerates the shrine.

The second celebratory mode found in *jinja uta* captures the bounteousness of nature and projects them onto the shrines. Fecundity, growth, and vegetal luxuriance are posed in opposition to depletion, death, and decay. Through this imagery the ever-increasing prestige, value, and well-being of the songs' subjects are solicited. The focus on the bounteous and copious in nature may also indicate a fertility cult at work.

RH 509   [KYISU, no. 65, Yūshi naishin ō ke no Kii (d. 1113?)]

yorozu yo o	The thick shadows
matsuno-o yama no	of Mount Matsuno-o
kage shigemi	wait as many worlds pass:
kimi o zo inoru	they pray that you will be
tokiwa kakiwa to	unchanging, like the rocks.[120]

RH 510   [SIS, no. 592, Kiyohara Motosuke (908–90)]

oishigere	Grow thick
hirano no yama no	green cypresses
ayasugi yo	of Mount Hirano,
koki murasaki ni	so thick you seem
tagawarubeku mo	dark purple![121]

RH 533   [GSS, no. 1371, Ki no Tsurayuki]

ōhara ya	Oh, the grove of small pines
oshio no yama no	on Mount Oshio in Ōhara,
komatsubara	you trees grow fast and thick,
haya ko dakakare	to show the colors
chiyo no kage mimu	of a thousand years![122]

The next song refers to the vitality of nature and its inexhaustible energy as a way of blessing the Kamo Shrine:

RH 506 [SGSIS, no. 1533, Ōe no Masafusa]

kamiyama no	In Mitarashi River, skirting
fumoto o tomuru	Mount Kamiyama's base,
mitarashi no	oh, the waves
iwa utsu nami ya	break against the rocks
yorozu yo no kazu	through ages beyond number.[123]

In the following song on the Iwashimizu Hachiman Shrine, the focus shifts to animal life. The sacredness and prosperity of the shrine are expressed through the image of doves, the messengers of the Hachiman divinity, which swarm in the shrine compounds, taking the pine trees as their nests:

RH 495[124]

yamabato wa	Where do the mountain-doves
izuku ka togura	roost?
iwashimizu	On the young pine branches
yawata no miya no	in the Yawata Shrine
wakamatsu no eda	of rock-clear water.

Some of the songs in this category express blessings and admiration by focusing on the very timelessness of nature. By alluding specifically to this constancy, the songs implicitly raise the converse notion of the passage of time and the potential for growth. In turn, the continuity between nature and humans can be discerned. With the establishment of such an affinity, the speaker hopes to apply auspicious natural signs to human affairs. The following song is a typical example. The wish for the prosperity of the Kamo Shrine is expressed through praise of the young pine trees, which symbolize longevity and endurance:

RH 501 [KKS, no. 1100, Fujiwara Toshiyuki (d. 901)][125]

chihayaburu	The young pine trees
kamo no yashiro no	at awe-inspiring
himekomatsu	Kamo Shrine
yorozu yo made ni	do not change color
iro wa kawaraji	till the end of time.

A similar technique is used to present wishes for a long imperial reign, by invoking the luxuriant vegetation on the sacred mountain of Matsuno-o:

RH 508   [GSIS, no. 1168, Minamoto Kanezumi (dates unknown)][126]

chihayaburu	To look at the shades
matsuno-o yama no	of the awe-inspiring pines
kage mireba	on Mount Matsuno-o
kyō zo chitose no	is to know that today begins
hajimenarikeru	a thousand years.

The following song makes use of the luxuriant image of *fuji* (wisteria), emblem of the Fujiwara clan, in full bloom and thereby expresses the speaker's loyal wishes for the good fortune of the clan:

RH 502   [SIS, no. 1235, Konoe (dates unknown)][127]

chihayaburu	The wisteria waves
kamo no kawabe no	on the bank of the river
fujinami wa	by the awe-inspiring Kamo Shrine
kakete wasururu	are not forgotten, but held in my heart,
toki no ma zo naki	where time does not pass.

The last poetic mode found in congratulatory songs is a straightforward statement of felicitation, stripped of rhetorical adornment. The inclusion in some of such formulas as *kimi ga yo* or *miyo* combined with *chihaya-buru* makes these songs sound elevated in tone but at the same time extremely ritualistic and perfunctory:

RH 511   [SIS, no. 264 by Ōnakatomi Yoshinobu (921–91)][128]

chihayaburu	Awe-inspiring
hirano no matsu no	Hirano pines
irokaezu	never change color;
tokiwa ni mamoru	ah, forever they keep watch
kimi ga miyo kana	over your sacred reign!

RH 528   [KYISU, no. 60, Ōe no Masafusa][129]

kimi ga yo wa	Boundless
kagiri mo araji	the world you rule,
mikasayama	as long as the morning sun
mine ni asahi no	returns to the peaks
sasamu kagiri wa	of Mount Mikasa.

RH 518   [KKRJ, no. 1080, Ise (877?–940?)]

inariyama	People coming and going
ukikō hito wa	on Mount Inari
kimi ga yo o	pray for your reign
hitotsu kokoro ni	ceaselessly
inori yawasenu	with a single heart. [130]

Jinja uta are largely direct quotations or adoptions with minor changes of *waka* that served the Shinto ritual purposes of the ruling classes. They are therefore quite limited in lyrical flexibility, with many remaining on a formulaic or strictly ceremonial level. The congratulatory songs reveal a conservative religious consciousness that is fundamentally inclined to preserving and maintaining the existing order by expanding it to its optimal state. In essence, they are endorsements and affirmations of the here and now.

The presence in *Ryōjin hishō* of *jinja uta* gives the anthology a comprehensive coverage in terms of Heian-period religious practices, showing the ritual life of the aristocracy as well as Buddhist evangelism and the folk observances of commoners. At the same time, these songs demonstrate how thoroughly the popular music of *imayō* penetrated the nobles' ceremonial activities, was fostered by the upper classes, and finally contributed to the enhancement of the critical moments in their celebration of life.

6 The Unrolling Human Picture Scroll in *Ryōjin hishō*

Folk Life

One of the more engaging aspects of *Ryōjin hishō* is its portrayal of common people—their aspirations, way of life, relationships, worries, and diversions. The people who populate this world are woodcutters, potters, common soldiers, peddlers, petty officials, shamans, and peripheral figures such as gamblers, jugglers, and *asobi*. No pretense of refinement or sophistication enters songs delineating the folk life. Rather, life is presented realistically, in all its beauty and ugliness, joy and heartache, fulfillment and frustration. Even animals—cows, snails, grasshoppers, dragonflies, butterflies, and lice—as well as such mundane objects as charcoal containers, washtubs, hooks, and flails—all subjects far outside the poetic lexicon and canon of *waka*—provide poetic inspiration to the singers of these *imayō*.

Humorous, roguish, and sometimes satirical elements play a vital role, as do folk wisdom and wit. At times songs are used as vehicles for critical commentary about contemporary society. The observations are usually only suggestive, but they nevertheless provide rare glimpses into the common people's perspective on some of the changes that were occurring at the end of the Heian period. These poetic sketches leave one with the impression of having unrolled an *emaki* and viewed a human landscape teeming with activity. It is significant that the majority of these songs belong to the categories of *shiku no kamiuta* and *niku no kamiuta*, where the influence of folk song is strongest.

OF MEN AND WOMEN

The *Ryōjin hishō* poets' unflagging fascination with human beings turns the anthology into a portrait gallery decked with realistic sketches of men and women of Heian society, usually at its lower levels. Significantly, a number of names or nicknames of people who appear in this folk world are quite esoteric, and were probably restricted to certain specific social groups; their meanings may have been obscure even to Heian citizens, not to mention a modern audience. This is particularly true in the case of courtesans and gamblers—the outcasts. Some of the pictures we encounter are sketched with empathy, but more often they are caricatures highlighting human foibles. In any event, a keen sense of observation and awareness of surroundings is palpable in these songs.

What we hear, though, is not the personal, individual lyric voice of the Heian commoner in general, but rather that of the professional singers— *miko*, *asobi*, and *kugutsu*—who assume the voices of others, filtering, interpreting, and stylizing. Since the singers adopt the posture of the object they describe, we often encounter a shift in the lyric voice from the third person to the first person. Hence, the proxy or representational function and contribution of the female singers is of critical importance to any appraisal of these songs.

In the following *shiku no kamiuta*, the physical strength of a wood-chopper and the rigor of his work are vividly captured. The focus of the song, however, appears to be the fearlessness of the protagonist, who dares to challenge authority. If we assume that songs of this nature were composed by *asobi* or other such women, the attraction expressed here toward masculine virility and indomitability takes on a suggestive overtone as well:

RH 399

kikori wa osoroshi ya	Oh that fierce woodchopper
arakeki sugata ni kama o mochi	with his rough look, clutching his sickle,
yoki o sage	carrying his axe!
ushiro ni shibaki mainoboru to ka ya na	On his back, oh, firewood piled high;
mae ni wa yamamori yoseji to te	in front, to fend off the warden,
tsue o sage	he swings his thick stick.[1]

Another song draws a group picture of woodchoppers, with a special eye turned on a novice among them:

RH 385

nishiyamadōri ni kuru kikori	On their way to Nishiyamadōri,
ose o narabete sazo wataru	the woodchoppers are wading;
katsuragawa	in single file they cross the Katsura,
shirinaru kikori wa shinkikori na	but look at that young one, the last,
nami ni orarete shirizue sutete	caught in the waves!
kaimotorumeri	He lost his staff, he's falling . . .[2]

The setting of this song—the western part of the capital near the Katsura River, which during the Heian period hosted a fair number of courtesans—suggests that the speaker is one such woman and that the woodcutters are making a difficult trip to find some diversion.[3] The young woodcutter, then, is not only new in his profession but also new to amorous adventure—making the *asobi's* attention on him all the more suggestive.

Ryōjin hishō frequently features men who seek physical enjoyment. In the following song, also set in the western outskirts of the Heian capital, the male protagonist is shown toying with the idea of having fun with women of pleasure—here suggested by the names of birds, often epithets for prostitutes:[4]

RH 388

nishi no kyō yukeba	On the west side of the capital,
suzume tsubakurame tsutsudori ya	that's where the birds are, oh yes,
sa koso kike	like sparrows, like swallows, like cuckoos.
irogonomi no ōkaru yo nareba	It's a world of men on the prowl, I hear,
hito wa toyomu to mo	which people make much of.
maro dani toyomazu wa	Well it doesn't faze me!

On the surface, the following three songs deal with catching shrimp and small fish. In reality, however, they are talking about men chasing women of questionable reputation. This becomes clear when we realize that Ōtsu along the Setagawa River, which flows from Lake Biwa, was a well-known area populated by courtesans.[5] But in any case, the entertainment context in which *asobi* performed these *imayō* songs for amorous provocation justifies taking songs of this kind other than literally.

RH 395

ebisui toneri wa izuku e zo	Hey, shrimper, where to?
saisui toneri gari yuku zo kashi	I'm going to the little fish catcher's.
kono e ni ebi nashi	No shrimp in this river;
orirare yo	let's try the other,
ano e ni zakō no chiranu ma ni	before those small fry slip away.

RH 396

iza tabe tonari dono	Neighbor, let's fish for small fry
ōtsu no nishi no ura e zako suki ni	in the bay west of Ōtsu.
kono e ni ebi nashi	In this river, no shrimp,
ano e e imase	but in the other river
ebimajiri no zako ya aru to	we'll discover a shoal of small fry and shrimps to feast on!

RH 441

awazu no kyōen wa	Pleasures of Awazu:
hingashi ōtsu no nishi ura e	drift to the western bay in eastern Ōtsu,
ebimajiri no zako tori ni	to search for shrimp and small fry.
ōtsu no nishi no ura wa waroshi	No, no, Ōtsu is bad;
nobori ōji zo nani mo yoki	everything's good on the wide streets of the capital![6]

This song, which seemingly is about a small sweetfish (*ayu*), may well describe the plight of *asobi* exploited by their customers:

RH 475

yodogawa no	In the Yodo's depths
soko no fukaki ni	the sweetfish baby
ayu no ko no	squeaks, pierced
u to iu tori ni	by the cormorant's beak
senaka kuwarete	from behind.
kirikiri meku	Writhing.
itōshi ya	How pitiful!

The following *shiku no kamiuta* may be about a man's sexual impotence, as symbolized by a dull sickle,[7] and his repeated inability to make sexual conquests. Here, the *kusa* (grass) suggests women, the objects of his unsuccessful amorous pursuits:

RH 370

seita ga tsukurishi karikama wa	How did Seita get that sickle
nani shini togikemu yakiken	sharpened hard in the fire?
tsukurikemu	Now he wants to toss it away;
sutetōnan naru ni	it just can't cut the grass,
ōsaka narazaka fuwa no seki	not in Ōsaka, not in Narazaka,
	not on Fuwa Barrier,
kurikomayama ni te kusa mo	not on Mount Kurikoma . . .[8]
ekaranu ni	

In contrast to the men about town in search of women, the next song narrates the farce of a young bridegroom who gets cold feet at the prospect of matrimony. The speaker plays the role of a village gossip, who in so many cultures epitomizes folk humor at its broadest; she does not fail to relay all the details of local scandal and thus titillate the curiosity of her audience:

RH 340

kaza wa memōke ni kinkeru wa	Well the young man came to take a wife,
kamaete futayo wa nenikeru wa	you know, and faked it through two nights,
miyo to iu yo no	but on the third, you know,
yonaka bakari no akatsuki ni	he took off at first light,
hakama torishite nigenikeru wa	clutching his, you know, trousers around him.[9]

During the Heian period, on the two nights just before the wedding a bridegroom was expected to visit his bride at her home under the cover of night. Only at the end of the third night, after the wedding ceremony, was the marriage made public, thus freeing the man from the inconvenience of nocturnal visits.[10] In this song the young bridegroom, knowing what is in store for him after the third night, beats a hasty retreat. The repetition of the verb ending -*keru*, used to report events, accentuated by the exclamatory particle *wa*, heightens the dramatic effect of the story.

A good marriage, and an upward one at that, is, however, the greatest dream of many parents—then as now. The following *shiku no kamiuta* voices this aspiration, focusing on the beautiful daughter of a lowly potter:

RH 376

kusuha no mimaki no	By the imperial pasture at
dokitsukuri	Kusuha

doki wa tsukuredo musume no kao zo yoki	the potter makes earthenware,
ana utsukushi ya na	but his daughter has a porcelain face.
are o mikuruma no yokuruma no	If only she could ride wedding carts, three or four,
aigyō teguruma ni uchinosete	drawn by hand, in procession,
zuryō no kita no kata to iwaseba ya	as the provincial governor's bride![11]

Provincial governors were officials dispatched by the central government to oversee the political and economic affairs of outlying regions. Toward the end of the Heian period, they frequently remained behind after the term of office was over. Gradually they emerged as regional economic potentates, amassing wealth in land and estates in the countryside, away from the watchful eyes of the central government. During the *insei* period, moreover, such men began to exercise political clout as they allied themselves with the warrior classes and gained a say in governmental affairs.[12] In the eyes of commoners, locked tightly within the class hierarchy of their day and lacking the economic means to escape it, the rising fortunes of the new classes must have been the object of envy. Marriage alliance, so often exploited by the aristocracy, was surely seen as a tempting way to climb out of poverty and low social status.

The onerous task of marrying a daughter is expressed in the following song, in which a mother-in-law faces a list of fashion preferences given by her future son-in-law, probably to be referred to in choosing wedding gifts for him. Presented in a combined dialogue-catalog form, the list reveals the rather finicky and presumptuous taste of the young groom. The song therefore pokes fun at the fastidious fashion consciousness and extravagance of the upper classes:

RH 358

muko no kaza no kimi	All right you, young man, son-in-law,
nani iro no nani zuri ka konōdō	what are your colors, what patterns
kimahoshiki	will you have for your robes?
kijin yamabuki tomezuri ni	Yellow-green, yellow-gold, indigo,
hanamurago mitsunagashiwa ya	spotted light blue, oh sure! and the patterns: triple oak-leaf,

ryugo wachigae sasamusubi	hand-drums, overlapping wheels, bamboo leaves bound together?
kōkechi maetari no hoya no	Why not a dye with white spots, or dye of sap,
ka no ko yui	or tie-dye dappled perfect, like the fur of a fawn![13]

The human interest in *Ryōjin hishō* does not, of course, attach only to songs about men. In fact, commentary on women is just as strong, sometimes overriding the interest shown for men. We have already seen this in the songs about *asobi* and *miko*; in addition, a number of songs expose the unseemly side of these women's lives, behavior, or deportment. But there is more humor than critique in the songs as a whole, perhaps because of the special relationships between the female singers/poets and their subject matter. The following one, for example, paints a humorous portrait of a young woman:

RH 402

tonari no ōiko ga matsuru kami wa	The gods the girl next door serves are
kashira no shijikegami masukami	hair gods: in curly hair, in frowzy hair,
hitaigami	in hair rolling to her shoulders;
yubi no saki naru tezutsugami	a bungling, messy god at her fingertips,
ashi no ura naru arukigami	the god who walks in her soles.

This song, most likely teasing a *miko*, plays on the word *kami*, which can mean either god or hair. Despite the conjunction in the first line of the words *kami* and *matsuru* (to worship), the *kami* turns out to be the woman's various hairdos—some of which are less than respectable. Especially, considering that during the Heian period straight hair was the fashion for women, the heroine's "curly," "frowzy" hairstyles suggest a certain freakishness on her part. At least two levels of wordplay are discernible in the word *tezutsugami* (an inept god). As a compound of *tezutsu* (clumsy or messy) and *gami* (*kami*, hair or god), the word suggests "the inept god in her messy hair." But *tezutsugami* can also be broken into *te* (hand), *zutsu* (or *tsutsu*, from *tsuku*, to be divinely possessed), and *gami* (god), resulting literally in "a hand possessed by a clumsy god"—an oblique reference to the woman's lack of skill. Thus the single word *tezutsugami* can be taken in an expanded sense to mean the sloppiness and ineptitude of the woman as a *miko*. Last but not least, a walking god (*arukigami*) in the soles—that is, a god who excites the woman to saunter around—implies yet further degradation of divinities. All this deliberate sport with the sacred fills out the humor in the song, while doubling as a commentary on a woman who deviates from the classical role of virtuous female—well groomed, good at sewing, and homebound.

Miko form an important topic in *Ryōjin hishō*, being the subject of a large number of songs. In one, the speaker is captivated by the sight of a *miko* in an ecstatic state; but the speaker's attention focuses on her personal appearance, which provokes an awed disdain: her hair is false, and the ceremonial robes she wears are not really hers. Even so, the *miko* is perfectly capable of carrying out her ritual possession. In the detail of the long tear in her robe, even a hint of eroticism is suggested:

RH 545

sumiyoshi no	At the outer gate
ichi no torii ni	to Sumiyoshi Shrine,
mau kine wa	a shrine-maiden dances,
kami wa tsuki gami	wigged, in a trance,
kinu wa kari ginu	in a borrowed robe
shirikeremo	slit high up behind.

Here again, the phrase *kami wa tsuki gami* functions on two levels. On one hand, it refers to the trancelike state of the *miko* as she becomes divinely possessed; on the other, it is a reference to her wig, worn for dramatic effect in her performance. Likewise, the phrase *kinu wa kari ginu* has a double suggestiveness. Her borrowed hunting robe (*kari ginu*), the ordinary court costume for males, evokes the image of a transsexual, signifying her asexuality, and hence her supramundane power. Yet it may indicate her poverty as well. This complex dimension of a *miko*'s existence between spirituality and profanity seems to be the source of her magnetism.

In the following song, the promiscuity of a *miko* living near a shrine is described quite openly. The words *sasakusa* (bamboo grass) and *koma* (horse) are used allegorically to refer to women and men, respectively, with the image of the horse eating the bamboo grass suggestive of erotic relationships. The woman's sexuality is made explicit in the last couplet:

RH 362

ōji no omae no sasakusa wa	Before the shrine the bamboo grass

koma wa hamedomo nao shigeshi	is lush, though the horses chomp it.
nushi wa konedomo yodono ni wa	Her real love never comes, but
toko no ma zo naki wakakereba	she is young, her bed is never empty.

Interest in the erotic life of *miko* continues in the next song, which expresses unreciprocated desire. As this song makes clear, the shrines were often sites for affairs between *miko* and men on pilgrimage—this time, specifically, at the Sumiyoshi Shrine:

RH 541

sumiyoshi wa	In the southern guest room
minami kyakuden	in Sumiyoshi Shrine,
nakayarido	the door latch
omoi kakegane	will not open,
hazushi ge zo naki	oh, to my desire.

The song makes skillful use of the pivot word *kake(ru)* (to hang or lock), which links *omoikake* (yearning) to *kakegane* (metal latches). It brings the tension between the *miko* and the amorous man into high relief: his strong yearning is bolted by the latch she uses to block the man's advance.

The topic of *miko* around the Sumiyoshi Shrine appears again in another song, marking the fact that the shrine was indeed a site for *miko's* double lives:

RH 273

sumiyoshi shisho no omae ni wa	She lives at Sumiyoshi Shrine,
kao yoki nyotai zo owashimasu	a beauty, with the body of an empress;
otoko wa tare zo to tazunureba	but there's her man (I checked), lover-man,
matsu ga saki naru suki otoko	right there on the cape of pines, Matsuga-saki.[14]

The song makes humorous use of the word *nyotai*, which can mean either "woman's body" or "empress." This double meaning is reinforced by the honorific verb *owashimasu* (to reside), which seemingly refers to an empress but in fact points to the *miko*/prostitute.

The following song may be the bantering of a *miko* around the shrine area, cajoling a male pilgrim into a tryst with the word *iro* (color, but also erotic love). Here, the double lives of both *miko* and pilgrims come to the forefront:

RH 360

omae ni mairite wa	Are you going home from the shrine
iro mo kawarade kaere to ya	without changing your colors?
mine ni okifusu shika dani mo	Even the mountain deer know enough
natsuge fuyuge wa kawarunari	to change their coats with the season.

We see a picture of women luring men into amorous adventure in the next song as well. The divinities mentioned are presumably aliases of these women, and it is in this unlikely link between the sacred and the profane that the humor of the song lies:

RH 555

uzumasa no	Though I'm heading for
yakushi ga moto e	the house of Yakushi at Uzumasa,
yuku maro o	sometimes
shikiri todomuru	the divine one at Konoshima
konoshima no kami	just stops me in my tracks.[15]

The following song is more somber, depicting the essentially desolate and lonely nature of a *miko*'s life. It could well be one such woman's own lament:

RH 514

inari naru	At the Inari Shrine,
mitsu mure garasu	three flocks of crows:
awarenari	their days full of love-play,
hiru wa mutsurete	but their lonely nights
yoru wa hitori ne	are desolate.[16]

Sometimes *Ryōjin hishō* songs are about young girls or courtesans inexperienced in male-female relationships, and so provide words of warning. Here, the image of an early spring bracken hints at affection on the part of speaker for the young woman:

RH 451

haru no no ni	In the fields of spring
koya kaitaru yō nite	you're a young bracken plant
tsuitateru kagiwarabi	ready for life,
shinobite tatere	but stand quiet, don't be plucked
gesu ni toraru na	by some vulgar knave!

Within the poetic setting of the *Ryōjin hishō*, where double entendre is plentiful, the following song cannot simply be taken as an innocuous list of foodstuffs. Rather, it may be another song of erotic suggestion.[17] Here, the names of fruits and vegetables seem to refer to women who may have had amorous relationships with Seita, whom we met in song no. 370, a man of few sexual ventures, and largely unsuccessful ones. Since the song mentions a shrine, these women may be *miko*:

RH 371

seita ga tsukurishi misonō ni	Seita made a shrine-garden
nigauri amauri no nareru kana	wih sweet pears and muskmelons,
	fruitful, yes, and pumpkins too.
akodauri	
chiji ni edasase naribisako	Spread yourself open, bottle gourds,
mono na notabi so egunasubi	and bitter eggplant, shut your mouth!

Humor plays an essential part in the treatment of women in *Ryōjin hishō*. The following song jokes about a homely woman who has lost the chance for marriage. Even so, the speaker may have his own secret designs on her, indicated by the word *tane* (seeds), meaning children:

RH 372

yamashiro nasubi wa oinikeri	Old, that Yamashiro eggplant,
torade hisashiku narinikeri	nobody ever plucked her,
akaramitari	all reddened.
saritote sore o ba sutetsubeki ka	So throw her away? No, leave her,
oitare oitare tane toramu	leave her, I'll reap her seeds.[18]

The bustling marketplace scene in the next song is reminiscent in its earthy and animated quality of the folk characters that have appeared in other *Ryōjin hishō* songs. The scene takes place in Suzaku Avenue, the border between the main part of the capital and its outskirts, where peddlers and shoppers swarm:

RH 389

kindachi suzaka haki no ichi	The nobles come to Suzaku market,
ōhara shizuhara nagatani iwakura	and from Ōhara, from Shizuhara, from Hase,

yase no hito atsumarite	the wood sellers come, from Iwakura, from Yase.
ki ya mesu sumi ya mesu	Here's charcoal! Here's wood!
taraibune shina yoshi ya	A wood basin! My wares are good!
hōshi ni kine kaetabe miyako no hito	City folk, this monk has a maiden mallet to trade.[19]

Ōhara was especially famous for its women peddlers, called *oharame* (women of Ohara), who came to the capital carrying bundles of firewood on their heads, hawking their goods as they walked the city streets.[20] Their voices must have contributed to the song's noisy scene. Humor is provided in the last line, where the word *kine* can be taken to mean either a wooden mallet or a shrine-maiden. On a literal level, then, the line describes a mountain monk asking if anyone is interested in trading for his wooden mallet; yet he may in fact be making a proposition of an entirely different sort. The market, in short, is not a place where only material commodities are exchanged. In a sense, the song serves as a fitting backdrop for the dramas that have been played out individually among the folk characters of the songs, conveying a sense of energy, multifariousness, and travesty of the folk life in the *Ryōjin hishō*.

LOVE

Love has long been a prominent theme in the Japanese poetic tradition. *Ryōjin hishō* is no exception. In the anthology, love songs are concentrated in the "miscellaneous" section of the *shiku no kamiuta* and in the untitled sections of the *niku no kamiuta*. None is found in the *hōmon uta*.

The love songs of *Ryōjin hishō* deal exclusively with the love affairs of commoners and those on the fringes of Heian society, addressing in particular emotions experienced on an instinctual or physical level and expressed with little reservation. The speakers are most frequently women, including courtesans, who tell of their desires, frustrations, vexations, and fears, as well as their flirtatious moods. Most of the songs are presented in an extremely fluid vernacular, which forms a sharp contrast to the *hōmon uta*, with their dominantly public, declarative mode of address.

In the performative context of *asobi* and other entertainers, the songs may have functioned to instruct the audience about the different kinds of love these women experienced. They may also have served as protests against inconstancy, cruelty, and desertion—all part of the love experience of these women. The graphic descriptions of sensual love likely aroused and satisfied erotic impulses of their male listeners as well, which in many cases, of course, was the entertainers' ultimate professional goal.

The next few songs represent a light mood of flirtation, which is achieved largely through repetition of similar phrases, alliteration, and the use of emphatic particles—rhetorical devices that in some cases lend an incantatory resonance as well:

RH 456

koishiku wa	If you love me,
tōtō owase	come quick;
waga yado wa	my house is in Yamato
yamato naru	at the foot of
miwa no yama moto	Mount Miwa;
sugi tateru kado	a cedar stands at my gate.[21]

RH 484

musubu ni wa	In the knots of love,
nani wa no mono ka	what can't be joined?
musubarenu	Against the blowing wind,
kaze no fuku ni wa	what wouldn't
nani ka nabikanu	be swayed?

RH 485

koishi to yo	I love you, you know,
kimi koishi to yo	you know I love you,
yukashi to yo	I long for you, you know.
awaba ya miba ya	I long to meet you, yes, see you, yes,
miba ya mieba ya	let you see me, watch you seeing me.

A kindred sense of amorous dalliance dominates the following song, which deals with a successful consummation by a pair of lovers, symbolized by the man's rush hat (*ayaigasa*) dropped into the river (the woman):[22]

RH 343

kimi ga aiseshi ayaigasa	That rush hat you loved so much,
ochinikeri ochinikeri	it fell in, and it fell in,
kamogawa ni kawa naka ni	into the middle of Kamo River;
sore o motomu to tazunu to seshi hodo ni	we look, we explore, and while we do
akenikeri akenikeri	dawn has come, dawn has come,
sarasara sayake no aki no yo wa	after a clear, rustling autumn night.

The artistry of this song is delightful. First, the echo of the verb ending
-*nikeri* in *ochinikeri* and *akenikeri* creates a pleasing, refrainlike effect.
This rhythmic cadence is then underscored by the alliterative pairing of
ai and *ayai* in the first line, *kamogawa* and *kawa* in the third, and *sarasara*
and *sayake* in the last line. To cap it off, an end rhyme is contrived by the
repetition of *ni* in the third and fourth lines, and an internal rhyme is
gained from the repetition of *to* in the fourth line. This intricate poetic
craftsmanship gives the song a lively sense of movement.

The following two songs are rare instances in which the lyric voice is
male, both expressing an erotic yearning for a woman. In the first song,
this yearning—metaphorically conveyed through the image of a small
flower—is one that cannot be gratified by sight only. In similar fashion,
in the second song the presumably male speaker vocalizes his sexual
fantasy by identifying himself with creeping and sinewy wild vines. His
strong desire, he says, is as inevitable as a karmalike destiny (*sukuse*)—
an exaggerated claim that produces a hint of whimsical humor:

RH 452

kaki goshi ni	I never tire of looking
miredo mo akanu	at a wild pink
nadeshiko o	across the fence;
ne nagara ha nagara	I wish the wind
kaze no fuki mo	would blow all of it to me,
kosekashi	from root to tip.

RH 342

binjō uchimireba	When I see a beautiful woman
hitomoto kazura ni mo narinaba ya	I want to be a clinging vine,
to zo omou	that's what I dream of.
moto yori sue made yorareba ya	Oh, I'd wind from her top to her bottom;
kiru to mo kizamu to mo	cut me, chop me, I won't come off easy,
hanaregataki wa waga sukuse	that's my karma.

Not all *Ryōjin hishō* love songs are so upbeat, however; some articulate
agonized feelings about unresponsive lovers. One such case is the following example, in which an intense desire to fuse with one's beloved is
voiced, underscored by the vehement accusation a young woman levels at
her feeble lover. The same expression as in the preceding song, *kiru to mo
kizamu to mo* (to try to cut or to chop), is used here, providing thematic

affinity through the lexical repetition. It is also a song of a lover's defiance against outsiders' meddling, especially that of parents or neighbors—also a favorite theme in *Man'yōshū* and *saibara* songs:[23]

RH 341

wanushi wa nasake na ya	Hard-hearted lover!
warawa ga araji to mo sumaji to mo	What if I said let's not be together,
iwaba koso nikukarame	not live together, wouldn't you hate it?
tete ya haha no saketamau naka nareba	My mother, my father want to rip us apart,
kiru to mo kizamu to mo yo ni mo araji	but the whole world can't split us, cannot, try as it will, cut down our love.

In the following two songs we are reminded of the more formal *waka*, in terms of both tone and poetic artistry. The first one captures a pensive mood grounded in a longing that knows no bounds, reaching out for the object of desire as far as Michinoku Prefecture—virtually the end of the world in Heian times:

RH 335

omoi wa michinoku ni	My longing goes as far as Michinoku,
koi wa suruga ni kayounari	as my love wanders Suruga;
misomezariseba nakanaka ni	if it had not been love at first sight,
sora ni wasurete yaminamashi	it would be easy to forget, fading into the distant air.[24]

Skillfully integrating *waka* and the folk song tradition, this song achieves layers of meaning by playing on pivot words. In the first line, *michi* is linked to *omoi* and *noku* to produce two phrases: *omoi wa michi(ru)* ("the heart is full") and *michinoku* (the name of a province). Then in the second line, *suru* is connected to both *koi* and *ga*, resulting in *koi wa suru* (to love) and *suruga* (the name of a province). This technique gives the first half of the song a *waka*-like sense of semantic control and subtlety. The second half, however, is totally free of rhetorical contrivances; the result is a straightforward and unreserved voicing of the speaker's state of mind.

In the second song, the focus is on a single-shelled abalone, which serves as a metaphor for the one-sided longing of a lover:

RH 462

ise no umi ni	Like the abalone shell,
asa na yū na ni	brought up morning and evening,
ama no ite	by the women divers
toriagunaru	in the sea at Ise:
awabi no kai no	my one-sided
kataomoinaru	love.[25]

A handful of love songs in *Ryōjin hishō* are uninhibited invitations to lovemaking. They evoke banquet scenes where unbridled revelry loosens erotic impulses, such as in the following song, in which an overture for a sexual union is rendered in a quasi-cataloging style:

RH 487

sakazuki to	Wine and
u no kuu io to	fish for the cormorants and
onnago wa	women:
hate naki mono zo	never enough. So!
iza futari nen	Let's go to bed!

The act of lovemaking is sometimes described explicitly, as in this song:

RH 460

koi koi te	Longing, and longing, then,
tamasaka ni aite	once in a while you meet her.
netaru yo no yume wa	When you sleep that night,
ikaga miru	what do you see in dreams?
sashisashi kishi to	The tight embrace, the thrusting,
daku to koso mire	oh yes, the thrusting.

Even the reluctance of lovers parting can be expressed in frank physical terms:

RH 481

iza nenamu	Come on, let's go back to bed!
yo mo akegata ni	Night ending, first light,
narinikeri	bells ringing.
kane mo utsu	We've been in bed since evening,
yoi yori netaru dani mo	but what else
akanu kokoro o ya	can I do
ikani semu	with my hungry heart?

As in both *waka* and folk songs, the theme of unrequited love stands out in *Ryōjin hishō*. Invariably, the pain of love—loneliness, regret, or the tragedy of betrayal—is expressed from the standpoint of women. The love relationships described in *Ryōjin hishō* usually end in estrangement, with promises more often broken than kept. This group of songs represents perhaps the most intense emotional outpouring in *Ryōjin hishō*.

RH 463

ware wa omoi	Oh I want him,
hito wa nokehiku	but he left me:
kore ya kono	oh! one-sided love,
nami taka ya	mine is,
ara iso no	like an abalone shell
awabi no kai no	in the high waves
kata omoi naru	on the rough shore.

This song, though reminiscent of no. 462, is more forthright in expressing the lover's desertion; the image of the rugged, wave-battered seashore is particularly evocative of the harshness of such an experience.

In the next song, as the speaker traces the flow of time from past to future, the void in her life created by her lover's leaving is brought into sharp relief. Without his visit, time hangs heavy on her hands, and life is dismal, drained of purpose:

RH 459

waga koi wa	Not yesterday,
ototoi miezu	not the day before,
kinō kozu	my love did not come.
kyō otozure nakuba	If today there's no visit,
asu no tsurezure	how can I face
ikani sen	the dead time tomorrow?

In another song we see the loneliness, shame, and muted agony of a woman whose love affair went wrong. Here, as in the last song, the speaker emphasizes the passage of time, in this case on the smaller scale of one night, and reveals the psychological shifts of her mind—from stoic patience in the early evening to frustration at dawn. Her feeling of abandonment is set off by the concrete image of the "desolate bed," alluding to the sexual nature of her love relationship:

RH 336

hyakunichi hyakuya wa hitori nu to	I'd rather sleep alone a hundred days, a hundred nights,
hito no yozuma wa naji shō ni hoshikarazu	than be someone's mistress—

yoi yori yonaka made wa yokeredomo	I'm fine, from evening through midnight,
akatsuki tori nakeba	but at first light, the cock crying,
toko sabishi	I wake in a desolate bed.

Some of the betrayed women in *Ryōjin hishō* songs do not suffer passively; they vent their anger. Songs of protest, like the following example, give a sharper edge to the anthology's spirited love songs. The speaker here may be a courtesan who lays out a plan of revenge for a fellow courtesan wronged by her lover:

RH 338

keshō kariba no koya narai	At the ornate hunting cabin
shibashi wa tatetare neya no to ni	it's only right to make him wait outside the bedroom,
koroshime yo yoi no hodo	and let the evening punish him
yobe mo yōbe mo yogareshiki	for not coming, last night, the night before.
keka wa shitari to mo shitari to mo	No matter how he repents,
me na mise so	don't let him glimpse you!

An element of humor is added to the song with the word *keka* (repentance), originally a Buddhist term referring to a rite of penitence.

The theme of jilted love receives unconventional treatment in another song, one of the most beloved in *Ryōjin hishō*. The speaker is an *asobi* of unusual pluck, who thrashes her fickle lover with a series of curses:

RH 339

ware o tanomete konu otoko[26]	The man who stole my trust but doesn't come:
tsuno mitsu oitaru oni ni nare	may he turn into a three-horned devil scorned by men;
sate hito ni utomare yo	may he be a bird
shimo yuki arare furu	on a rice paddy in the frost,
mizuta no tori to nare	in the hail, the falling snow,
sate ashi tsumetakare	may his feet freeze;
ike no ukikusa to narinekashi	may he be a drifting duckweed on a lake,
to yuri kō yuri yurare arike	tossed this way, tossed that way, tossed!

The song centers on three images—a three-horned devil (symbol of ugliness as well as terror), a bird, and a floating weed—all non- or subhuman entities.²⁷ Vitality and power are successively diminished, from the relative mobility of the devil to the total passivity of a drifting weed. Since the *uki* in *ukikusa* (drifting duckweed) also implies melancholy or sadness, the speaker wills that to be part of her lover's lot. The poignancy of the song lies in the fact that the speaker, in her diatribe, projects her own feared destiny onto her lover: loss of beauty, privation, and loneliness from an uprooted existence.²⁸

In practical terms, some of the love songs in *Ryōjin hishō* must have been created to entice male customers into the arms of *asobi*. In addition, songs such as nos. 338 and 339, discussed above, may be intended to declare the dignity of these women, even though they are basically at the mercy of their patrons. Despite moments of amorous elation, on the whole the songs communicate the harsh reality of love relationships—their risks, unpredictability, and pain—especially for *asobi*. The lot of these women, we learn, was ultimately one of deep sadness.

Any discussion of love in *Ryōjin hishō* would be incomplete without mention of the following song, at once the best known and one of the most controversial in the anthology:

RH 359

asobi o sen to ya umarekemu	Was I born to play?
tawabure sen to ya mumareken	Was I born to frolic?
asobu kodomo no koe kikeba	As I hear the children playing,
waga mi sae koso yurugarure	even my old body starts to sway.

The controversy involves the identity of the speaker and the meaning of the words *asobi* and *tawabure*. Some say that the song is an old *asobi's* lament over her life spent in sin, while others see it as the wistful reflection of an old person about his or her own life.²⁹ When we consider the song in the context of women performers and their professional life, which often included prostitution, the meaning is much clearer: here we encounter the nostalgia of an *asobi* who, though limited in her entertaining activities by her age, still finds the music and performance (symbolized by the young children's frolicking) exciting and magical. Her life of flirtation and pursuit of love will end in time, but the delight she finds in songs and entertainment will continue to live on.

OLD AGE

The subject of old age, like love, is a recurrent theme in *Ryōjin hishō*. Fear and sadness at its inevitable approach seize the imagination of the *imayō* poets, stimulating them to produce compelling songs. Their perceptions are rendered in various manners—sometimes frivolous, sometimes doleful, sometimes sardonic. Altogether, however, they present old age as an unavoidable and problematic part of life, especially for *asobi*, whose livelihood depends on youth and beauty. As a consequence, the lyric voice in the songs about old age, as in those about love, is predominantly female.

Lament—one of the most predictable responses to old age—is the subject of the following song. Here the inevitability of human aging is contrasted with the power of self-renewal in nature, seen in the image of the moon, which, though ever changing, is each month born anew:

RH 449

tsuki mo tsuki	The moon is
tatsu tsuki goto ni	the same moon,
wakaki ka na	each month it's new!
tsukuzuku oi o	What about
suru waga mi	my old body,
nani naruramu	slowly on the wane?

In another song, the same concern with old age, represented by facial wrinkles—the "waves beating on the shore of the forehead"—takes the form of an envious look back at one's youthful years:

RH 490

oi no nami	The waves of age
isohitai ni zo	beat on the shore
yorinikeru	of the forehead;
aware koishiki	oh, I mourn for
waka no ura ka na	the beloved bay called Youth.

The poetic complexity of this song hinges on wordplay involving two phrases, *oi no nami* (waves of old age) and *waka no ura* (young bay; also the proper name Waka Bay).[30] On the literal level, the phrases may simply describe the waves breaking against the beach of Waka Bay. But on a metaphorical level, they dramatize the contrast between the youth of the bay and human old age. In addition, the *engo* relationships among the words *nami* (waves), *iso* (beach), and *ura* (bay) bind the song into a tight unit, with each word anticipating and referring to the others.

The feeling of helplessness at the aging process is expressed in the following song about an old barrier-keeper. An ironic tone is achieved through the discrepancy between the guard's power to ward off unwelcome intruders and his inability to avert the stealthy encroachment of old age:

RH 328

tsukushi no moji no seki	At Tsukushi's Moji gate
seki no sekimori oinikeri	the barrier guard has aged,
bin shiroshi	his sideburns turning white.
nani tote suetaru seki no	If the barrier he keeps
sekiya no sekimori nareba	is a good one,
toshi no yuku o ba	why can't he stop the years?[31]
todomezaruran	

The pathos of the barrier-keeper's situation is enhanced by the word *seki* (barrier), the sixfold repetition of which seems to echo the futility of combating the invisible but unavoidable assault of time.

Indeed, the effect of time and old age can be devastating. It is felt most acutely in human relationships, especially between men and women. While fickleness may cause some heartache, far more destructive is the havoc that time works on a woman's beauty, and consequently on men's love for her. In the following song, the uncared-for mirror, which was called "the soul of women" and which in ancient times needed periodic polishing to keep it from tarnishing,[32] suggests the sad reality of an aged woman, once beautiful. It is also an apt image to convey human reflection on the intricate relationships between women, beauty, youth, and the heart, all of which are subject to the workings of time:

RH 409

kagami kumorite wa	As my mirror clouds,
waga mi koso yatsurekeru	so my body has grown gaunt;
waga mi yatsurete wa	as my body grew gaunt,
otoko nokehiku	so men become distant.

The fact that all created beings and man-made objects inevitably disintegrate may be the theme of the following catalog song, which evokes a strong sense of mutability, *mujōkan*.[33] But as the last-line clincher in the Japanese original indicates, the most pitiful case is that of childless court ladies in old age:

RH 397

miru ni kokoro no sumu mono wa	Sights that cool the heart:
yashiro koborete negi mo naku	a broken shrine, no priests, no acolytes,
hafuri naki	the palace fallen in the middle of the field,

| nonaka no dō no mata yaburetaru | the last years of a lady of the court, |
| ko umanu shikibu no oi no hate | her children never born. |

The word *shikibu* in this song is a general term for court ladies or ladies-in-waiting, but it is also suggestive of particular women—Izumi Shikibu, Murasaki Shikibu, or Sei Shōnagon, the most illustrious of the Heian female court attendants. The legends depicting Sei Shōnagon as a decrepit old nun begging favors from courtiers in her old age seem especially pertinent here.[34] The unexpected juxtaposition of the ruined buildings and the old court lady is jarringly powerful, conveying both the ruthlessness and power of time, which makes no distinction between sentient human beings and inanimate objects.

Old age is not always a topic of gloomy sadness in *Ryōjin hishō*. In the following song, an old man supporting himself on a staff is perceived as grimly funny, though at the heart of the remark an aversion to old age may well be lurking:

RH 391

okashiku kagamaru mono wa tada	Eye-catching, curved things are:
ebi yo kubichi yo	shrimps! traps!
meushi no tsuno to ka ya	and also cow's horns! And the tips
mukashi kaburi no koji to ka ya	of old-time hats! And the bent back
okina no tsue tsuitaru koshi to ka ya	of the old man stooped on his stick![35]

This catalog song, like the one above, jolts us with the sudden transition from small, negligible curved items to a human being—which in effect objectifies the old man, placing him on the same level as the other animate and inanimate things listed.

A much lighter, tongue-in-cheek treatment of age in women appears in the following song, which, depending on the gender and age of the speaker or singer, can have several interpretations—self-praise, bantering self-mockery, humorous jesting at women, or disdain for the fickleness of men:

RH 394

| onna no sakarinaru wa | Women peak at fourteen, fifteen, sixteen, |
| jūshigoroku sai nijūsanshi to ka | twenty-three, twenty-four, and so on; |

sanjūshigo ni shi narinureba	by thirty-four or -five, oh no, they are
momiji no shitaba ni kotonarazu	like autumn leaves on bottom branches.

WIT AND HUMOR

The wit and humor of many *Ryōjin hishō* songs are truly a delight. Concentrated mostly in the *shiku no kamiuta*, such songs involve various wordplays, compact aphorisms, and, sometimes, sharp comments on how the world works. Structurally, most of the songs take the catalog format and function as revealing guides to what their authors found pleasing, exciting, ridiculous, or surprising.

The objects of these observations, however, are not those usually found in *waka*; instead we encounter ordinary and comparatively drab images drawn from the everyday world of commoners. *Ryōjin hishō* poets, in fact, seemed to shun refined or elegant images; they found the commonplace uncommon, the ordinary extraordinary, and the seemingly meaningless full of meaning. This break from *waka* practice reveals an important aspect of the *Ryōjin hishō* poets' attitude toward life: they could find joy and beauty even in the smallest things in nature and in the most insignificant facets of human activity. The alert sense of perception, immediacy, and flair for waggishness that these songs demonstrate gives credence to the description of the anthology as a Heian depository of commoners' exercises in witticism, ingenuity, and poetic sensibility.

The delight in finding little equivalences in people's immediate living environment is characteristic of these songs. The poet (re)discovers for us the possibilities of things we would likely overlook as interesting objects of poetic perception:

RH 435

sugunaru mono wa tada	Straight things are simply:
karasao ya nodake	flails, yes, bamboo arrows,
kanna no shi moji	the letter *shi* in *kana*,
kotoshi haetaru mumezuhae	thin plum branches newly grown,
hatahoko saitoridake to ka ya	flag-decked halberds, bird-catching bamboo poles, and so on.

In pointing to the *shi* letter as something straight—an ingenious perception—and comparing it to more tangible items, the wit of the poet flashes.

The next two companion songs also reveal an elevated pleasure in ordinary things. This time, the scope moves beyond nature to take in the human realm:

RH 330

yokuyoku medetaku mau mono wa	Things that dance superbly well:
kōnagi konaraha kuruma no dō to ka ya	shrine-maidens, oak leaves, cart axles, and so on
yachikuma hikimai tekugutsu	spinning tops, acrobats, puppets;
hana no sono ni wa chō kotori	and in the blooming garden, butterflies whirl with tiny birds.

RH 331

okashiku mau mono wa	Eye-catching dancers are:
kōnagi konaraha kuruma no dō to ka ya	shrine-maidens, oak leaves, cart axles, and so on
byōdōin naru mizuguruma	the water wheel at Byōdōin;
hayaseba maiizuru ibōjiri katatsuburi	and when they feel the beat and dance, the praying mantis and the snail.[36]

These songs are refreshing precisely because of the unexpected yoking of human elements to a list of objects of slim significance. Notice, incidentally, the continuing interest in *miko* and other performing artists, a sign of their importance to commoners' diversion and entertainment.

The same technique of juxtaposing human and natural elements is used to explore a more poetically inclined topic:

RH 333

kokoro no sumu mono wa	Things that cool the heart:
kasumi hanazono yowa no tsuki	mist, flower gardens, the midnight moon,
aki no nobe	the fields of autumn,
jōge mo wakanu wa koi no michi	love that knows no class distinction,
iwama o morikuru taki no mizu	the waterfall escaping through the rocks.

The abrupt and unexpected introduction of human love in the midst of the list of natural images suspends the smooth flow of association and offers a new context and way of looking at the power of such unconventional love—as something arresting, refreshing, and free.

Another song achieves a similar jolting poetic effect by inserting a human element amid a list of things all natural. Here, the unexpected reference to courtesans brings such women into sharp relief as the focal point of the song, thus delivering a surprising twist. Indeed, the skill with which this is accomplished suggests that the cataloging technique required considerable imagination and went far beyond a simple mechanical enumeration of similar images and thoughts:

RH 334

tsune ni koisuru wa	Always in love:
sora ni wa tanabata yobaiboshi	in the sky, the Weaver Maiden and shooting stars;
nobe ni wa yamadori aki wa shika	pheasants in the fields, the autumn deer;
nagare no kyūdachi fuyu wa oshi	women of the floating world; in wintertime, mandarin ducks.[37]

As we have seen, some catalog songs begin with a harmless list of things, and only toward the end—usually in the last line—does one realize that the song is not an innocuous compendium after all, but a vehicle of curt messages. In this way folk wit, wisdom, and sometimes satire come in to teach—and outsmart—the audience, whose mental reaction to the punch lines approaches "sudden enlightenment." The following famous example capitalizes on the technique, in conjunction with wordplay based on homonyms:

RH 382

fushi no yōgaru wa	Funny knotty things:
ki no fushi kaya no fushi	tree knobs, the joints of reeds,
wasabi no tade no fushi	horseradish lumps, and smart weeds;
mine ni wa yamabushi	hermits sleeping in the mountains,
tani ni wa ka no ko fushi	fawns nestled in the valleys,
okina no binjō marienu hitori fushi	the naughty old man lying alone without a pretty woman of his own.

The song is built on puns on the word *fushi* (knot or knob), as set forth in the first line. By the end of the third line, however, *fushi* is no longer a noun, but a form of the verb *fusu* (to lie down); it is in fact linked to the word *yamabushi* (*yama* + *fushi*), which literally means "those who lie down on the mountains." This image of rugged *yamabushi* on the mountain is then contrasted with the gentler image of fawns resting (*fusu*) in the valley. Yet the most striking turn of the song comes in the last line, where an old man, having failed to win the favor of a young woman, lies in bed alone. His "lying down" (*fushi*) is neither spiritual, like that of the *yamabushi*, nor natural, like that of the fawns. Thus the song ridicules an old man who has passed his season but is still preoccupied with things of the flesh.

Sharp observation of the disparities, contradictions, and absurdities of human life is apparent in the next example. In its forcefulness and directness, this song is perhaps the most striking of its kind:

RH 384

shaba ni yuyushiku nikuki mono	This world's most disgusting things:
hōshi no aseru agari uma ni norite	a monk on horseback, the restless horse
kaze fukeba kuchi akite	rearing in the wind, mouth open wide;
kashira shirokaru okinadomo no wakame gonomi	old greybeards hot for young girls;
shūtome no amagimi no mononetami	a jealous mother-in-law, mama nun.

The characters in the song are far from exemplary, though they ought to be. For that reason, they are here the objects of caricature, with revulsion at their lack of self-knowledge the main theme. Like the preceding song, this one condemns old men with inordinate sexual desires, probably revealing the female singers' loathing detestation of old age.[38]

The time-honored theme of *waka*, autumn, also receives poetic attention in the following *shiku no kamiuta*:

RH 332

kokoro no sumu mono wa	Things that cool the heart:
aki wa yamada no io goto ni	clappers to frighten the deer in autumn,
shika odorokasuchō hita no koe	sounding from every mountain watchman's hut;
koromo shide utsu tsuchi no oto	the sound of fulling blocks beating cloth.

The clappers and fulling blocks were well-established *waka* images evoking autumnal melancholy. The clappers were mentioned in *Man'yōshū*,[39] but their first use in this specific sense is found in *Goshūishū*, poem no. 369. Since then, along with deer and insects, they have been staple symbols for the sad mood of autumn. The sound of the fulling block was first used by Ki no Tsurayuki in a poem (no. 187) included in the autumn section of *Shūishū*, and thereafter became almost synonymous with both autumn and the longing felt for a loved one away from home.[40] In the present song, however, these images, set as they are in the commoner's working life, have a different aesthetic effect, conveying something close to the existential loneliness that seems to pervade all sentient beings.

Several songs in *Ryōjin hishō* display a refined sense of beauty equal to that of any *waka*, with the larger poetic space provided by the *shiku no kamiuta* form giving more room for imagination. For example:

RH 373

kaze ni nabiku mono	Things that sway in the breeze:
matsu no kozue no takaki eda	high pine branches,
take no kozue to ka	and topmost bamboo leaves;
umi ni ho kakete hashiru fune	ships running on the seas with sails raised high;
sora ni wa ukigumo	in the sky, the drifting clouds;
nobe ni wa hanasusuki	in the fields, spiked pampas grass.

The most radical departure from the decorum of *waka* and an outstanding example of folk humor is found in the following *shiku no kamiuta* about lice. Not only the images but also the verbs used indicate a playful mind at work:

RH 410

kōbe ni asobu wa kashira-jirami	On my head the head-lice frolic,
onaji no kubo o zo kimete kuu	then snack on the nape of my neck;
kushi no ha yori amakudaru	but the comb's tooth drags them down to earth;
ogoke no futa nite mei owaru	on the clothes chest's lid, a tragic death.

Usually, *amakudaru* refers to the descent of the heavenly *kami* to earth, as in the well-known case of Ninigi no Mikoto, the grandson of the Sun Goddess, Amaterasu, reported in *Kojiki*.[41] And the phrase *mei owaru* (a partial Japanese reading of *myōjū*) is often used in the Buddhist sutras to allude to the death of an illustrious personage.[42] The humor comes from the use of these lofty verbs to describe such lowly creatures as lice.

On the whole, the wit found in *Ryōjin hishō* relies on comparatively down-to-earth perceptions, whether these involve natural phenomena, fellow human beings, or society as a whole. What is operative in this exercise is an analytical power avidly engaged in sorting out, distinguishing, or comparing objects close at hand. It then classifies and puts them in order, usually in catalog form. This technique, perfected by Sei Shōnagon in *Makura no sōshi* to preserve her perceptions, found a poetic heir in *Ryōjin hishō*.

Signs of the Times

The chaotic political developments in the latter part of the Heian period were transforming Japanese society in a manner inconceivable even for the main agents of the changes. The warrior class, never before a major force in shaping Japanese politics or culture, now became the prime mover. Unprecedented armed conflicts among the warrior clans, unlike localized power struggles at court, dragged even commoners into the fray. Military control led to the replacement not only of the political system but also of basic ways of life and outlook, creating a whole new array of values. It was a time of massive social upheaval; and for many, the world really seemed to be falling apart.

Contemporary literature, such as *Hōjōki* (The Ten-Foot-Square Hut, 1212) by Kamo no Chōmei (1155–1216) and *Heike monogatari*, reflected these convulsive currents. *Ryōjin hishō* songs also capture the disturbing symptoms of the changing world, helping their readers understand what it was like to be part of history in the making. Unlike the prose chronicles, the contents of *Ryōjin hishō* offer only a glimpse of the new signs and mood, but they do make it very clear that ominous and disturbing shifts were well under way.

What caught the attention of the *Ryōjin hishō* poets most was the undeniable presence of warriors in Heian society. Their wealth, life-style, and power are viewed with mixed feelings of envy, wonder, and occasional derision. In one example, we find a survey of the kinds of diversions that warriors enjoyed. The song's speaker, obviously an outsider and not of the warrior class, is awestruck by the spectacles unfolding in the compounds of a warlord's mansion—the riches and power evident in the large number of horses and the garishness of the unusual entertainment:

RH 352

jōme no ōkaru mitachi kana	Look, a mansion: with all those fine horses,
musa no tachi to zo oboetaru	yes, it must be a warrior's place.

| jushi no kozushi no kataodori | On the big acrobats, little acrobats leap, |
| kine wa hakata no otoko miko | and a shaman dances, a man, from Hakata.[43] |

The acrobats (*jushi*) described in the song were associated with *sarugaku* players. Their repertoire included juggling, gymnastics, and magical tricks; colorful costumes as well as superb performing skills contributed to their popular appeal.[44] During the Heian period, acrobats were often invited to perform at the banquets of nobles. When the warriors began to gain power, the *jushi* became an essential part of their entertainment program as well.[45] Another noteworthy sight is the male shaman dancer. Given the fact that *miko* were ordinarily women, a male shaman impersonating a female would be an aberration. Through the speaker, who may represent the collective attitude of the common people, the song expresses a sense of uneasiness tinted with wonder about the warriors and what they represent.

The impression that warriors make on their onlookers is also the subject of the next song, in catalog form, which uses the same formulaic expression we encountered in chapters 5 and 6, *konomu mono*. The detailed inventory of the splendid regalia and arms reveals a fascination with the warriors' physical appearance on the part of the speaker, who may be someone familiar with the taste and ways of the warriors:

RH 436

musa no konomu mono	Warriors' favorite things:
kon yo kurenai yamabuki	navy blue, crimson, gold,
koki suhō akane hoya no suri	dark red, madder red, *hoya* dye;
yoki yumi yanagui muma kura	fine bows, quivers, horses, saddles,
tachi koshigatana	long swords, short swords,
yoroi kabuto ni wakidate kote gushite	helmet, and armor complete with side-bucklers and arm-guards.[46]

The dark blue (*kon*) was a color used for the outfits of low-ranking warriors and was consciously avoided by Heian aristocrats, never appearing in works such as *Genji monogatari* to describe the nobility's clothes.[47] The fact that it tops the list in the present song clearly signifies a new aesthetic taste ushered in by the warrior class.

The power and spirited life of the rising military classes are suggested in the following song, undergirded by the playful suggestion that, to keep up with the times, one should join the warrior culture:

RH 327

musa o konomaba koyanagui	If you admire warriors, get a quiver;
kari o konomaba ayaigasa	if you like hunting, a rush hat
makuri agete	with a rolled brim.
azusa no mayumi o kata ni kake	Sling the catalpa bow on your shoulder
ikusa asobi o yo ikusagami	and let's play war, you war gods.

Some songs in *Ryōjin hishō* confirm the indisputable arrival of warriors in Heian society by listing the Shinto shrines dedicated to the gods related to warfare. The following two companion pieces, for example, using the Ōsaka Barrier in Ōmi as the demarcation line, divide the Japanese country in two, east and west, and suggest how far the sphere of the warriors' activities and power had spread—to include virtually the whole of the country. The shrines, in a sense, embody the mythico-political history of Japan, which is replete with military expeditions and conquests. The first song enumerates warrior shrines in the east:

RH 248

seki yori hingashi no ikusagami	These gods of war live east of the barrier:
kashima kandori suwa no miya	Kashima, Katori, Suwa no Miya,
mata hira no myōjin	and Hira Myōjin;
awa no su tai no kuchi ya otaka myōjin	also Su in Awa, Otaka Myōjin in Tai no Kuchi,
atsuta ni yatsurugi ise ni wa tado no miya	Yatsurugi in Atsuta, and Tado no Miya in Ise.

The main god of Kashima Shrine in Ibaraki Prefecture is Take mikazuchi no Mikoto, who helped Emperor Jinmu during his conquest of the Kumano region; his sword is a special object of veneration at the shrine.[48] Katori Shrine in the same prefecture enshrines Futsu nushi no Mikoto, another god who helped Jinmu in his expedition through the Yamato basin. These two shrines, Kashima and Katori, were once the most powerful shrines in the eastern part of Japan.[49] Located in Nagano Prefecture, the main divinity of Suwa no Miya Shrine is Take mina kata no Kami, who settled in Suwa after being defeated by Take mikazuchi no o no Kami.[50] The Hira Myōjin (Shirahige Shrine) in Shiga Prefecture venerates Saruta hiko no Okami, who, after serving as the vanguard of Ninigi no Mikoto on his descent to earth, settled in the Lake Biwa area.[51] The song's Su Shrine is in fact Awa Shrine in Chiba Prefecture, where Ame no futotama no Mikoto, who served the Sun Goddess Amaterasu in controlling the Inbe (the Shinto ceremonial lineage group), is worshiped.[52] Otaka Myōjin, or simply Otaka Shrine, is located nearby in Tai no Kuchi.[53] Yatsurugi, another name for the Atsuta Shrine in Nagoya, houses the sword that Yamato Takeru supposedly used during his expedition to the eastern region.[54] Tado no Miya, or Tado Shrine, in Mie Prefecture worships Amatsu hikone no Mikoto, a son of Amaterasu, and for this reason has a close relationship with the Ise Shrine.[55]

The next song lists warrior shrines in the west, beginning in the Chūgoku area:

RH 249

seki yori nishi naru ikusagami	These gods of war live west of the barrier:
ippon chūsan aki naru itsukushima	Ippon Chūsan, Itsukushima in Aki,
bichū naru kibitsumiya	Kibitsumiya in Bichū,
harima ni hiromine sōsanjo	Hiromine and Sōsanjo in Harima;
awaji no iwaya ni wa sumiyoshi nishi no miya	across from Iwaya in Awaji are Sumiyoshi and Nishi no Miya.

Ippon Chūsan is in fact Kibitsu Shrine, located on Mount Chūsan in Okayama Prefecture, where the general Ōkibitsu hiko no Mikoto pacified provincial disturbances during the reign of Emperor Sujin (r. 97–30 B.C.).[56] Next, the song makes due note of Itsukushima Shrine, the tutelary shrine of the Taira clan. To the east, in Himeji in Hyōgo Prefecture, the Hiromine Shrine worships Susano o no Mikoto as its main god,[57] while Sōsanjo (the Idatehyōju Shrine) has two warrior gods: Idategami (the god of arrow and shield) and Hyōjugami (the god of arms).[58] Iwaya is Iwaya Shrine, also located in Hyōgo Prefecture, whose main divinities are Izanami and Susano o no Mikoto.[59] The next two shrines, Sumiyoshi and Nishi no Miya (Hirota Shrine), likewise in Hyōgo Prefecture, are grouped together as centers of veneration for the gods who assisted Empress Jingū (r. 201–69) on her legendary expedition to Korea.[60]

Different from the preceding songs, the following one dwells specifically on an individual warrior's achievement; he is Minamoto Yoshiie (1039–1106), popularly known as Hachiman Tarō.[61] The eldest son of Yoriyoshi, Yoshiie fought with his father in the Early Nine Years War (1051–62), which marked the beginning of the Minamoto ascendancy in the eastern provinces. He also became a hero in another war, the Later Three Years War (1083–87), crushing the rebellion of Kiyohara Iehira (d.

1087).[62] In the present song, the allusion to the eagle exalts both Yoshiie's military prowess and the Minamoto's increasing prominence:

RH 444

washi no sumu miyama ni wa	In the mountain retreats where eagles dwell,
nabete no tori wa sumu mono ka	can lesser birds live?
onajiki genji to mōsedomo	Though he bears the common Genji name,
hachiman tarō wa osoroshi ya	oh, how terrifying, that Hachiman Tarō!

The Hōgen Disturbance was not only the tragedy of the imperial family but also a turning point in Japanese history.[63] Its victim, Emperor Sutoku, seems especially to have impressed himself on the popular mind, as his destiny was so extraordinary and appalling. The next song, which is considered to allude to Sutoku, uses a warped pine tree to convey his consuming grief in Sanuki, the place of his exile:

RH 431

sanuki no matsuyama ni	On Mount Matsuyama in Sanuki,
matsu no hitomoto yugamitaru	a single crooked pine,
mojirisa no sujirisa ni	tortured and bent,
soneudaru ka to ya	they say it's raging.
naoshima no sabakan no	Even on the Island called Straight,
matsu o dani mo naosazaruran	they can't put this one right.[64]

Notice the play on the word *naosu* (to straighten), which is found in both *naoshima* (straight island) and *naosazaruran* (seems unable to be straightened). The imagery is a metaphor for the depth and intensity of Sutoku's unredressable grudge against his brother, Go-Shirakawa—ironically the recorder of the song.

Signs of the changing times were found not only in sensational events involving the highborn, but also in the lives of the commoners. The troubled state of the country and apprehension about its future are expressed in the following song about a young man drafted into the army. Scenes such as this were likely all too common as the country found itself swept into the Genpei War:

RH 393

ashiko ni tateru wa nani bito zo	Who is standing there?
inari no shimo no miya no tayū	Isn't it the priest's son,
mimusuko ka	from the Lower Inari Shrine?
shinjichi no tarō na ya	Yes, the oldest son,
niwaka ni akatsuki no	suddenly a soldier;
hyōji ni tsuisasarete	they came for him at dawn,
nokori no shujōtachi o	to keep the people in peace—
heian ni mamore to te	that's why.[65]

The Inari shrines in general were associated with rice cultivation, and the one at Fushimi, mentioned here, was the center of such shrines—the core of the life of farmers. If the son of the shrine priest were drafted, especially the eldest one who would continue the priestly line, the situation in the capital must have been grave indeed. The fact that he was taken away at dawn makes the situation all the more fearful and ominous.

The civil war, which necessitated moving soldiers from one region to another, provided the Heian residents with opportunities to learn about manners and customs other than their own. But the cultures outside the capital—especially those to the east—were usually perceived as unpalatable or even objectionable and thus often became the object of derision. The two following songs betray this attitude of disdain. In the first one, contempt for the reprehensible behavior of a common soldier from the east (Azuma) is highlighted, focusing on his violation of the basics of marriage protocol:

RH 473

azuma yori	Just got in yesterday
kinō kitareba	from Azuma—
me mo motazu	haven't had time to get a wife;
kono kitaru kon no	how about trading
kariao ni musume	your daughter
kaetabe	for this here dark blue cloak?

The dark blue (*kon*) color of the man's cloak and the man's proposal of marriage in exchange for a mean article of clothing convey the scandalized feelings of the ceremonious Heian capital residents and their sense of outrage not just at boorish easterners but at warriors in general.

In the second song, the strange customs of the east are on view as the speaker comments scornfully on the aberrant performances of male *miko*:

RH 556

azuma ni wa	Are there no women
onna wa naki ka	in the east?
otoko miko	Only male shamans there,
sareba ya kami no	but even so,
otoko ni wa tsuku	the god sweeps down on them.

Yet even in the capital, things are not as they once were. New trends, not always desirable, prevail. And what happens in the capital, whether it be frivolous or serious, is interpreted as an index of the state of the nation as a whole. The following two companion songs detail the latest fashion vogue in the capital—the disturbing symptom of an age steeped in flimsy fads while serious political crises brew:

RH 368

kono goro miyako ni hayaru mono	Up-to-date fashion in the capital:
kataate koshiate ebōshitodome	stiff shoulder pads, waist pads, hat pins,
eri no tatsu kata sabiebōshi	high collars, lacquered caps,
nuno uchi no shita no hakama	cotton under trousers, narrow outer trousers
yono no sashi nuki	not four-*no* wide![66]

The basic feature of this list of trendy fashion items for men is the *kowasōzoku*, meaning "stiffened costume." It emphasized an angular, hard look achieved by starching and padding the clothes.[67] The result was a striking contrast to the *naesōzoku* (softer costume), characterized by rounded and flowing lines, which had been popular among courtiers up to mid-Heian times. On the whole, the new men's fashion reflects a shift from the effusive taste of the aristocracy to the more stern, controlled, and action-oriented functionalism of the warrior class. These disturbing trends arise again in the second song, concerning women's fashion:

RH 369

kono goro miyako ni hayaru mono	Up-to-date fashion in the capital:
ryūtai kamigami esekazura	eyebrows penciled willow-thin, all sorts of hairdos, hairpieces,
shioyuki ōmime onnakaza	*shioyuki*, Ōmi women, women dressed like men;

naginata motanu ama zo naki   not a nun without a halberd,
                                    none!

During the Heian period, it was customary for women to shave their natural eyebrows and draw on thick ones on the forehead. The fad laid out here, however, stresses a very thin line like a willow branch—obviously a new style.[68] The meaning of *shioyuki* is unclear, but it may refer to courtesans.[69] The Ōmi women are likely *asobi* or *kugutsu* who settled around the Setagawa River in the vicinity of Lake Biwa in Ōmi.[70] "Women in male costumes" may be *shirabyōshi*, women who danced in men's clothing. On the whole, the fashionable items for women outlined here are marked by affectation and sham; those who wore such things would hardly have been considered commendable or of good breeding. The flourishing of various types of female entertainers is also notable. Most striking is the image in the last line of nuns armed with halberds parading through the streets of the capital, which certainly suggests great social unrest and insecurity.

In another song, the deteriorating situation of women during these times finds expression in the figure of a nun. Despite her assertion that she has respectable relatives (all male) to rely on, she is obviously in reduced circumstances. It is possible that songs such as these were originally beggars' songs:

RH 377

ama wa kaku koso saburaedo	I may look like an old drab nun, but
taianji no ichimanhōshi mo oji zo kashi	Ichiman, the priest at Taianji Temple,
oi mo ari	he's my uncle. Also there's a nephew,
tōdaiji ni mo shugakushite ko mo motari	also a son studying at Tōdaiji Temple.
amake no saburaeba	It looks like rain,
mono mo kide mairikeri	so I dressed really plain.[71]

Some *Ryōjin hishō* songs register the conditions of hard-pressed families in the lower classes. In the following song—one of the longest in *Ryōjin hishō*—we find a grievous protest raised against the callousness of the elites in Heian society, through the lyric voice of a mother wailing about her broken family. The speaker of the poem, probably a female shaman at Wakamiya Shrine in the Iwashimizu Hachiman Shrine complex, pours out her woes to the *kami* she serves:[72]

RH 363

ōna ga kodomo wa tada futari	Only two children for this old lady.
hitori no onnago wa	They called my girl
nii no chūjō dono no	to be a kitchen maid
kuriya zōshi ni meshishikaba	for the middle general.
tatemateki	I gave her up.
ototo no onokogo wa	They wanted my boy, the younger one,
usa no daiguji ga hayafune	to be an oarsman on the sloop
funako ni koishikaba	of the high priest at Usa.
madaiteki	I served him up.
kami mo hotoke mo goranze yo	Oh gods, oh buddhas, bear witness!
nani o tataritamau wakamiya no omae zo	God of Wakamiya, what is my sin?[73]

The old mother's acute sense of the wrongs inflicted on her family by the powerful represents a social indictment rarely seen in the poetry of the times.

Another indication in *Ryōjin hishō* of the unstable social atmosphere that then prevailed was the depiction of gamblers. Although as a poetic topic gamblers have appeared in literary works from *Man'yōshū* on, they are featured six times in *Ryōjin hishō* , which suggests their conspicuous presence at least among the singers of these songs.[74] Their uprooted and marginal life-style comes to light in the following song, in which a mother prays for her son's success in gambling. Given that in the late Heian period the government took action to quash gambling as a socially disruptive activity, arresting bands of gamblers wholesale on the streets of the capital,[75] the mother's concern takes on a compelling significance:

RH 365

waga ko wa hatachi ni narinuran	My son must be in his twenties now—
bakuchi shite koso arikunare	I hear he's a wandering gambler
kuniguni no bakutō ni	in a provincial gambling gang.
sasugani ko nareba nikukanashi	Well, he's mine, I can't hate him!
makaitamau na	Gods of Sumiyoshi and Nishi no Miya,
ōji no sumiyoshi nishi no miya	I beg you, don't let him lose the game.[76]

The following song deals with the hidden area of gamblers' practices and preferences, phrased in the familiar formula *konomu mono*, which we have seen used for the esoteric world of *asobi, hijiri*, and warriors as well. The list concerns dice playing; in addition, several skillful gamblers are named, likely by aliases:

RH 17

bakuchi no konomu mono	A gambler's favorite things:
hyōsai kanasai shisōsai	*hyō* dice, steel dice, the die faces four and three;
sore o ba tare ka uchietaru	hands skilled in the toss:
monsan gyōsan tsukizuki seiji to ka	Monsan, Gyōsan, Tsukizuki Seiji, so they say.[77]

In the next song, too, the gamblers mentioned are probably identified by aliases. Interestingly, most of their names have a Buddhist ring to them, representing another striking combination of sacred and profane in *Ryōjin hishō*. While we cannot know whether these were assumed or real names, some contemporary sources suggest that priest-gamblers did exist during the Heian period; perhaps, then, the men named here belonged to such a group:[78]

RH 437

hōshi bakuchi no yōgaru wa	Strangest of the priestly gamblers:
jizō yo kasen jirō terashi to ka	Jizō, Kasen, Jirō, Terashi, so it's said,
owari ya ise no mimizu shimochi	Mimizu from Owari or Ise, and Shimochi;
muge ni waroki wa keisokubō	but the wildest knave of all is Priest Keisoku.

The names with definite links to Buddhism are Jizō, Kasen (the Japanese reading of Mahākātyāyana, one of the Buddha's Four Great Disciples), Terashi (another reading of *jishu*, a temple secretary), Shimochi (a word meaning a new Buddhist convert), and Keisoku (the Japanese reading of Mount Kukkuṭapāda, on which Mahākāśyapa is supposedly to have entered into nirvanic meditation). The meaning of Mimizu is not clear, but it could be a variant of *mikuzu*, a scum on the water or an ugly person with a mean demeanor.[79] The man identified as Shimochi may be a novice priest who has just had a religious awakening (*hosshin*).[80] In this subculture, the profane simply appropriates the sacred, which leads to a quality of wry humor.

The confused and decadent mood of the times comes into full view in the lament of a mother whose children seem to epitomize the moral lapses of the folk world depicted in *Ryōjin hishō*:

RH 366

ōna no kodomo no arisama wa	This old lady's children, how they act!
kaza wa bakuchi no uchimake ya	My elder son's a gambler, born to lose;
katsu yo nashi	the time of his winning is never.
zenshi wa madakini yakō konomumeri	The younger son's a young monk, but given to wandering the night.
hime ga kokoro no shidoke nakereba	As my daughter's heart is wild as well,
ito wabishi	how miserable their mother![81]

A summary of late-Heian decadence and hedonism is presented in the following song, which is filled with jestful irreverence:

RH 426

hijiri o tateji wa ya	Why bother to be holy men?
kesa o kakeji wa ya	Why wear the stole,
zuzu o motaji wa ya	why carry the beads?
toshi no wakaki ori tawaresen	The years of youth are the time to play!

Thus the troubled yet gay mood of the period leaves its imprint in the songs of *Ryōjin hishō*, telling that life may be painful, imperfect, and often irksome, but at the same time it remains energizing, exciting, and colorful.

Quasi-Children's Songs

When we speak of the wide variety of topics in *Ryōjin hishō*, a handful of songs ostensibly for children are invariably mentioned. Admittedly, these songs, in their utter simplicity, do at first glance appear to be ones that young children might sing. Yet when they are considered in the performative context of *asobi* entertainment, it becomes clear that they are in fact anything but children's songs.

This song, presumably voicing a child's threat to a snail, illustrates the point:

RH 408

mae mae katatsuburi	Dance, snail, dance!
mawanu mono naraba	If you fail, snail,
muma no ko ya ushi no ko ni	I'll have colts kick,
kuesaseten fumiwaraseten	calves stamp, smash you flat.
makoto ni utsukushiku	But dance pretty and
mautaraba	
hana no sono made asobasen	you can dance among flowers in
	my garden.

The song may originally have been sung in conjunction with *monomane mai* (mimic dances), a dance form that imitated the movement of people at work, animals, and insects in a humorous or even lewd manner and was staged as entertainment during banquets.[82] Once it became an *imayō* performed by female entertainers, however, the song may have taken on a meaning very different from that of children playing with insects. Uttered in a disguised children's voice and in children's language, the song can easily imply men's suggestive exhortations for an *asobi* to display her skills—both as a musical entertainer and as a prostitute.

The following song, because it focuses on a dragonfly, long a popular motif in children's songs, has usually been understood to belong to that genre.[83] But here again, when we view the ditty in the context of an *asobi's* performance, another meaning presents itself. Especially with the words *warawabe* and *kaza*, which mean young men rather than children, and *asobase*, meaning to let someone have fun and carrying a clear erotic undertone, the song could easily be a strong, provocative utterance spoken to *asobi* during physical contact with a customer:[84]

RH 438

iyo iyo tōbō yo	Stay, dragonfly, stay,
katashio mairan sate itare	I'll salt your tail to make you
	stay,
hatarakade	hey, don't move a muscle!
sudareshino no saki ni	I'll tie you up with a horsehair
	rope,
muma no o yoriawasete	hitched to a bamboo pole;
kaitsukete	and then
warawabe kaza bara ni	the boys, the young men, I'll let
	them
kurasete asobasen	spin you around and have their
	fun.[85]

Similarly, the next song is anything but a children's song, although it may be interpreted as a dialogue between a toy top and its owner, usually assumed to be a boy. However, the street names and the references to the festival at Jōnanji Shrine hint at a more multivalent meaning. Most likely, *komatsuburi* (literally, a spinning top) is the name of a courtesan, and the song represents her coy refusal of an invitation to go to the outskirts of the capital with a customer, presumably for a tryst. The "horses" may well allude to men around the Toba Palace area (possibly warriors) with whom the woman had an unpleasant experience she does not want to repeat:

RH 439

izare komatsuburi	Let's go, my spinning top,
toba no jōnanji no matsuri mi ni	to see the fair in Toba, at Jōnanji!
ware wa makaraji osoroshi ya	Oh no I won't, for I'm afraid,
korihatenu	I've learned my lesson:
tsukurimichi ya yotsuzuka ni	too many restless horses rearing up
aseru agari uma no ōkaru ni	on the Tsukurimichi and Yotsuzuka roads.[86]

As these songs make clear, it is important always to keep the performative context and the females' role as lyricists, singers, and entertainers in mind when engaging in interpretation. Indeed, an important part of the entertainment purpose is achieved only when the audience decodes the symbolic or implied meaning of the songs, appreciating the messages on more than one level. This is true of numerous other seemingly simple songs in *Ryōjin hishō* as well: when looked at closely, they reveal qualities not apparent at first or even second glance. And it is these qualities that give the songs their appeal.

Conclusion

Because the *Ryōjin hishō* was lost for so many centuries, its influence on premodern Japanese literature is slight. But it has had a noticeable impact, perhaps as much as other classical texts, on many modern Japanese poets and novelists and even on the general public. Twentieth-century readers have found the anthology appealing because of its fresh insights into Heian realities, its frank and open character, its comprehensive coverage of poetic subjects, and because of the symbolic significance of its survival and recovery after centuries of obscurity.

The *imayō* genre as seen in *Ryōjin hishō* represents a synthesis of the Japanese song tradition, a tradition that extends back to the folk songs of ancient Japan including *kiki kayō* (songs from the *Kojiki* and *Nihonshoki*), songs in *Man'yōshū*, *kagurauta*, *saibara*, and *fuzoku*. And by integrating Buddhist songs into the native song tradition, *imayō* became a genre in which seemingly incompatible elements of Heian culture could coexist and interact. In a sense, it reflected the total poetic configuration of Heian Japan. The breadth of its themes is matched only by its diversity of poetic form and prosody, comparable to that in *Man'yōshū*.

The fact that the main creators and performers of *imayō* were female singers of marginal social status cannot be overemphasized. Women began to contribute to Japanese literature and performing arts as early as the period of the *Kojiki* and *Man'yōshū*. In the late Nara period, some women performing artists were employed by the Naikyōbō, a government office specifically charged with providing and supervising female musical entertainment and dance at the court.[1] This official tradition of female entertainment continued well into the Heian period, reaching its peak during the Fujiwara regency.[2]

The female *imayō* singers—*miko, asobi,* and *kugutsu*—however, provided a private form of performing arts, developing and regulating their artistry and methods of musical transmission within their respective groups and complementing the government-managed female entertainment programs. The *kugutsu* were most seriously committed to *imayō* as a dignified form of high art, cultivating it with keen aesthetic sense and controlling the training and the transmission of songs through kinship lines. Both *miko* and *asobi* used *imayō* largely as an auxiliary medium in their life of prostitution. The fact that groups of these female entertainers became the principal arbiters of popular music during the late Heian period, even penetrating court culture with their songs, demonstrates their consummate artistry. In a few cases, their artistic accomplishments even afforded them occasional or temporary upward social mobility.

The *imayō* genre, however, never achieved the status of a recognized state art or craft as *kagurauta* had, nor did its singers in general receive the public patronage of the court. Their recognition by Emperor Go-Shirakawa stands as a significant exception. Go-Shirakawa's interest in *imayō* was grounded in a personal, religio-aesthetic understanding of the power of music, derived from Buddhist dialectical thought and the concept of *kyōgen kigyo* (see chapter 3). Go-Shirakawa's unorthodox pursuit and championing of the art of *imayō* has thus preserved at least some of these songs for posterity in the extant fragments of *Ryōjin hishō.*

Go-Shirakawa suffered much political adversity during his career and, most tragically, was haunted by the specter of his wronged brother, Emperor Sutoku. Nevertheless, he is credited for his efforts to reassert royal prestige and power, long eclipsed by the Fujiwara regentship. Notable among these activities are his commissioning of the *waka* collection *Senzaishū* as well as lavish picture scrolls and his unparalleled frequent pilgrimages to outlying regions.

Ryōjin hishō may be counted as one of the most telling expressions of Go-Shirakawa's expansive cultural projects, a product born of his riveting interest in *imayō* music of plebeian origin. It is a complex and multifaceted work, containing diverse viewpoints, richly evocative observations, and far-ranging sentiments. Its themes cover religion, society, human relationships, and even nature; they touch upon the old and the new, the high and the low, the center and the periphery, the sacred and the profane. This expanded vision of the plurality of Heian society is conspicuously absent from contemporary aristocratic *waka,* where insistence on homogeneity, uniformity, and conformity to received models are of paramount concern. The songs in *Ryōjin hishō* in this sense embody the consciousness of a new age in the making, where difference was more tolerated, class boundaries were more fluid, and a fresh synthesis of differing traditions was appreciated. The anonymous singer-poets of *Ryōjin hishō* seem to have captured in their songs this transition from aristocratic exclusivism to populist participation in the creation of a new national culture.

The sense of the passing of one age and the advent of another is first evinced in the *hōmon uta*, chiefly through religious reflection. Even in this rather homogeneous section there is some diversity, for the songs deal not only with orthodox Tendai doctrines but also with the newly burgeoning Amida pietism. Tendai metaphysics is set against the pleas for salvation of fishermen and hunters; and public praise of Buddhist divinities shares space with monologues by common women aspiring to spiritual emancipation. The abstruse, transcendental realm of the buddhas and bodhisattvas is rendered in the simple storytelling style of popular *setsuwa*. In the cultic worship of the Lotus Sutra and the divinities in the Buddhist pantheon, the trend is clearly toward easy access.

In the *shiku no kamiuta* virtually every area of human activity is touched upon: religion, love, society, men and women, and the surrounding environment. This wide assortment of subjects is often named as the source for the colorfulness and diversity of *Ryōjin hishō*. Through detailed examination of these spheres we learn much about the mundane existence as well as the aspirations of many distinctive groups in Heian society, especially those living on the margins. The folk characters display the perennial foibles of humankind; their keen observations provide a rare panorama of contemporary social change, and their sparkling wit brings into relief the tragicomedy in which they play out their roles. In this sense, the *shiku no kamiuta* section can be characterized as the most enlivening and entertaining element of *Ryōjin hishō*.

The theme of love proves as powerful in kindling the imagination of *Ryōjin hishō* poets as it does for *waka* poets, but the emphasis here shifts dramatically from subtle evocation to frank expression of physical love. Parental love is also expressed, signifying a more comprehensive coverage of human love than in traditional lyrical poetry. *Ryōjin hishō* songs exhibit a keen awareness of the social and political changes that were taking place at the end of the Heian period. Disturbing trends symptomatic of the instability of Heian society are acutely observed and reported; human behavior and social mores in all their anomaly, hypocrisy, and incongruity become the subject of biting commentary. Some events, viewed as ominous portents of larger historical developments of disastrous consequence, are regarded with a sense of awe and apprehension; the rise of the warrior classes is particularly called to our attention. Yet at the same time, the ability and even need to laugh in the face of adversity remain clearly evident.

Themes on Shinto religious practices appear, all concentrated in *jinja uta* in the *niku no kamiuta* section. These songs are often stylized Shinto prayers for the enduring prosperity of the sovereign and aristocratic clans. Most of them are celebratory, stressing the bright, joyful side of human life.

In the final analysis, Go-Shirakawa's *Ryōjin hishō* is a kind of photo album, preserving colorful snapshots of Heian society as it faced radical changes. It stands as faithful witness to the throes of those times, registering the confusion, turbulence, movement, and excitement that accompany any such upheaval. The anthology embraces life in its entirety, traditional and innovative, whole and broken, beautiful and unseemly. No single set of values is advocated exclusively over the others. That an emperor, surrounded by an elitist and exclusive court culture, should have played a catalytic role in the birth of this mosaic anthology is remarkable. *Ryōjin hishō* stands as an enduring testament to his unorthodox poetic vision.

Notes

The basic annotated texts of the *Ryōjin hishō* used for this study are the following: Kawaguchi Hisao and Shida Nobuyoshi, eds., *Wakan rōeishū, Ryōjin hishō*, Nihon Koten Bungaku Taikei, vol. 73 (Iwanami Shoten, 1965) [hereafter cited as NKBT 73]; and Usuda Jingorō and Shinma Shin'ichi, eds., *Kagurauta, Saibara, Ryōjin hishō, Kanginshū*, Nihon Koten Bungaku Zenshū, vol. 25 (Shōgakkan, 1976) [hereafter cited as NKBZ 25]. Occasional references are made to Enoki Katsurō, ed., *Ryōjin hishō*, Shinchō Nihon Koten Shūsei, vol. 31 (Shinchōsha, 1979).

INTRODUCTION

1. Konishi Jin'ichi, *Ryōjin hishō kō* (Sanseidō, 1941), pp. 51, 81.
2. NKBZ 25:182–83.
3. NKBT 73:345. It must be noted that Han Ê was a female singer.
4. An implicit reference to this "dancing dust," signifying the power of superb singing, appears in *Tosa nikki*. See Suzuki Tomotarō et al., eds., *Tosa nikki, Kagerō nikki, Izumi Shikibu nikki, Sarashina nikki*, Nihon Koten Bungaku Taikei, vol. 20 (Iwanami Shoten, 1965), p. 30.
5. See sec. 14 in Nishio Minoru, ed., *Hōjōki, Tsurezuregusa*, Nihon Koten Bungaku Taikei, vol. 30 (Iwanami Shoten, 1964), p. 102.
6. Sasaki Nobutsuna, *Ryōjin hishō* (Iwanami Bunko, 1933), p. 194.
7. Konishi Jin'ichi, Preface to his *Ryōjin hishō kō*.
8. Shinma Shin'ichi, *Kayōshi no kenkyū: sono ichi—imayō kō* (Shibundō, 1947), pp. 244–67.
9. See song no. 314. It has fourteen lines with highly irregular prosody.
10. The most extreme case is song no. 410, which is on the topic of lice.
11. Arthur Waley, "Some Poems from the *Manyoshu* and *Ryojin Hissho*," *Journal of the Royal Asiatic Society*, 1921, pp. 193–203. More recent

translations of *Ryōji hishō* are "Thirty-two Songs from the *Ryōjin hishō*," in Hiroaki Sato and Burton Watson, eds. and trans., *From the Country of Eight Islands: An Anthology of Japanese Poetry* (New York: Anchor Books, 1981), pp. 157–62; and Yasuhiko Moriguchi and David Jenkins, trans., *The Dance of the Dust on the Rafters: Selections from Ryojin-hisho* (Seattle: Broken Moon Press, 1990).

CHAPTER 1. EMPEROR GO-SHIRAKAWA AND *IMAYŌ*

1. Go-Shirakawa, the seventy-seventh sovereign, was the fourth son of Emperor Toba and his principal consort, Taikenmon-in (Fujiwara Shōshi, 1101–45). He became emperor in 1155 on the death of Emperor Konoe (1139–55), his younger half-brother, born of the union between Toba and his favorite secondary consort, Bifukumon-in (Fujiwara Tokushi, 1117–60). His becoming emperor at the age of twenty-nine makes him a late-comer in Heian politics, where infants were frequently elevated to the throne.

2. The remark is reported by Jien (1155–1225) in his *Gukanshō* (Tracts of Foolish Views) (1219–20). See Okami Masao and Akamatsu Toshihide, eds., *Gukanshō*, Nihon Koten Bungaku Taikei, vol. 86 (Iwanami Shoten, 1967), p. 216.

3. See Watanabe Shōgo, *Ryōjin hishō no fūzoku to bungei* (Miyai Shoten, 1981), pp. 7–8.

4. Go-Shirakawa's thirty-five-year rule as a retired emperor (*insei*) was record-breaking. The five emperors under his *insei* were his son Nijō (r. 1158–65), grandson Rokujō (r. 1165–68), son Takakura (r. 1168–80), grandson Antoku (r. 1180–83), and grandson Go-Toba (r. 1183–98). Emperor Shirakawa (1053–1129) is credited with the establishment of *insei*.

5. Sutoku was known as a son born of the illicit liaison between Emperor Shirakawa, Go-Shirakawa's great-grandfather, and Taikenmon-in, Shirakawa's adopted daughter and Toba's consort. Therefore, Sutoku was the half-brother of Go-Shirakawa; however, he passed as the putative son of Emperor Toba. The disturbance—a succession dispute, in essence—occurred in the wake of the death of senior ex-Emperor Toba, when junior ex-Emperor Sutoku (1119–64), forced to abdicate by Toba in favor of Konoe, tried to restore his line on the throne.

6. This marked the first time that the death penalty was revived since the Kusuko Disturbance in 810 during the reign of Emperor Saga (r. 809–23). Shinzei is said to have recommended to Go-Shirakawa the execution of the culprits involved in the incident. See Iida Yukiko, *Hōgen, Heiji no ran* (Kyōikusha, 1979), p. 116.

7. Okami and Akamatsu, eds., *Gukanshō*, p. 335.

8. Quoted in Enoki, ed., *Ryōjin hishō*, p. 281.

9. See Iida, *Hōgen*, p. 138.

10. NKBT 73:444.

11. *Saibara* refers to folk songs arranged to court music. *Rōei* is the practice of chanting or singing Japanese poems in the manner of recited Chinese poems. *Shōmyō* is a general term for Buddhist vocal music usually performed by priests during temple ceremonies. Emperor Toba himself was an expert in *saibara* singing, and Go-Shirakawa's skill was equal to his father's. Go-Shirakawa underwent training in the Minamoto school of *rōei* and is also listed in the lineage chart of the transmission of *shōmyō* as the disciple of the priest Kakan. See Shinma, *Kayōshi*, pp. 46–50.

12. Emperor Juntoku (1197–1242), Go-Shirakawa's great-grandson and Go-Toba's son, attests in his work *Yakumo mishō* (His Majesty's Yakumo Treatise, 1234), that Go-Shirakawa was an accomplished *imayō* singer. See Konishi, *Ryōjin hishō kō*, p. 1.

13. Shinma, *Kayōshi*, pp. 89–93, 149–56.

14. Kure Fumiaki, *Imayō kō* (Risōsha, 1965), p. 31. *Fuzoku (uta)* refers to country folk songs in a general sense. More narrowly, it refers to folk songs incorporated into the court entertainment repertoire. Some fifty such song lyrics are extant. See Tsuchihashi Yutaka and Konishi Jin'ichi, eds., *Kodai kayōshū*, Nihon Koten Bungaku Taikei, vol. 3 (Iwanami Shoten, 1957), pp. 277–78.

15. See NKBT 73:469.

16. At least two scenes in different sections of *Murasaki Shikibu nikki* describe court nobles' enjoyment in singing *imayō* at their gatherings; see Ikeda Kikan, Kishigami Shinji, and Akiyama Ken, eds., *Makura no sōshi, Murasaki Shikibu nikki*, Nihon Koten Bungaku Taikei, vol. 19 (Iwanami Shoten, 1958), pp. 445, 503. In *Makura no sōshi*, Sei Shōnagon briefly mentions *imayō* as "songs with long melodies"; see ibid., sec. 280, p. 301.

17. Geinōshi Kenkyūkai, ed., *Nihon geinōshi*, 7 vols. (Hōsei Daigaku Shuppankyoku, 1981–90), 2:113. Genshin is best known for his major work, *Ōjōyōshū* (Essentials of Salvation); Mount Kinbu (also known as Mount Ōmine or Mount Mitake), a famous site for mountain asceticism, is in the southern part of Nara Prefecture.

18. See Mitani Eiichi and Sekine Yoshiko, eds., *Sagoromo monogatari*, Nihon Koten Bungaku Taikei, vol. 79 (Iwanami Shoten, 1965), pp. 429–30. *Sagoromo monogatari*, a tale of the love adventures of the hero, Sagoromo, is ascribed to Rokujō saiin baishi naishinnō no Senji (1022?–92).

19. For instance, Go-Shirakawa's *imayō* teachers in his youth were Akomaro, from Kagami no Yama in Ōmi Province, who served at the Bureau of Palace Maintenance; and Kane from Kanzaki, a personal attendant of Taikenmon-in, Go-Shirakawa's mother. See NKBT 73:443.

20. Kure, *Imayō kō*, pp. 121–24. Also valuable as a source regarding *imayō* performances at court is *Kokon chomonjū* (Stories Heard from Writers Old and New, 1254), one of the major *setsuwa* (tales) collections

in Japan, by Tachibana Narisue (dates unknown), a literary and musical figure of the Kamakura period.

21. See Kure, *Imayō kō*, p. 149. *Bunkidan*, compiled by Ryūen (dates unknown), a *biwa* expert of the Kamakura period, is a valuable music reference containing materials on *biwa* music and various song forms, including *imayō*.

22. Ibid., pp. 124–26.

23. Ibid., pp. 124–38; Shinma, *Kayōshi*, pp. 189–94.

24. G. Cameron Hurst maintains that the *insei* period represented the time when emperors exercised real political power, having weakened the influence of Fujiwara regentship; see *Insei: Abdicated Sovereigns in the Politics of Late Heian Japan, 1086–1185* (New York: Columbia University Press, 1976), pp. 212–13.

25. Nakayama Tarō, *Nihon mikoshi* (Ōokayama Shoten, 1930), pp. 580–83.

26. Ibid., pp. 92–114.

27. Yamagami Izumo, *Miko no rekishi* (Yūzankaku Shuppan, 1981), pp. 123–25.

28. See Baba Mitsuko, "*Ryōjin hishō* mikouta," *Nihon kayō kenkyū* 17, no. 4 (1978): 16.

29. See Ogihara Asao and Kōnosu Hayao, eds., *Kojiki, jōdaikayō*, Nihon Koten Bungaku Zenshū, vol. 1 (Shōgakkan, 1973), pp. 81–83. See also Matsumae Takeshi, "The Heavenly Rock-Grotto Myth and the *Chinkon* Ceremony," *Asian Folklore Studies* 39, no. 2 (1980): 9–22.

30. Konishi, *Ryōjin hishō kō*, p. 150.

31. Tago Bay, famous for its scenic beauty with a view of Mount Fuji, is located at the present-day Fuji City in Shizuoka Prefecture. The phrase *tago no ura* was often used in *waka* as *utamakura*, a place-name with poetic association.

32. For details, see Matsumae, "Heavenly Rock-Grotto Myth."

33. Joseishi Sōgō Kenkyūkai, ed., *Nihon joseishi* (Tōkyō Daigaku Shuppankai, 1982), 2:109.

34. Nakayama, *Nihon mikoshi*, pp. 214–20. For further details, see Gorai Shigeru, "Asobi-be kō," *Bukkyō bungaku kenkyū* 1 (1963): 33–50; Akima Toshio, "The Songs of the Dead: Poetry, Drama, and Ancient Death Rituals of Japan," *Journal of Asian Studies* 41 (1982): 485–509; and Yung-Hee Kim Kwon, "The Female Entertainment Tradition in Medieval Japan: The Case of *Asobi*," in *Performing Feminisms: Feminist Critical Theory and Theatre*, ed. Sue-Ellen Case (Baltimore: Johns Hopkins University Press, 1990), pp. 316–27.

35. Gorai, "Asobi-be kō," p. 46.

36. Yamagishi Tokuhei et al., eds., *Kodai seiji shakai shisō*, Nihon Shishō Taikei, vol. 8 (Iwanami Shoten, 1981), p. 154. The "Yūjoki" is by far the most detailed document on *asobi* available from the Heian period.

37. Takigawa Masajirō, *Yūgyōnyofu, yūjo, kugutsume* (Shibundō, 1965), p. 121. A scene in *Hōnen Shōnin eden*, a picture scroll from the Kamakura period on the life of the priest Hōnen (1133–1212), depicts an *asobi* trio in their boat appoaching the ship carrying the priest to exile in Tosa from the Muro no Zu port in Harima Province. See Komatsu Shigemi and Kanzaki Mitsuharu, eds., *Hōnen Shōnin eden*, Zoku Nihon Emaki Taisei, vol. 2 (Chūō Kōronsha, 1981), pp. 150–51.

38. Yamagishi et al., eds., *Kodai seiji shakai shisō*, pp. 154–55.

39. Takigawa Masajirō, *Miko no rekishi* (Shinbudō, 1981), p. 53.

40. Takigawa, *Yūgyōnyofu*, pp. 115–119; Watanabe, *Ryōjin hishō*, p. 35.

41. Takigawa, *Miko no rekishi*, p. 41. At first the Hyakudaifu may have been represented by young female dolls; see ibid., pp. 130–32.

42. Yamagishi et al., eds., *Kodai seiji shakai shisō*, p. 155.

43. Ibid. The Hirota Shrine is located in the present-day city of Nishi no Miya in Hyōgo Prefecture, to the west of Eguchi and Kanzaki. The Sumiyoshi Shrine is located in present-day Osaka, to the south of Eguchi and Kanzaki.

44. Shimae is presumably the name of a place on the lower Yodo River.

45. Ivan Morris, trans., *As I Crossed a Bridge of Dreams: Recollections of a Woman in Eleventh-Century Japan* (New York: Dial Press, 1971), p. 115.

46. See Ōe no Masafusa, "Yūjoki," in Yamagishi et al., eds., *Kodai seiji shakai shisō*, p. 155; and Takigawa, *Yūgyōnyofu*, pp. 168–69, 192, 196.

47. Similar information may be found in Fujiwara Akihira's (989–1066) *Meigō ōrai* (Meigō's Correspondence, 1066), a collection of exemplary letters. See Takigawa, *Yūgyōnyofu*, pp. 161–64, 181.

48. On a visit in 1023 to Eguchi, Emperor Ichijō bestowed 100 *koku* (500 bushels) of rice on the groups of *asobi* that crowded around the imperial barge. In 1000, during Michinaga's visit to Eguchi, the Empress Dowager Tōsanjō-in granted 100 *koku* of rice to *asobi*, while Michinaga gave 50 *koku*. Yorimichi distributed 200 skeins of silk and 200 *koku* of rice on his visit to the Eguchi and Kanzaki areas in 1031. See Watanabe, *Ryōjin hishō*, pp. 37–40.

49. See NKBT 73:454. Tanba no Tsubone's father seems to have been an aristocrat, but her mother was obviously an *asobi*. See Watanabe, *Ryōjin hishō*, p. 43.

50. The Tennōji Temple is located in Osaka. This episode found its way as well into such *setsuwa* collections as *Senjūshō* (Selected Stories, 1183) and *Kojidan*. Finally, the same story was dramatized in the Noh play "Eguchi," attributed to Kan'ami (1333–84), where in the finale the *asobi* reveals herself as the Bodhisattva Fugen. See Yokomichi Mario and Omote Akira, eds., *Yōkyokushū*, 2 vols., Nihon Koten Bungaku Taikei, vols. 40–41 (Iwanami Shoten, 1964), 1:49–56. For a detailed discussion on impli-

cations of the poetic exchange between Saigyō and the *asobi*, see William R. LaFleur, "Inns and Hermitages: The Structure of Impermanence," in *The Karma of Words: Buddhism and the Literary Arts in Medieval Japan* (Berkeley and Los Angeles: University of California Press, 1983), pp. 60–79.

51. Shōkū Shōnin (910–1007) is the founder of Enkyōji Temple on Mount Shosha in Harima Province. The priest, therefore, is also known as Shosha Shōnin. *Kojidan* also relates a story of Shōkū Shōnin's encounter with an *asobi* in Kanzaki, who turns out to be the Bodhisattva Fugen. See Kure, *Imayō kō*, pp. 94–95.

52. Fujiwara Nakazane (1057–1118) was a leading figure in the *waka* circle of Emperor Horikawa (r. 1086–1107).

53. The lineage chart of the *imayō* transmission attached to "Imayō no ranshō" (Origin of *Imayō*), a Kamakura document concerning the genealogy of singers, is included in Konishi, *Ryōjin hishō kō*, pp. 610–13. It shows that many *kugutsu*, who are mentioned in the *Kudenshū*, belong to this lineage group.

54. See NKBT 73:446–52. For an English translation of *Kudenshū*, see Yung-Hee Kwon, "The Emperor's Songs: Go-Shirakawa and *Ryōjin hishō Kudenshū* Book 10," *Monumenta Nipponica* 41 (1986): 277–82.

55. Yamagishi et al., eds., *Kodai seiji shakai shisō*, p. 158.

56. Ibid., p. 159.

57. Morris, trans., *As I Crossed a Bridge of Dreams*, pp. 47–48. Apparently, here, the author of the diary did not make a distinction between *asobi* and *kugutsu*.

58. Konishi, *Ryōjin hishō kō*, p. 149.

59. Takigawa, *Yūgyōnyofu*, p. 231. It has been noted that Mino Province used to be the major center of the *katari-be*, a hereditary lineage of reciters, which dispatched the largest number of its members (relative to other reciter groups) to the imperial court to take part in the enthronement ceremony. See Inoue Tatsuo, *Kodai ōken to kataribe* (Kyōikusha, 1979), p. 16. Some scholars even suggest that the *imayō* singers from Mino were descendants of the *katari-be* of the region; see, for example, Sekine Kenji, "Aohaka no bungaku, geinō," *Kokubungaku: kaishaku to kanshō* 45, no. 12 (1980): 182.

60. Morris, trans., *As I Crossed a Bridge of Dreams*, pp. 51–52.

61. NKBT 73:452. Hatsukoe served as Go-Shirakawa's *imayō* teacher in the early stages of his *imayō* studies; see ibid., pp. 444–45.

62. Ibid., p. 451. Fujiwara Ienari (1107–54) was an ardent patron of *imayō*. The terms beginning with *ashigara* are various song forms within *imayō*, but their exact meanings are unknown.

63. Nabiki may be the same woman, who headed the third generation of the Mino *imayō* lineage. See Konishi, *Ryōjin hishō kō*, p. 616.

64. According to Nose Asaji, the term *shirabyōshi* originally referred

to both a form of dance and the music that accompanied it. Later it came to be used for the dancers themseves. It is generally believed that *shirabyōshi* dance and music contributed to the evolution of Noh drama. For further details on the etymology and development of *shirabyōshi*, see Nose, "Shirabyōshi ni tsuite," *Kokugo kokubun* 1, no. 3 (1931): 6–22. See also Konishi, *Ryōjin hishō kō*, pp. 159–61. For sources on the origin of *shirabyōshi*, see Ichiko Teiji, ed., *Heike monogatari*, 2 vols., Nihon Koten Bungaku Zenshū, vols. 29–30 (Shōgakkan, 1973–75), 1:50; and sec. 225 of *Tsurezuregusa* in Nishio, ed., *Hōjōki, Tsurezuregusa*, p. 271, which suggests the rise of the *shirabyōshi* sometime during the reign of Emperor Go-Shirakawa.

65. See Ichiko, ed., *Heike monogatari* 1:49–64; Kajihara Masaaki, ed., *Gikeiki*, Nihon Koten Bungaku Zenshū, vol. 31 (Shōgakkan, 1971), pp. 257–70.

66. See Geinōshi Kenkyūkai, ed., *Nihon geinōshi* 2:164.

67. Konishi, *Ryōjin hishō kō*, p. 160.

68. NKBT 73:447–51.

69. Ibid., pp. 444–45.

70. Ibid., p. 442.

71. Ibid., pp. 442–43. *Zōgeishū* is believed to have been an *imayō* collection, no longer extant, that preceded *Ryōjin hishō*. The title is also mentioned in *Sengohaykuban utaawase* (The Poetry Match in Fifteen Hundred Rounds, ca. 1201) and *Genpei jōsuiki* (or *seisuiki*, A Record of the Genpei War, ca. 1247). *Hōmon* (or *hōmon uta*) are songs on Buddhism. *Hayauta* are presumed to be *imayō* with a fast tempo.

72. See Robert H. Brower and Earl Miner, *Japanese Court Poetry* (Stanford: Stanford University Press, 1961), p. 257; and Konishi Jin'ichi, "Michi and Medieval Writing," in *Principles of Classical Japanese Literature*, ed. Earl Miner (Princeton: Princeton University Press, 1985), pp. 181–208.

73. See NKBT 73:443. Some scholars believe, therefore, that Go-Shirakawa's interest in *imayō* may have first been inspired by his mother, Taikenmon-in. See Ogawa Hisako, "Goshirakawa-in no 'imayō netsu' to Taikenmon-in Shōshi: nyoin inshi to imayō," *Nihon kayō kenkyū* 19 (April 1980): 12–17.

74. The remark is entered under the heading "Unsuitable Things" in her *Makura no sōshi*; see sec. 45 in Ikeda, Kishigami, and Akiyama, eds., *Makura no sōshi*, p. 93.

75. NKBT 73:444.

76. Otomae was brought to Go-Shirakawa's attention by his retainer, Shinzei. At first she refused to accept the invitation, saying that she was no longer good at *imayō* and that she was unpresentable, an indirect reference to her old age. According to *Kudenshū*, when Otomae was twelve or thirteen years old her musical talent caught the attention of Minamoto

Kiyotsune, inspector of finances at the Ministry of Central Affairs, who came to the Mino area on business and was entertained by this young disciple of Mei, a well-known *imayō* singer of the region. At Kiyotsune's suggestion, both Mei and Otomae came up to the capital and received his patronage. Kiyotsune, the maternal grandfather of the priest Saigyō and presumably an authority in *imayō*, maintained an intimate personal relationship with Mei until her death and also may have been instrumental in Otomae's development into an accomplished *imayō* singer. The *Kudenshū* also reports that a circle of minor-courtier *imayō* patrons—including Fujiwara Atsuie (1032–90), his son Atsukane (dates unknown), and Fujiwara Akisue (1055–1123)—formed around Mei a generation before Emperor Go-Shirakawa initiated his patronage of the art form. See NKBT 73:445–51.

77. The song is identical to *Ryōjin hishō* no. 32. According to Buddhist eschatological tradition, Buddhism was predicted to decline continuously through three stages after the Buddha's decease. The first period, called the "Correct Dharma" (*shōbō* in Japanese), would last five hundred to one thousand years, during which Buddhist doctrines, practices, and enlightenment all exist. In the second period, known as the "Imitation Dharma" (*zōbō*), also lasting five hundred to one thousand years, both doctrines and practices still exist, but enlightenment is no longer possible. The last period, called the "Degenerate Dharma" (*mappō*), spans ten thousand years, and during it only doctrines survive. In Japan, it was believed that the *mappō* period would begin in the year 1052.

78. NKBT 73:452–53.

79. Ibid., p. 453. The Rishu Sutra ("Sutra of the Principle of Wisdom") emphasizes the compassionate actions of Dainichi (Mahāvairocana), the central divinity in Shingon practice, and is recited daily in the sect as its main scripture. The Ninnaji Temple is a Shingon center located in western Kyoto; its abbots were traditionally imperial princes.

80. Ibid., p. 454.

81. Ibid.

82. Ibid.

83. Ibid., pp. 469–70. Suketoki was the son of Sukekata (1113–88), Go-Shirakawa's early *imayō* teacher. Formerly an officer in the Left Gate Guards, Suketoki became a priest in 1186. Besides being an expert in *imayō*, he was also skilled in playing the flute and lute, as he came from a renowned family of musicians. Moronaga, an expert *biwa* player, was the second son of Yorinaga (1120–56), one of the leading insurgents of the Hōgen Disturbance. Appointed prime minister in 1177, he was later deposed and exiled by Taira Kiyomori to Owari, where he adopted the title Myōon-in, after the name of the bodhisattva of music, Myōon.

84. Shinma, *Kayōshi*, pp. 36–43. The twenty-two-volume *Kikki* is an important source for the study of late Heian cultural developments. Some

other records that mention this event are *Hyakurenshō* (Seasoned Selections), an anonymously compiled seventeen-volume history based on court nobles' diaries and other sources from the period 968–1259, and *Yoshino Kissuiin gakusho* (Musical Record Kept at Yoshino Kissuiin), a mid-thirteenth-century collection of information on musical genres, performances, and events of earlier periods.

85. Shinma, *Kayōshi*, pp. 42–43.

CHAPTER 2. GO-SHIRAKAWA AS A PATRON OF HEIAN CULTURE

1. Taniyama Shigeru, *Senzaiwakashū to sono shūhen*, Taniyama Shigeru Chosakushū, vol. 3 (Kadokawa Shoten, 1982), p. 247.

2. NKBT 73:446–47, 458–60.

3. The following discussion owes much to Taniyama, *Senzaiwakashū*, pp. 7–36.

4. Ibid., pp. 20–21.

5. Reportedly Munemori vowed that the Taira would fight to the last man to carry out Kiyomori's dying wish—an injunction to his sons to capture Yoritomo, behead him, and hang the head over Kiyomori's grave before they perform his funeral. See Ichiko, ed., *Heike monogatari* 1:452.

6. See Nagazumi Yasuaki and Shimada Isao, eds., *Hōgen monogatari, Heiji monogatari*, Nihon Koten Bungaku Taikei, vol. 31 (Iwanami Shoten, 1986), p. 181. To appease Sutoku's maligned spirit, a shrine for him was finally built in the fourth month in 1184 on the banks of the Kasuga River, at the site of the battle of the Hōgen Disturbance.

7. *Kyūan hyakushu* includes one hundred *waka* poems composed by fourteen poets, including Sutoku and Shunzei. It is considered the best of the poems produced by the poetic circle under Sutoku's leadership and served as the basis for *Senzaishū*. See Taniyama, *Senzaiwakashū*, pp. 19–20.

8. Some of these poems are included in Shunzei's collection of *waka*, *Chōshū eisō* (Shunzei's Collection for Her Former Majesty, 1178), compiled at the request of Princess Shokushi (d. 1201), daughter of Go-Shirakawa and a renowned *waka* poet.

9. Taniyama, *Senzaiwakashū*, pp. 19–20.

10. *Shokushikashū* never became an imperial anthology owing to the death of Emperor Nijō in 1165.

11. Taniyama, *Senzaiwakashū*, p. 11.

12. Ichiko, ed., *Heike monogatari* 2:94–97.

13. The choice of Sukemori is considered to have been a conciliatory gesture to placate Taira. See Taniyama, *Senzaiwakashū*, pp. 28–30.

14. Ibid., pp. 25–26.

15. For instance, a poem by Taira Tokitada (the elder brother of Kiyomori's wife) and three poems by his younger brother, Chikamune, are

included in *Senzaishū* and identified by the poet's name. Other poems by more prominent members of the Taira, however, are listed as anonymous: Tadanori, no. 66; Tsunemasa, nos. 199 and 245; Yukimori, no. 519; and Tsunemori, no. 667. All of these poets had been Shunzei's disciples.

16. The poem was originally included in *Kyūan hyakushu*, and later Shunzei selected it for inclusion in his *Koraifūteishō* (Poetic Styles Past and Present, 1197), which indicates that the poem was one of his favorites. See Kubota Jun and Matsuno Yōichi, eds., *Senzaiwakashū* (Kasama Shoin, 1970), pp. 44–45.

17. This poem was also included in both *Kyūan hyakushu* and *Koraifūteishō*. It is regarded as one of Shunzei's best poems, embodying the essence of *yūgen* (feelings of mystic depth). See ibid., pp. 53–54.

18. Both Shiga and Mount Nagara are located in Ōmi. This poem is the one that Tadanori presumably entrusted to Shunzei before retreating from the Heian capital. See Ichiko, ed., *Heike monogatari* 2:94–97.

19. See Taniyama, *Senzaiwakashū*, pp. 195–97.

20. The anecdote is found in the entry on the seventeenth day of the sixth month in 1184. Fujiwara Mitsunaga (or Tokiwa no Genji Mitsunaga) heard the story from Taira Yorimori (1131–86), a brother of Kiyomori. See Komatsu Shigemi, "Ōchō emaki to Goshirakawa-in," in *Genji monogatari emaki, Nezame monogatari emaki*, ed. Komatsu Shigemi, Nihon Emaki Taisei, vol. 1 (Chūō Kōronsha, 1977), pp. 117–18.

21. Ibid., pp. 132–33.

22. See ibid., p. 127.

23. Komatsu Shigemi, "*Nenjūgyōji emaki* tanjō," in *Nenjūgyōji emaki*, ed. Komatsu Shigemi, Nihon Emaki Taisei, vol. 8 (Chūō Kōronsha, 1977), p. 116.

24. See ibid., p. 106.

25. Motofusa, who is the elder brother of Kanezane, was a well-known expert in official matters. See ibid., p. 127.

26. Ibid., p. 109.

27. Ibid., p. 110.

28. Ibid., p. 114.

29. Ibid., p. 115.

30. Komatsu, "Ōchō emaki to Goshirakawa-in," p. 118.

31. Ibid., p. 125.

32. See Komatsu, "Nenjūgyōji emaki tanjō," p. 120.

33. See Komatsu, "Ōchō emaki to Goshirakawa-in," p. 133.

34. See Tanaka Hiroshi, "Pilgrim Places: A Study of the Eighty-eight Sacred Precincts of the Shikoku Pilgrimage, Japan" (Ph.D. diss., Simon Fraser University, 1975), p. 12.

35. Saichō traveled to T'ang China during the years 804–5 and studied on Mount T'ien-t'ai. Upon his return to Japan he founded the Tendai sect on Mount Hiei. Kūkai, a contemporary of Saichō, also studied in China

from 804 to 806. Ennin, one of Saichō's disciples, is best known for his *Nittō guhō junrei gyōki* (The Record of a Pilgrimage to China in Search of the Dharma), an account of his sojourn in China from 838 to 847. Enchin stayed in China for six years, 853–58, studying on Mount T'ien-t'ai and in Ch'ang-an.

36. W. G. Aston, trans., *Nihongi: Chronicles of Japan from the Earliest Times to A.D. 697* (Rutland, Vt.: Charles E. Tuttle, 1972), pp. 21–22.

37. Murayama Shūichi, *Honji suijaku* (Yoshikawa Kōbunkan, 1974), p. 149.

38. Aston, trans., *Nihongi*, pp. 115–16.

39. Shinma, *Kayōshi*, p. 53. Emperor Sutoku, who made only one pilgrimage to Kumano, is the sole exception during the *insei* period. The exact number of Go-Shirakawa's pilgrimages to Kumano is disputed; I have followed Shinma, who provides a detailed biographical chronology, pp. 290–360.

40. The years he did not go to Kumano are 1161, 1176, 1181–85 (the Genpei War period), and 1189.

41. The years in which two trips took place are 1167, 1168, 1169, 1171, 1173, 1174, 1175, and 1177. In the years 1167, 1169, and 1175, Go-Shirakawa's favorite consort, Kenshunmon-in, accompanied him on one of the two trips.

42. Shinma, *Kayōshi*, p. 54.

43. See Hashigawa Tadashi, *Nihon bukkyō bunkashi no kenkyū* (Chūgai Shuppan Kabushiki Kaisha, 1924), pp. 261–63; and Murayama, *Honji suijaku*, p. 156. One of the memorable episodes in *Heike monogatari* relates the drowning of Taira Koremori (1158–84), a grandson of Kiyomori, off the shore of Nachi in 1184; see Ichiko, ed., *Heike monogatari* 2:326–31.

44. Murayama, *Honji suijaku*, p. 164.

45. An example of the extreme austerities endured by ascetics is found in the story of the priest Mongaku at the Nachi Falls in Kumano, who, in winter, repeatedly submerged himself in the pool of the waterfall; see Ichiko, ed., *Heike monogatari* 1:379–83.

46. Murayama, *Honji suijaku*, pp. 152–53.

47. See Miyaji Naokazu, *Kumano sanzan no shiteki kenkyū* (Kokumin Shinkō Kenkyūkai, 1954), pp. 462–67.

48. NKBT 73:460–63; the years were 1160, 1162, and 1169.

49. The figure in an ascetic's white robe illustrated on the "Kumano mandala," preserved in Saikyōji Temple in Ōtsu City, is believed to be Emperor Go-Shirakawa on his pilgrimage to Kumano. See Shinma Shin'ichi, "Goshirakawa-in to bukkyō," *Chūsei bungaku ronsō* 3, no. 1 (1980): 11.

50. Anzu Motohiko, *Shintō jiten* (Osaka: Hori Shoten, 1968), p. 298.

51. NKBT 73:463–67.

52. Shinma, *Kayōshi*, p. 51. This ceremony of anointment, called *kanjō*, was performed in esoteric Buddhism. The rite conferred higher status to the recipient than did a regular tonsure. It sometimes was administered for special reasons such as to provide relief from illnesses or to prepare one for the next life.

53. NKBT 73:461–62. Minamoto Michiie (d. 1167) was the son of Sukekata. He died five years after accompanying Go-Shirakawa on this pilgrimage to Kumano. Kakusan, a priest from Onjōji Temple, served as the guide on this pilgrimage.

54. Ibid., p. 464.

55. Shirai Eiji and Toki Masanori, eds., *Jinja jiten* (Tōkyōdō Shuppan, 1979), p. 44.

56. Ibid., pp. 43–44.

57. Shinma, *Kayōshi*, p. 55.

CHAPTER 3. GO-SHIRAKAWA AND *RYŌJIN HISHŌ*

1. NKBT 73:442.

2. The *Zuinō* is also known as *Toshiyori kuden(shū)*, *Toshiyori mumyōshō*, and *Toshi hishō*. The two-volume book elucidates different *waka* forms, prosody, topics, styles, techniques, rhetoric, and ideals. It reinforces the critical contents by selecting examples of superior poems under each heading. The work is characterized by its structurally loose, rambling narrative.

3. In the conversation with his son Teika, Fujiwara Shunzei praised Toshiyori as a poetic genius in his use of poetic dictions; see Ichiko Teiji, ed., *Nihon bungaku zenshi*, 6 vols. (Gakutōsha, 1978), 2:494. It is no wonder, therefore, that Shunzei selected in *Senzaishū* fifty-two poems by Toshiyori, the largest number by any single poet represented in the anthology.

4. *Zuinō* contains fifty such poems based on historical or legendary narratives from China or Japan, as well as nineteen poems that share similar story origins with *Konjaku monogatari*; see Ikeda Tomizō, *Minamoto Toshiyori no kenkyū* (Ōfūsha, 1973), pp. 906–10, 989.

5. Ibid., pp. 903–5.

6. NKBT 73:469.

7. Ibid., p. 470. It was only in 1178 that *imayō* transmission began in earnest with Minamoto Suketoki and Fujiwara Moronaga.

8. The following observation owes much to Walter Ong's insights into oral tradition and literacy as presented in his book *Orality and Literacy: The Technologizing of the Word* (London: Methuen, 1982).

9. NKBT 73:440. Nothing is known about *mononoyō*. *Tauta*, rice planting songs, also belong to the folk song genre.

10. NKBZ 25:22. The regent Fujiwara Michinaga is supposed to have written the text himself.

11. Ibid., p. 117. One notable textualization of *saibara* was done by Fujiwara Moronaga, Go-Shirakawa's *imayō* successor. The *saibara* texts are preserved in his musical score collections: *Inchiyōroku* (Compendium of Benevolence and Wisdom) for *koto* and *Sangoyōroku* (Compendium of Fifteen Eras) for *biwa*.

12. Between the reigns of Emperor Seiwa (r. 858–76) and Emperor Daigo (r. 897–930), the court *kagurauta* repertoire was believed to have been fixed; see ibid., pp. 16–17.

13. NKBT 73:467.

14. Ibid., pp. 467–68.

15. Two legends explain the circumstances of Atsuie's death in 1090. According to one, he died on Mount Kinbu on a pilgrimage; the other relates that he died on a pilgrimage to Kumano, because the deities there wished to keep him with them, so impressed were they by his music. See NKBT 73:467.

16. Fujiwara Michisue (d. 1128), assistant middle councillor, was an elder brother of Taikenmon-in and, therefore, Go-Shirakawa's maternal uncle. The song he sang is the same as no. 160 in *Ryōjin hishō*.

17. Kōryūji Temple is located in the western part of Kyoto.

18. The song may have been no. 235 of *Ryōjin hishō*. The story of Tonekuro is included in well-known Buddhist *setsuwa* collections such as *Hōbutsushū* (A Collection of Treasures), compiled by Taira Yasuyori (fl. 1190–1200), and *Jikkinshō* (A Treatise of Ten Rules, ca. 1252) compiled by Rokuhara Jirōzaemon (fl. mid-Kamakura). According to these sources, an *asobi* named Tonekuro from Kanzaki was mortally wounded in an ambush by pirates on her way to Tsukushi by boat in the company of a male companion. Before she died, she reportedly sang this song and achieved rebirth in the Pure Land. See NKBT 73:468.

19. Shirōgimi was probably an *asobi* from Takasago, a seaside village in Hyōgo Prefecture.

20. The Kumano pilgrimage tops the list, with such incidents happening on three occasions, in 1160, 1162, and 1169. On pilgrimages to the following shrines, such an incident occurred once: Kamo Shrine in 1169, Itsukushima Shrine in 1174, and Yawata Shrine in 1178. See NKBT 73:460–67.

21. See ibid., p. 463. In fact, Go-Shirakawa's recital of *imayō* on this occasion included thirteen of the twenty known *imayō* forms. This variety indicates how seriously he took the occasion: as if to display the best of his performing art as well as to experience the climax of his musical career as a layperson, he seems to have covered as exhaustively as possible the ground he had cultivated for so many years.

22. NKBT 73:463. *Ichiko* is one form of *imayō*, but nothing is known

about it. Fujiwara Chikanobu (dates unknown), chief of the Right Bureau of Horses, was dismissed from his post during Kiyomori's coup in 1179. The original sentence beginning "It may be the flapping sound . . . " is garbled, making it difficult to decipher the exact meaning.

23. Ibid., p. 468–69.

24. Suzuki Hideo and Fujii Sadakazu, eds., *Nihon bungeishi*, vol. 2 (Kawade Shobōshinsha, 1986), p. 333. The group comprised forty members, half of whom were poets and half priests from Enryakuji Temple on Mount Hiei. The first meeting was held in 964 at Gatsurinji Temple in Nishisakamoto. Although subsequent meetings were occasionally disrupted, they continued until 1122 at various locations. Yasutane was a famous scholar of Chinese studies during the reign of the Emperor Kazan. Shitagō was the compiler of *Wamyō (ruijū)shō* (Japanese Names for Things Classified and Annotated, ca. 931–37), the first Japanese dictionary of encyclopedic scope. Tamenori was Shitagō's disciple and the compiler of *Sambōe(kotoba)* (Illustrated Words on the Three Treasures, 984), a *setsuwa* collection.

25. The passage is included in the section titled "Hsiang Shan ssu pai shih luo chung chi chi" (Preface to *Luo chung-chi* by Po Chü-i Dedicated to the Hsian Shan-ssu Temple) in book 71 of his *Pai shih wen chi* (The Collected Writings of Po Chü-i). At the Kangaku-e gathering, the members chanted the phrase *kyōgen kigyo* along with Po Chü-i's poems. A detailed description of the Kangaku-e meetings is included in *Sambōe* by Minamoto Tamenori. See Ichiko, ed., *Nihon bungaku zenshi* 2:258–59.

26. See Kikuchi Ryōichi, "Bungei daiichigitei o enzu: kyōgen kigyo sokubutsudō," *Bukkyō bungaku kenkyū* 11 (1972): 9–10. The *Muryōjukyō* Sutra (Amitayūs Sutra) condemns false words and showy language as one of the ten vices.

27. Among them, the Parable of the Burning House in the Lotus Sutra is usually taken as the most effective illustration of this point. For an English translation, see Leon Hurvitz, trans., *Scripture of the Lotus Blossom of the Fine Dharma* (New York: Columbia University Press, 1976), pp. 49–83.

28. Kikuchi, "Bungei," p. 47.

29. In the preface to his *Koraifūteishō*, Shunzei advocates the *kyōgen kigyo* ideal; Saigyō in his *Sankashū* (Collection from a Mountain Hut) also talks about the same concept. See Kikuchi, "Bungei," pp. 24–26.

30. See poem no. 588, NKBT 73:200.

31. *Kudenshū*, book 1, NKBT 73:440; italics added.

32. A similar concept is echoed in the preface to *Kanginshū* (Songs for Leisure Hours), a mid-Muromachi collection of popular songs. See NKBZ 25:384. In some popular song genres such as *wazauta*, songs were considered to have prophetic or premonitory power, usually warning of events

of grave political consequence. See Misumi Haruo, *Geinōshi no minzokuteki kenkyū* (Tōkyōdō Shuppan, 1976), p. 42.

33. Ōbayashi Taryō, ed., *Ensha to kankyaku: seikatsu no naka no asobi*, Nihon Minzoku Bunka Taikei, vol. 7 (Shōgakkan, 1984), p. 90.

34. Geinōshi Kenkyūkai, ed. *Nihon geinōshi* 1:215.

35. Ibid.

CHAPTER 4. POETIC FORMS AND TECHNIQUES

1. Six such examples are found in *Ryōjin hishō*: no. 18 is the same as no. 194; no. 19 = no. 25; no. 20 = no. 23; no. 21 = no. 22; no. 30 = no. 237; and no. 324 = no. 414.

2. Konishi, *Ryōjin hishō kō*, pp. 151–53.

3. A handful songs in *hōmon uta*, such as nos. 67, 95, 100, 221, and 227, deviate from this norm. The 8-5 syllable line is more common than that of 7-5 in *hōmon uta*. See Shinma Shin'ichi and Shida Nobuyoshi, eds., *Kayō II: Ryōjin hishō, Kanginshū*, Kanshō Nihon Koten Bungaku, vol. 15 (Kadokawa Shoten, 1979), p. 73.

4. See Enoki Katsurō, "Hōmon uta," *Kokugo kokubun* 18 (1949): 83–86; Shinma, *Kayōshi*, pp. 165–67.

5. NKBT 73:468.

6. The song is from the parable of the burning house in chapter 2 of the Lotus Sutra, "Hōbenbon" (Expedient Means).

7. The song is based on the story of a prodigal son and his father featured in "Shingehon" (Belief and Understanding), chapter 4 of the Lotus Sutra.

8. The song is taken from the parable of a jewel sewn into the robe of a drunken man, included in "Gohyaku deshihon" (Receipt of Prophecy by Five Hundred Disciples), chapter 8 of the Lotus Sutra.

9. Geinōshi Kenkyūkai, ed., *Nihon geinōshi* 2:103.

10. Taya Raishun, *Wasanshi gaisetsu* (Kyoto: Hōzōkan, 1933), p. 44.

11. Ibid., p. 50. Part of this *kansan* appears as poem no. 591 in *Wakan rōeishū*; see NKBT 73:201. Tomohira also wrote another *kansan* called "Fugen bosatsu san" (Praise of Fugen Bodhisattva).

12. Enoki, "Hōmon uta," p. 89.

13. Taya, *Wasanshi gaisetsu*, p. 92. The *wasan* genre that developed on Mount Hiei was cultivated largely by priests inclined toward the Pure Land school. This close relationship may account for the fact that *wasan* was the major form used in Pure Land liturgy and that the majority of extant *wasan* are related to Pure Land Buddhism.

14. Ibid., pp. 4, 27.

15. Takeishi Akio, *Bukkyō kayō* (Hanawa Shobō, 1973), p. 27. This

wasan is on the Tendai doctrines, beginning with those elaborated by Ennin.

16. Ibid., pp. 24–28. "Gokurakukoku mida wasan" is supposed to have been popularly sung, rather than used in solemn Buddhist ceremonies.

17. Taya, *Wasanshi gaisetsu*, pp. 30–36. Most of these are included in Takano Tatsuyuki, ed., *Nihon kayō shūsei*, 12 vols., rev. ed. (Tōkyōdō Shuppan, 1960), vol. 4.

18. Konishi, *Ryōjin hishō kō*, p. 104.

19. Two songs, nos. 296 and 303, in the *shiku no kamiuta* section are also from "Tendai Daishi wasan."

20. Yōkan was the eighth patriarch of the Pure Land sect. He had long been associated with the Tōdaiji Temple in Nara and the Zenrinji Temple in Kyoto.

21. Taya, *Wasanshi gaisetsu*, pp. 86–87.

22. Mount Sumeru is the center in Indian cosmology and is thought to be composed of gold, silver, emerald, and crystal and surrounded by a great ocean in the four cardinal directions.

23. Early *wasan* were simply Japanese reading of *kansan*, with occasional insertions of Japanese particles such as *wa, ga, o, ni*, or *no*; see Geinōshi Kenkyūkai, eds., *Nihon geinōshi* 2:104.

24. See Shinma Shin'ichi, "Imayō ni miru bukkyō," *Bukkyō bungaku kenkyū* 2, no. 2 (1964): 80–85. *Kungata*, which consist of a quatrain, are Buddhist songs used in temple rituals and have closest affinity with *hōmon uta*. *Kyōke* are another form of Buddhist song performed in temple ceremonies and are much longer than *kungata*.

25. Konishi, *Ryōjin hishō kō*, p. 133.

26. The clappers were made of small bamboo stalks attached to a piece of wooden board; when pulled by a rope, they would make jingling noises. This device was used to scare away animals from damaging the crops in the fields or rice paddies.

27. The Day of the Rat refers to the First Day of the Rat in the New Year, when people would go to the fields to transplant small pine trees and pluck young shoots. The peach blossom refers to a Chinese legend in which a fairy offered Emperor Wu of the Han dynasty a large peach, the harvest from a blossom that bloomed but once in three thousand years; see NKBZ 25:313.

28. Yokawa is one of the major areas in the Enryakuji Temple compound on Mount Hiei. Chishō Daishi (Enchin), after returning home from his studies in China, was appointed in 866 as head priest of the Miidera (Onjōji) Temple in Ōtsu, Ōmi Province. Kōbō Daishi founded the Kongōbuji Temple on Mount Kōya.

29. No. 58 demonstrates spatial progression in much the same way as *michiyuki*, while no. 100 is limited to enumerating the names of a series

of palaces. See Tsuchihashi and Konishi, eds., *Kodai kayōshū*, pp. 73–74, 99–100.

30. Ibid., p. 187.

31. Song no. 13 on gambling is partly in catalog form; no. 22, titled "Kubo no na," lists names of female sexual organs. See NKBZ 25:132, 227–38.

32. See Konishi, *Ryōjin hishō kō*, p. 152. By the time *imayō* appeared in the Heian period, *waka* poems were already being sung.

33. The song is based on *Goshūishū* poem no. 1166 by the priest Egyō (dates unknown). The "three jeweled fences" refer to the three major shrines that make up the Inari Shrine complex.

34. Nagato is an old name for the Kurahashijima Island in Hiroshima Prefecture. A buddha supposedly has thirty-two primary body marks, one of which is "golden-colored" skin; in addition, he has eighty secondary body marks. For the detailed list of these marks, see Leon Hurvitz, *Chih-i (538–597): An Introduction to the Life and Ideas of a Chinese Buddhist Monk*, Mélanges chinois et bouddhiques, vol. 12 (Brussels: L'Institut Belge des Hautes Études Chinoises, 1962), pp. 353–60.

35. Konishi, *Ryōjin hishō kō*, p. 85.

36. Ibid., p. 152.

37. Ibid., p. 108.

38. Anzu, *Shintō jiten*, pp. 522–23. In times of grave national crisis, it was standard court procedure to dispatch special envoys to these shrines to present offerings and prayers for the nation. The origins of the system go back to ancient times, but the names and ranks (high, middle, or low) of the twenty-two shrines were fixed during the reign of Emperor Go-Suzaku (r. 1036–45). Except for the Ise Shrine, all the shrines are concentrated in the capital area.

39. The identity of Amatsuyuwake is unknown, but there is a theory that it is in fact not a shrine name but a Shinto god worshiped in the Kiyomizu Temple. Konoshima is a shrine located in the Uzumasa area of Kyoto. See NKBZ 25:341–42.

40. This may reflect the close association of *imayō* singers, such as *asobi* and *kugutsu*, with that shrine.

41. *Kokin (waka)rokujō* is a manual in six parts for *waka* composition, presumably compiled by Minamoto Shitagō and Prince Kaneakira (914–87). It includes 4,370 exemplary *waka*, more than half of which are from *Man'yōshū, Kokinshū,* and *Gosenshū. Kaya no in shichiban utaawase* is a collection of seventy *waka* composed during the poetry competition held in 1094 at Kaya no In, the mansion of the former chancellor Fujiwara Morozane (1042–1101). *Horikawa-in hyakushuwaka* is a collection of one hundred *waka* poems by sixteen poets, compiled by Minamoto Toshiyori and dedicated to Emperor Horikawa in 1105.

42. The poem was composed by the emperor on his pilgrimage to the Sumiyoshi Shrine in the third month of 1073, three months after his abdication. Two months later, the emperor died at the age of thirty-nine.

43. The song is based on two poems by Kakinomoto Hitomaro, nos. 1244–45 in *Shūishū*.

44. Konishi, *Ryōjin hishō kō*, p. 16.

45. See Enoki, *Ryōjin hishō*, p. 187.

46. The conch shell was used like a bugle by *yamabushi* (mountain ascetics) to communicate as they roamed in the mountains.

47. See Enoki, *Ryōjin hishō*, pp. 190–91.

CHAPTER 5. THE WORLD OF RELIGION IN *RYŌJIN HISHŌ*

1. Of a total 220 *hōmon uta*, 218 are on Buddhism, the exceptions being nos. 193 and 229; about 40 of the 204 *shiku no kamiuta* are on the same topic; while *niku no kamiuta* and the *imayō* in book 1 contribute minimally, with six and four songs, respectively. In fact, all four such songs in book 1—nos. 18, 19, 20, and 21—duplicate the *hōmon uta* nos. 194, 25, 23, and 22, respectively.

2. Shinma and Shida, eds., *Kayō II*, p. 33.

3. Monju is usually depicted riding a lion, while Fugen is shown riding a white elephant with six tusks. Fudō, who is known for his power to destroy the devils who interfere with Buddhist practice, is represented as a wrathful figure, holding a sword in his right hand, to smite the wicked, and a rope in his left, to catch and bind them, as flames rage around him. Kongōsatta is the second of the first eight patriarchs of the Shingon school, to whom Dainichi directly transmitted the esoteric teaching. Myōken was worshiped in Japan for his power to cure eye diseases.

4. These are the flowers of two of the four trees in Indra's paradise; see NKBZ 25:213.

5. The verse refers to a scene in the chapter where the jeweled stūpa decorated with seven gems—gold, silver, lapis lazuli, giant clam shell, coral, pearl, and carnelian—emerges from the earth and hangs suspended in midair. Although the verse does not specify, the stūpa contained in it the Buddha of Many Jewels (Tahō Nyorai; Prabhūtaratna), a bodhisattva who had once lived in the land of Pure Jewel and had entered nirvana after making a vow that he would appear in the jeweled stūpa wherever the Lotus Sutra was preached.

6. King Śuddhodana was the ruler of the Śākya tribe in Kapilavastu, and Suprabuddha was a rich elder from the city of Devadarśita nearby.

7. Both the horse and Chandaka are supposed to have been born on the same day as the prince. Mount Dantaloka is located in Gandhāra in the northern part of India.

8. This sutra is an important scripture in both the Tendai and Shingon schools.

9. See Mochizuki Shinkō, *Bukkyō daijiten*, 7th ed. (Sekai Seiten Kankō Kyōkai, 1972), 2:1446–47.

10. See Gary L. Ebersole, *Ritual Poetry and the Politics of Death in Early Japan* (Princeton: Princeton University Press, 1989), pp. 74–75, 165, 174–75, 257–61.

11. See Tsuchihashi and Konishi, eds., *Kodai kayō*, pp. 239–47. For an English translation and study, see Roy Andrew Miller, *"The Footprints of the Buddha": An Eighth-Century Old Japanese Poetic Sequence* (New Haven: American Oriental Society, 1975).

12. Actually the prince's father ruled in Kapilavastu, not the Magadha Kingdom. Magadha, the most powerful kingdom in India during Śākyamuni's time, was ruled by King Bimbisāra.

13. Mount Gayā was located in the Magadha Kingdom.

14. The song is based on the story of the magnanimous faith of Sudatta (Anāthapiṇḍika), a wealthy merchant of the Śrāvastī Kingdom, who became an early convert to Buddha's teaching. According to the story, the elder, to offer a place of retreat for the Buddha, attempted to buy a park owned by Prince Jeta of Śrāvastī Kingdom by covering the ground with gold, as he was told to by the prince. But the prince stopped his prank and donated the land to the Buddha, which later became the Jetavana Monastery, the Buddha's favorite resort where he spent summer rainy seasons for the last twenty-five years of his life. See Edward J. Thomas, *The Life of Buddha as Legend and History* (London: Kegan Paul, Trench, Trubner, n.d.; reprint New York: Alfred A. Knopf, 1927), p. 104.

15. Legend says, for example, that Ānanda, to protect the Buddha from harm from animals, kept fires lit through the night on their journeys in the wilds.

16. Ānanda is considered especially responsible for reciting the Buddha's teaching, which later became the basis of various sutra texts. See Thomas, *Life of Buddha*, pp. 166–67.

17. Pāvā was within a day's journey from Kuśinagara, the site where the Buddha died. See ibid., p. 149.

18. The full name of the River Vatī is Hiraṇyavatī. The actual site where the Buddha took the meal was in the mango grove of Cunda, rather than on a seat between the twin Śāla trees. See "The Book of the Great Decease: Mahā-parinibbāna-sutta," in *Buddhist Suttas*, trans. T. W. Rhys Davids, The Sacred Books of the East, vol. 11 (Oxford: Clarendon Press, 1881; reprint New York: Dover, 1969), pp. 70–72.

19. See Thomas, *Life of Buddha*, pp. 149–51.

20. The Buddha is said to have passed away at midnight on the bed prepared by Ānanda between twin Śāla trees; see ibid., pp. 151–53.

21. The assembly, which had five hundred participants, was held at the

Pippala Cavern in Rājagṛja, the capital of the Magadha Kingdom; see W. Woodville Rockhill, *The Life of the Buddha and the Early History of His Order* (London: Kegan Paul, Trench, Trubner, 1907), p. 151.

22. Two persons were mostly responsible for forming the canon: Upāli, known for his knowledge of monastic rules, contributed to the formation of the Vinaya (regulations for the Sangha); and Ānanda, through his recitation of the Buddha's oral teaching, laid the foundation for the sutras. See N. A. Jayawickrama, trans., *The Inception of Discipline and the Vinaya Nidāna: Bāhiranidāna of Buddhaghosa's "Samantapāsādikā,"* Sacred Books of the Buddhists, vol. 21 (London: Luzac & Co., 1962), pp. 11–13.

23. The *arhats* are Buddhist saints. It is not clear who these sixteen saints are, but they are believed to have promised to propagate the Buddha's teaching eternally. See NKBT 73:500.

24. See Rockhill, *Life of the Buddha*, pp. 152–57.

25. Mochizuki, *Bukkyō daijiten* 1:842–43.

26. The Dragon-flower tree is said to be the site where Maitreya will be preaching the Buddha's Dharma.

27. Shida Nobuyoshi, *Kayōkenshi*, 4 vols. (Shibundō, 1982), 4:376–90. Kawabata Yoshiaki sees wider implications of the interest in *setsuwa* expressed in *hōmon uta*; he points out that *Ryōjin hishō* shares a trend similarly reflected in *Konjaku monogatari*, a *setsuwa* collection presumably compiled during the reign of Emperors Shirakawa and Toba. See Geinōshi Kenkyūkai, ed., *Nihon geinōshi* 2:127–30.

28. The Triple Body, *sanjin* (Tri-kāya) is a Tendai interpretation of the identity of the Buddha as existing simultaneously in three dimensions. The first, the "Body of the Dharma" (*hosshin*; Dharma-kāya), sees the Buddha as the eternal metaphysical principle, transcending all human perceptions. This aspect of the Buddha can be termed the universal Buddha-soul, embodied in his teachings; it may be roughly equated with the divine logos in Christian theology. The second, the "Body of Manifestation" (*ōjin*; Nirmāna-kāya), refers to the historical Buddha, manifested in physical form to make the Dharma accessible to human sense perceptions and to save the people. The third, the "Body of Reward (or Bliss)" (*hōjin*; Sambhoga-kāya), means a nirvanic state of celestial wisdom obtained through enlightenment. See Anesaki Masaharu, *History of Japanese Religion* (Rutland, Vt.: Charles E. Tuttle, 1963), pp. 113–18.

29. The ten evils are killing, stealing, adultery, lying, flattery, defaming, duplicity, greed, anger, and stupidity or perverted views. The five vices vary depending on the sutra cited, but the most commonly accepted are patricide, matricide, killing an *arhat*, injuring a Buddha, and causing disunity in the community of believers. Transgression of any of these will cause one to fall into a hell of eternal suffering.

30. The content of this song is based on an Amidist convention that

allows a dying person to hang threads in five colors on the hands of Amida's statue and hold the end of them in the hope of salvation in the Pure Land. The song is based on poem no. 1925, *Shinkokinshū*, composed by the priest Hōen of the early eleventh century.

31. Amida, being supernatural, is endowed with forty teeth instead of the usual thirty-two.

32. "The eastern gate of the Pure Land paradise" in the song refers to the Tennōji Temple in Osaka, founded by the Prince Shōtoku. See NKBZ 25:244, note to song no. 176.

33. Mochizuki, *Bukkyō daijiten* 1:802.

34. Among Yakushi's twelve vows, the seventh is his pledge to gratify mundane needs such as curing illnesses and providing clothes and household supplies.

35. This song is the same as the one sung by Go-Shirakawa at Otomae's sickbed; see chapter 1.

36. Jizō, known to live on Mount Karavīka, is credited with power over the hells. He is devoted to saving all creatures during the period between the death of the historical Buddha and the advent of Maitreya, the future Buddha.

37. The four major disciples are Subhūti, Maudgalyāyana, Mahākā-tyāyana, and Mahākāśyapa; in some groupings, Subhūti is replaced by Śāriputra. This *hōmon uta* was sung by Enju, an accomplished female *imayō* singer of *kugutsu* origin, when she was praised by Emperor Go-Shirakawa for her superior command in *imayō* singing. See NKBT 73:459–60.

38. Shinma and Shida, eds., *Kayō II*, p. 85. The fascination with cormorant fishermen appears already in *Man'yōshū*—Kakinomoto Hito-maro touched upon cormorant fishermen in passing (no. 38; Kojima Noriyuki, Konoshita Masatoshi, and Satake Akihito, eds., *Man'yōshū*, 4 vols., Nihon Koten Bungaku Zenshū, vols. 2–5 [Shōgakkan, 1971–75], 2:84) and Ōtomo Yakamochi has two poems on the subject (nos. 4011 and 4156, ibid., 5:221, 302). *Heike monogatari* also includes a remark on a fisherman's killing a turtle to feed his cormorant (Ichiko, ed., *Heike mono-gatari* 1:466). Later in the medieval period, the same topic is given a new Buddhist interpretation in the Noh drama "Ukai," attributed to Zeami; see Yokomichi and Omote, *Yōkyokushū* 1:174–80.

39. See Takagi Yutaka, *Heian jidai hokke bukkyōshi kenkyū* (Kyoto: Heirakuji Shoten, 1978), pp. 248–50; also p. 224 for further details.

40. They are nos. 35, 110–19, 208, 231, 291–93, 424, and 492.

41. The enmity between the cousins is believed to have begun when Śākyamuni, as a twelve-year-old boy, took care of a goose wounded by an arrow shot by the mischievous Devadatta. The five charges against De-vadatta were (1) destroying the harmony in the Sangha, (2) injuring the Buddha with a stone, shedding his blood, (3) inducing a king to let loose

a rutting elephant to trample the Buddha, (4) killing a nun, and (5) putting poison on his own fingernails and saluting the Buddha with his hands, intending to kill him. See Mochizuki, *Bukkyō daijiten* 4:3352.

42. The Buddha could obtain the privilege of transmission of the Lotus Sutra from Asita by serving him for a thousand years. His service included picking fruits, drawing water, gathering firewood, preparing food, making a couch for him of his own body—and being patient under all circumstances. See Hurvitz, *Scripture*, p. 195.

43. The Dragon King, a ruler in his ocean palace in Sāgara, north of Mount Sumeru, is said to possess priceless pearls; see Mochizuki, *Bukkyō daijiten* 3:2117.

44. The notion of the five obstacles refers to women's inherent inability to become any one of the following five beings: (1) the Brahmā King, a god who resides on Mount Sumeru and rules this world; (2) the Indra King, another god who protects this world; (3) the King of Māra, a devil king; (4) the wheel-turning Cakravartī King, the preacher king; and (5) the buddhas.

45. See Nancy Auer Falk, "The Case of the Vanishing Nuns: The Fruits of Ambivalence in Ancient Indian Buddhism," in *Unspoken Worlds: Women's Religious Lives in Non-Western Cultures*, ed. Nancy Auer Falk and Rita M. Gross (San Francisco: Harper & Row, 1980), p. 216.

46. Diana Y. Paul, *Women in Buddhism: Images of the Feminine in Mahāyāna Tradition*, 2d ed. (Berkeley and Los Angeles: University of California Press, 1985), p. 5.

47. Kasahara Kazuo, *Nyonin ōjō shisō no keifu* (Yoshikawa Kōbunkan, 1975), pp. 5–6.

48. Ibid., p. 6. The *Shinjikankyō* (or *Daijōhonjō shinjikankyō*, Sutra of the Contemplation on the Base of Mind) has as its central theme the achievement of buddhahood by renouncing the world and by discarding all delusions through meditation.

49. Ibid., p. 11.

50. "This chapter" refers to the Devadatta chapter.

51. According to Diana Paul, "the Nāga princesses in general were especially renowned for their beauty, wit and charm, and were claimed to be the female ancestors of some South Indian dynasties. They were delicate water-sprite creatures similar to mermaids" (*Women in Buddhism*, p. 185).

52. Hurvitz, *Scripture*, p. 264.

53. Takagi, *Heian jidai hokke bukkyōshi kenkyū*, pp. 192–93. Among the five recommended activities, the first ever undertaken were lectures by Prince Shōtoku in 605, during the tenth year of the Empress Suiko's reign (592–628).

54. Ibid.

55. A good number of songs extol the value of listening to the Lotus

Sutra; examples are nos. 32, 64, 65, 66, 67, 69, 81, 85, 87, 117, 122, 133, 134, 138, 149, and 154. Besides these songs, close to ten songs in *hōmon uta* stress the importance of listening to the sutras in general.

56. There are nine songs on the efficacy of reading, three on chanting, two on expounding, and only one on copying.

57. The Medicine King (Bhaiṣajya-rāja) is a bodhisattva who cures all illnesses. He is the central figure in chapter 23 of the Lotus Sutra, "Yakuō" (Medicine King), which recounts the austerities he endured in his previous life in order to aquire such healing power.

58. Arjaka trees grow in India and other tropical regions. It is said that when a branch of this tree falls to the ground it splits into seven pieces. NKBZ 25:240.

59. The following discussion is based largely on Takagi, *Heian jidai hokke bukkyōshi kenkyū*, pp. 196–250.

60. Several such events are worthy of note. *Hokke hakkō* (eight recitations of the Lotus Sutra) is a ritual in which the eight scrolls of the Lotus Sutra are recited, usually in association with the memorial service. *Hokke jikkō* (ten recitations of the Lotus Sutra), first established by Saichō in 798 on the anniversary of death of Chih-i, covers the opening and closing scrolls in addition to the eight main scrolls of the sutra. *Hokke sanjūkō* (thirty recitations of the Lotus Sutra) is based on the chanting of the twenty-eight chapters of the sutra plus its closing and opening chapters. And *hokke chōkō* (long recitation of the Lotus Sutra), a ritual performed first by Saichō in 809, is in essence a prayer for the country's security accomplished by reading selected parts from the sutra. See Takagi, *Heian jidai hokke bukkyōshi kenkyū*, pp. 202–5.

61. He collaborated on a sequence of *waka*, titled "Ei hokkekyō nijū-hachi hon ka" (Songs in Praise of the Twenty-eight Chapters of the Lotus Sutra), in 1002 with such nobles as Fujiwara Kintō, Fujiwara Tadanobu, Fujiwara Yukinari, and Minamoto Toshikata (960–1027); the work was dedicated to the memory of his sister, Tōsanjō-in. Together with *Hosshin wakashū* (Collection of Poems on Religious Awakenings, 1012) by Princess Senshi dai Saiin, this work is considered to be the harbinger of the *shakkyōka*, *waka* on Buddhist themes. See ibid., p. 209.

62. Ibid., pp. 233–42.

63. Ibid., pp. 244–47.

64. Ibid., pp. 247–50.

65. The six roots refer to the six sensory organs of eyes, ears, nose, tongue, body, and mind, which are regarded as the source of earthly desire, attachment, and spiritual defilement.

66. Joseph M. Kitagawa, *Religion in Japanese History* (New York: Columbia University Press, 1966), pp. 69–70.

67. Murayama, *Honji suijaku*, pp. 212–19, 251–302.

68. Mount Tendai is in fact Mount Hiei, on which Enryakuji Temple,

the center of the Tendai school, is located. The Eastern Shrine means the Hie Shrine complex, located at the foot of Mount Hiei, to the east of the Heian capital.

69. The term comes from Lao-tzu's *Tao-te ching* (The Way and Its Power), where it refers to the value of self-effacement as a moral precept. Chih-i first borrowed the aphorism and gave it a Buddhist twist in his work *Mo-ho chih kuan*. See Sekiguchi Shizuo, "Wakō dōjin: *Ryōjin hishō* to honji suijaku shisō," *Nihon kayō kenkyū* 17 (April 1978): 10.

70. Besides the songs so far discussed, nos. 242, 243, 245, and 417, among others, are also related to the Tendai-Hie syncretism.

71. For details of the ranks and syncretic identities of these shrines, see Okada Yoneo, *Jinja*, Nihonshi Kōhyakka, vol. 1 (Kindō Shuppansha, 1977), pp. 172–74. The Sannō syncretism was presumably designed to win over to Buddhism the peasantry in the Mount Hiei area, who were closely tied to the *kami*, believed to govern their agrarian existence. See Daigan Matsunaga and Alicia Matsunaga, *Foundation of Japanese Buddhism*, 2 vols. (Los Angeles: Buddhist Books International, 1976), 2:294.

72. It was under the Bodhi tree that Śākyamuni is reported to have attained his enlightenment.

73. The interest in the Hie syncretic *mandala* is proved by the fact that among extant *mandala* on Shinto shrines, those dealing with the Hie complex outnumber all others. See Murayama, *Honji suijaku*, p. 283.

74. The Mount Kinbu compound is divided into forty-one quarters, just like Maitreya's Tuṣita Heaven is supposed to be. See NKBZ 25:266–67.

75. Murayama Shūichi, *Shinbutsu shūgō shichō* (Kyoto: Heirakuji Shoten, 1957), pp. 79–80.

76. For a complete list of these divinities, see Okada, *Jinja*, p. 226.

77. The Nagusa Beach and Waka Bay are located near Mount Nagusa in Wakayama City, Kii Province. An almost identical song was sung by Emperor Go-Shirakawa at the Nagaoka Shrine on his first Kumano pilgrimage in 1160. See NKBT 73:461.

78. Murayama, *Honji suijaku*, pp. 169–70.

79. "Buddhist Pilgrimage in South and Southeast Asia," in *The Encyclopedia of Religion*, ed. Mircea Eliade (New York: Macmillan, 1987), 11:348.

80. Joseph M. Kitagawa, *On Understanding Japanese Religion* (Princeton: Princeton University Press, 1987), p. 129.

81. Ichiro Hori, *Folk Religion in Japan: Continuity and Change* (Chicago: University of Chicago Press, 1968), pp. 159–60.

82. Laurence Bresler, "The Origins of Popular Travel and Travel Literature in Japan" (Ph.D. diss., Columbia University, 1975), p. 39.

83. The Kamo River, originating in the north of Kyoto, flows southward through the eastern part of the capital and empties into the Katsura

River. The Yodo ford was at the site where the Katsura and Uji rivers joined, to the southwest of Kyoto. Yawata, where the Iwashimizu Hachiman Shrine is located, is where the three tributary rivers, the Katsura, Uji, and Kizu, converge to form the Yodo River.

84. Hachiman was given the title of "Great Bodhisattva," a shortened form of "Great Bodhisattva of National Protection with Miraculous and Divine Power," in 781 by the Nara court. For details of Hachiman's Buddhistic deification, see Murayama, *Honji suijaku*, pp. 60–61.

85. The Saikoku circuit pilgrimage covers thirty-three temples that have Kannon as their main object of worship, the number coming from the thirty-three different forms Kannon is believed to take. The pilgrimage begins at Seigantoji Temple at Nachi Falls in Kumano and ends at Kegonji Temple in Gifu Prefecture. The Shikoku pilgrimage, undertaken in memory of Kūkai, is confined to the island of Shikoku and covers eighty-eight sites. It begins at Ryōzenji Temple and ends at Ōkuboji Temple. For detailed explanations and lists of the temples on these two circuit routes, see Nakao Takashi, *Koji junrei jiten* (Tōkyōdō Shuppan, 1979), pp. 90–107, 112–51. The Shikoku pilgrimage was supposedly established during the twelfth or thirteenth century; see Kitagawa, *On Understanding Japanese Religion*, pp. 133–34.

86. For a discussion on the development of this circuit, see James H. Foard, "The Boundaries of Compassion: Buddhism and National Tradition in Japanese Pilgrimage," *Journal of Asian Studies* 41 (1982): 231–51.

87. They were called *goeika* (holy chant) or *junreika* (pilgrim's chant); see Kitagawa, *On Understanding Japanese Religion*, p. 131.

88. Kiyomizu Temple in Kyoto is the sixteenth stop; Ishiyama Temple, located in Ōtsu, Shiga Prefecture, is the thirteenth; Hase Temple, in Sakurai City, Nara Prefecture, is the eighth; Kogawa Temple, in Wakayama Prefecture, is the third; and Rokkakudō Temple (Chōhōji), in Kyoto, is the eighteenth. Hikone Temple, in Shiga Prefecture, does not, however, belong to this pilgrimate route.

89. Many sites quoted in the song no longer exist as such or are unidentifiable. The following are those that have been identified. Kyōgoku is the street that ran from north to south in the eastern end of the Heian capital, while Gojō Street is one of the major east-west streets through the middle of the capital. Rokuharadō refers to Rokuharamitsuji Temple, founded by Kūya Shōnin and located in Higashiyama-ku in Kyoto; Otagidera is located to the north of Rokuharamitsuji. Yasaka Temple is in fact Hōkanji Temple, one of the seven major temples in the Heian capital; most of its buildings are gone now except for the five-story pagoda popularly known as the Yasaka Pagoda. Gion Shrine refers to the Yasaka Shrine, famous for the Gion festival. The "curious waterfall" is Otowa Falls, a small cascade emerging from Mount Otowa at the back of Kiyomizu Temple. An interesting feature of the falls is its three-forked stream

issuing from the rocks, as noted in the song. See NKBZ 25:280–81; Kanaoka Shūyū, *Koji meisatsu jiten* (Tōkyōdō Shuppan, 1970), pp. 87–88.

90. Uchi no Dōri refers to the area where the imperial palace was located. Nishi no Kyō is the area to the west of Suzaku Ōji Street, which ran down the middle of the capital, dividing it into the eastern and western sections. The Tokiwa forest was to the west of the capital, near Kōryūji Temple. The Ōi River passes along the Arashiyama area, where courtesans often gathered. NKBZ 25:278; Kanaoka, *Koji meisatsu jiten*, p. 305.

91. The Ima-Kibune Shrine mentioned here may be one located in the village of Fusamoto in Isumino District, Chiba Prefecture, though there were many Ima-Kibune shrines throughout Japan (see NKBT 73:516). Just as the divinites at the Kumano and Hie shrines were invoked and moved to new shrine sites called Ima-Kumano and Ima-Hie, the deities worshiped in the Kibune Shrine must have been transferred and enshrined at sites other than the main site in the Heian capital. See NKBZ 25:269.

92. Most Japanese scholars use the terms *yamabushi*, *shugenja*, and *shugyōja* interchangeably.

93. Ichiro Hori, "On the Concept of *Hijiri* (Holy-Man)," *Numen* 5 (1958): 134, 199, 229. Gyōgi's public service work for lower-class people included founding a charity hospital, a charity dispensary, an orphanage, and an old people's home; the establishment of free rooming houses; the excavation of canals for navigation and for irrigation; reservoir building; and bridge and harbor construction. For his work, Gyōgi was popularly called "Bodhisattva" during his lifetime.

94. Hori, *Folk Religion in Japan*, pp. 177–78.

95. According to legend, En no Gyōja, after a one-thousand-day confinement on Mount Kinbu, received magical power from Kongōzaō gongen, who revealed himself to the ascetic, bursting from the depths of the earth with flames emanating from his back. See Miyake Hitoshi, *Yamabushi: sono kōdō to soshiki* (Hyōronsha, 1973), pp. 29–30.

96. Ibid., pp. 21, 29–30, 175.

97. See Nakao Takashi, *Koji junrei jiten*, p. 104.

98. See Kanaoka, *Koji meisatsu jiten*, pp. 61, 65; and Okada, *Jinja*, p. 211.

99. See Kanaoka, *Koji meisatsu jiten*, pp. 321–22.

100. See Joseph M. Kitagawa, "Three Types of Pilgrimage in Japan," in *On Understanding Japanese Religion*, pp. 127–36.

101. See Okada, *Jinja*, pp. 272, 277; Kanaoka, *Koji meisatsu jiten*, pp. 150, 214, 264–65; and Nakao, *Koji junrei jiten*, p. 124.

102. Shida, *Kayōkenshi* 4:390–91.

103. The "Kumano sankei" (Kumano pilgrimage), a *sōka* (a fast-tempoed song or *enkyoku*, banquet song—a song genre that flourished during

the Kamakura and Muromachi periods) included in *Enkyokushō* (Selected *Enkyoku*, ca. 1296) by Myōkū, a prolific Kamakura-era composer of songs, lists a number of subshrines on the Kumano pilgrimage route and obliquely refers to the difficulties involved in the long journey. For the text of the song, see Takano, ed., *Nihon kayō shūsei*, 5:71–75.

104. Murakami Toshio, *Shugendō no hattatsu* (Unebō Shobō, 1943), pp. 196, 304–18.

105. Miyake Hitoshi, *Shugendō: yamabushi no rekishi to shisō* (Kyōikusha, 1978), p. 112.

106. The Suzu Cape, located at the tip of the Noto Peninsula in Ishikawa Prefecture, is one of the most rugged areas in northeastern Japan. The Koshi (or Hokuriku) Road, in one of Japan's roughest regions, covers the area from Wakasa and Echizen in Fukui Prefecture to Echigo and Sado in Niigata Prefecture.

107. A stole is made of small pieces of cloth sewn together and worn over a monk's robe; it stands for his ability to withstand insults and persecutions. See NKBZ 25:277, 519. The wicker basket contains various items, including small icons, clothing, and foodstuffs. An ascetic with the basket on his back stands for an embryo; that is, he is a spiritual child about to be born. See Miyake, *Yamabushi*, pp. 147–48. The complete Shikoku circuit required about sixty very difficult days on foot, and sometimes resulted in deaths owing to its severity; see Nakao, *Koji junrei jiten*, p. 113.

108. Carmen Blacker, *The Catalpa Bow: A Study of Shamanistic Practices in Japan* (London: George Allen & Unwin, 1975), p. 92. The practice was also highly valued in the Kumano pilgrimage and performed as often as circumstances allowed en route; see Miyaji, *Kumano sanzan no shiteki kenkyū*, p. 403.

109. See Mircea Eliade, *The Sacred and the Profane* (New York: Harcourt Brace Jovanovich, 1959), pp. 183–84. The hardship of "walking" in pilgrimage is also the topic in *shiku no kamiuta* nos. 258 and 300.

110. The tree knots are hollowed out and used as begging bowls; see NKBZ 25:278. The deer horns are used as a decoration on top of the ascetic's staff. The dotted deerskin is worn over the ascetic's outer garment. His staff has six metal rings inserted into its head; their clanking noises when shaken are used to beat rhythms for chanting or to warn off harmful animals in the mountains. See Miyake, *Yamabushi*, p. 146.

111. At least sixteen items constituted the typical *yamabushi* necessities: headband, hat (or headgear), robe, stole, bugle, rosary, a staff decorated with metal rings, a wicker basket in which a wooden box is inserted, a wooden stick, a piece of cloth or animal skin, leggings, fan, knife, ropes, and straw sandals. For the esoteric meaning of each, see ibid., pp. 21, 141–53.

112. Murakami, *Shūgendō no hattatsu*, p. 132.

113. Mount Hira, located to the north of Mount Hiei, is one of the eight scenic views of the Ōmi region. Horsetails are plants related to ferns.

114. Hori, "On the Concept of *Hijiri*," p. 228.

115. For details of their associations, see Nakayama, *Nihon mikoshi*, pp. 425–41.

116. Most of the *jinja uta* are taken from "Congratulations," "Shinto," or "Miscellaneous" sections of the imperial or private anthologies.

117. For the related subject of poems of praise, see Ebersole, *Ritual Poetry*, pp. 34–50.

118. In this section, bracketed references following the *Ryōjin hishō* song number identify the source *waka* on which the songs were based.

119. The literal meaning of the name of Iwashimizu Shrine, "rock-clear water," supposedly originates from the water that gushed out of the rocks at the front of the shrine. See *Nihon chimei daijiten*, 7 vols. (Asakura Shoten, 1967), 1:726.

120. Mount Matsuno-o, where the Matsuno-o Shrine stands, is located to the south of Mount Arashiyama in the western outskirts of the Heian capital.

121. The poet was one of the compilers of *Gosenshū*. The headnote says that the poem was composed to celebrate the birth of a son in a Minamoto family. The Hirano Shrine is located to the north of the capital. The Imaki no Kami, one of the divinities worshiped in the shrine, is the tutelary divinity of the Minamoto clan. See NKBZ 25:331.

122. The headnote to this *waka* says that it was composed for the coming-of-age ceremony in 935 at the residence of Fujiwara Saneyori (900–970), one of the powerful Fujiwara regents. Mount Oshio is located to the west of the capital, and the Ōharano Shrine stands at its foot. The shrine was regarded with great respect by both the imperial family and the Fujiwara clan.

123. The Mitarashi River flows through the middle of the Kamigamo Shrine and then joins the Kamo River. Kamiyama refers to Mount Kamo, located to the east of the shrine.

124. No source poem has been identified for this song.

125. The headnote says that the poem was written during the winter festival at Kamo Shrine.

126. The headnote says that the poem was composed on the occasion of Emperor Ichijō's first visit to Matsuno-o Shrine in 1004.

127. The headnote says that the poet composed the poem on the morning of the winter Kamo festival, for which she was chosen as a messenger. She attached the poem to the decorative wisteria blossoms and sent them to the wife of Fujiwara Michinaga.

128. The headnote says that the poem was composed when the poet served as a messenger at the Hirano festival for the first time.

129. The poem was composed during the *waka* competition on the congratulatory theme held at the mansion of Fujiwara Morozane (1042–1101). Mount Mikasa is located near Kasuga Shrine in Nara, which is the Fujiwara main tutelary shrine.

130. Inari Shrine is located in the Fushimi-ku, to the south of the Heian capital.

CHAPTER 6. THE UNROLLING HUMAN PICTURE SCROLL

1. Mountain wardens guarded the mountains against the unlawful felling of trees. A line-by-line parallel between this song and no. 284, which describes the physical features of the Fudō, can be noted. The precision of duplication is striking, allowing the possibility of an intended parody of Fudō. See NKBZ 25:305.

2. The Nishiyamadōri is near Mount Arashiyama to the west of the Heian capital; the Katsura River flows past this area.

3. From the mid-Heian period, the western section of the capital began to deteriorate, and by the end of the period it was populated only by the poor. The area, especially along the Katsura and Ōi rivers, was known as a gathering place for prostitutes. See Watanabe, *Ryōjin hishō*, pp. 144–46.

4. See ibid., p. 146. Song no. 387 is a list of birds—which may also be names of courtesans.

5. See NKBZ 25:297.

6. Awazu refers to the area southeast of Ōtsu.

7. Watanabe, *Ryōjin hishō*, p. 226.

8. Ōsaka refers to the barrier west of Ōtsu city; Narazaka is a hill north of Nara city; the Fuwa Barrier is in Gifu Prefecture; and Mount Kurikoma is located in Uji, south of Kyoto.

9. The word *kaza* originally meant a young male between twelve and sixteen years of age who had completed the coming-of-age ceremony.

10. NKBZ 25:288.

11. Kusuha was located in Hirakata City in Osaka-Fu; a kiln is believed to have existed once nearby. See NKBZ 25:298.

12. Watanabe, *Ryōjin hishō*, pp. 137–38.

13. Pale yellow-green (*kijin* or *kikujin*) was one of the colors reserved for the coats for emperors, not to be used by courtiers without court permission; see NKBT 73:408.

14. Since the Sumiyoshi Shrine consists of four major shrines, it is called *Sumiyoshi shisho* (Sumiyoshi four shrines). The location of Matsuga-saki is unclear.

15. Konoshima Shrine is located in Uzumasa, an area in the western part of Kyoto.

16. "Three" here refers to the three divisions of the Inari Shrine system, into lower, middle, high.

17. For similar interpretations, see Watanabe, *Ryōjin hishō*, pp. 224–29.

18. Yamashiro refers to the present-day Kyoto-Fu; the area was noted for its eggplants. See ibid., p. 228.

19. All the places mentioned are located in the same mountainous area just northeast of the Heian capital. They were famous for firewood, charcoal, and wood products. See ibid., p. 205.

20. The *oharame* were known as one of the remarkable sights in the capital; see *Fūzoku jiten* (Tōkyōdō Shuppan, 1957), p. 80.

21. Mount Miwa is located in Sakurai City in Nara Prefecture. The song is a variation of *Kokinshū* poem no. 982.

22. Enoki (*Ryōjin hishō*, p. 145) takes the rush hat to be a symbol for the male sexual organ. A rush hat was wide-brimmed, with a small cone-shaped part protruding from its center to accommodate topknots. It was worn by warriors while hunting, traveling, or during archery exercises on horseback. See *Kokugo daijiten* (Shōgakkan, 1981), p. 77.

23. See *Man'yōshū*, nos. 2606, 2911, 2912; and *saibara* song no. 5, "Nuki kawa," in NKBZ 25:127.

24. Michinoku refers to the present-day Aomori Prefecture, located in northeastern Honshū. Suruga is the present-day Sizuoka Prefecture.

25. The song is adapted from *Man'yōshū* poem no. 2798.

26. The word *otoko* (man) used here is rarely found in *waka* to refer to one's lover; here it indicates that the couple's relationship was mainly physical. Saigō Nobutsuna, *Ryōjin hishō*, Nihon Shijinsen, vol. 22 (Chikuma Shobō, 1976), p. 9.

27. Devils were ordinarily believed to have one or at most two horns; see Enoki, *Ryōjin hishō*, p. 143.

28. This song may have been the same *imayō*, "Ike no ukikusa" (A Floating Duckweed on a Lake), that the nobles sang during the party described in *Murasaki Shikibu nikki*; see Ikeda, Kishigami, and Akiyama, eds., *Makura no sōshi, Murasaki Shikibu nikki*, pp. 503–4.

29. For some different interpretations of the song, see Enoki, *Ryōjin hishō*, p. 151; Konishi, *Ryōjin hishō*, p. 468; Saigō, *Ryōjin hishō*, pp. 20–25; Shida Nobuyoshi, *Ryōjin hishō hyōkai*, rev. ed. (Yūseidō, 1977), pp. 172–73; and Shinma and Shida, *Kayō II*, pp. 88–89.

30. Waka no Ura is the bay at Wakayama City and is a famous place for poetic association. See also song no. 259.

31. The Moji Barrier, a checkpoint located in what is today Kitakyūshū City, was the most important gateway to the Kyushu region during the Heian period.

32. Watanabe, *Ryōjin hishō*, p. 162. In ancient times, mirrors were

made of metal, usually bronze, and so required periodic polishing to keep them from tarnishing.

33. See Baba Mitsuko, *Imayō no kokoro to kotoba: "Ryōjin hishō" no sekai* (Miyai Shoten, 1987), p. 48.

34. Book 2 of *Kojidan* is the source of the story about the wretched last days of Sei Shōnagon; see Ichiko, ed., *Nihon bungaku zenshi* 2:272.

35. The *kubichi* (or *wana*, trap) refers to circular snares made of rope or strips of bamboo in which food was placed to lure birds or animals. See *Kogo jiten* (Iwanami Shoten, 1974), p. 413; *Kokugo daijiten*, p. 2521.

36. The Byōdōin in Uji was the residence of Fujiwara Yorimichi, built in 1052.

37. The Weaver Maiden, a tragic heroine in Chinese mythology, is in love with the Ox Herder, whom she can meet only once a year on the seventh day of the seventh month by crossing over the Milky Way. A pun is implied in *yobaiboshi* (shooting star), centering on the word *yobai*, which originates in the verb *yobu* (to call) but later came to mean secret visits to women at night and, eventually, a marriage proposal (*Kogo jiten*, p. 1354). It is said that male and female pheasants (*yamadori*) stay together during the day but sleep apart at night, each on the different side of a hill (*Kogo jiten*, p. 1318); from this, the word *yamadori* also means sleeping alone (*Kokugo daijiten*, p. 2384). As for the significance of "autumn dear," it is well known that the bucks cry out to attract the does during their autumn mating season. And mandarin ducks have long been used to symbolize conjugal love because they remain mated for life.

38. Baba Mitsuko, "*Ryōjin hishō* 'oi' kō—so no ichi," *Chūsei bungaku ronsō* 1 (1976): 69–71.

39. Kojima, Konoshita, and Satake, *Man'yōshū* 2:365 (no. 1634).

40. In *Wakan rōeishū*, the topic even became an independent section (see nos. 345–51, NKBT 73:135–36). The Noh play "Kinuta," attributed to Zeami, also elaborates on this theme of a woman's death after a long period of longing for her absent husband; see Yokomichi and Omote, *Yōkyokushū* 1:331–39.

41. See Ogihara and Kōnosu, eds., *Kojiki, jōdaikayō*, pp. 129–30.

42. Saigō, *Ryōjin hishō*, p. 101.

43. Hakata may refer to the Hakata Shrine in Izumi City, Osaka-Fu; see NKBT 73:525.

44. Nihon Geinōshi Kenkyūkai, ed., *Nihon geninōshi* 2:35, 48.

45. Konishi, *Ryōjin hishō kō*, p. 462.

46. Precisely what *hoya* dye was we no longer know, but it may have been a kind of indigo blue dye made with sap squeezed from parasitic plants; see NKBZ 25:314. The colors listed are those of silk or leather cords that were used to sew the pieces of metal or leather together to make a suit of armor.

47. Watanabe, *Ryōjin hishō*, p. 129.

48. Shirai and Toki, eds., *Jinja jiten*, p. 91.

49. Ibid., p. 98.

50. Ibid., p. 191.

51. Ibid., p. 174.

52. Ibid., pp. 19–20.

53. NKBZ 25:263.

54. Shirai and Toki, eds., *Jinja jiten*, p. 13.

55. Ibid., p. 218.

56. Ibid., p. 117.

57. Ibid., p. 297.

58. Ibid., p. 38.

59. See *Shinto daijiten* 1:167.

60. Shirai and Toki, eds., *Jinja jiten*, pp. 187, 296.

61. The nickname Hachiman Tarō is reportedly based on two legends: one is that Yoshiie was conceived soon after his father, Yoriyoshi (988–1075), had a dream in which the warrior god Hachiman gave him a sword; the other is that Yoshiie's coming-of-age ceremony when he turned seven was performed at the Iwashimizu Hachiman Shrine. See *Nihon rekishi daijiten*, 2d ed., vol. 9 (Kawade Shobō, 1969), p. 78.

62. Yoshiie's valor was praised in a story stating that even thieves were scared away or surrendered simply upon hearing his name; see NKBZ 25:316.

63. See chapter 1 for details on the Hōgen Disturbance.

64. Sutoku was at first placed in Mount Matsuyama in Sanuki and then was moved to Naoshima Island.

65. The "soldier" (*hyōji*) here refers specifically to those charged with guarding the capital.

66. The caps or headgear (*ebōshi*) worn by men in the earlier Heian period were made of cloth, and the aristocrats used a soft lacquer coating on them. Toward the end of the Heian period, however, it became fashionable to stiffen them with thick lacquer varnish. (*Kokugo daijiten*, p. 294). Here, *no* refers to a unit for measuring the width of cloth, one *no* being about twelve inches. Formerly, outer trousers (*sashinuki*), worn over the under trousers (*shita no hakama*), had required six or eight *no* of cloth; one made with only four *no*, therefore, is a tighter garment with narrower breeches, better suited to action and movement. See NKBZ 25:296.

67. This new fashion is attributed to Emperor Toba and his favorite retainer, Minamoto Arihito (1103–47), who was particularly interested in matters of costume and manners. See *Heianchō fukushoku hyakka jiten* (Kōdansha, 1975), p. 370.

68. Watanabe, *Ryōjin hishō*, p. 141.

69. Ibid., p. 143.

70. NKBZ 25:297.

71. Taianji and Tōdaiji were two of the seven leading temples in Nara.

72. Enoki, *Ryōjin hishō*, pp. 153, 201.

73. A middle general is the second-ranking officer in the headquarters of the Inner Palace Guards (Konoe-fu) charged with protecting the imperial palace. Usa Shrine refers to the Usa Hachiman Shrine, located in Ōita Prefecture, Kyushu. The influential position of the head priest was hereditarily assumed by members of the Nakatomi and, later, Fujiwara families. See Anzu, *Shintō jiten*, p. 482. A speed sloop had many oars on both sides of the gunwale and was used for urgent business transactions; it is known that the priests of Usa Shrine came all the way to the capital through the Inland Sea on board these fast boats. See Shida, *Ryōjin hishō hyōkai*, p. 173; Saigō, *Ryōjin hishō*, p. 67.

74. See *Man'yōshū*, poem no. 3827; in *Ryōjin hishō*, nos. 17, 365, 366, 367, 437, and 442 are related to gamblers. For other works dealing with gamblers, see a *saibara* song titled "Ōzeri" (Large Parsley), no. 13, in NKBZ 25:132–33; Fujiwara Akihira, *Shinsarugakuki* (ca. 1052), annot. Kawaguchi Hisao (Heibonsha, 1983), pp. 62–69; and a *sōka* titled "Sugoroku" (Backgammon) in *Enkyokushō*, in Takano, ed., *Nihon kayō shūsei* 5:79–80.

75. Such action was taken in 1114, during the reign of Emperor Toba; see Watanabe, *Ryōjin hishō*, p. 121.

76. The Nishi no Miya Shrine may be the one in the Hirota Shrine complex; see song no. 249.

77. Just what *hyō* dice are remains unclear. The *shisōsai* (four-three dice) refers to the spots that appear when a pair of dice is thrown. See NKBZ 25:200–220.

78. In an entry for the eighth month of 1019 in *Shōyūki* (Record from Little Right), Fujiwara Sanesuke (957–1046) records a street brawl in the western part of the capital that involved priest-gamblers; see NKBT 73:534. The aforementioned Kamakura-period *sōka* "Sugoroku" shows how gambling penetrated into temples, catching priests in a vicious cycle of gambling and debt. See Takano, ed., *Nihon kayō shūsei* 5:80.

79. Shida, in NKBT 73:534; Enoki, *Ryōjin hishō*, p. 181.

80. Enoki, *Ryōjin hishō*, p. 181.

81. A similar family is depicted in Fujiwara Akihira's *Shinsarugakuki*, where the household headed by Uemon no Jō includes gamblers, *sumo* wrestlers, a priest, and courtesans.

82. Saigō, *Ryōjin hishō*, p. 78.

83. Ibid., pp. 72–73.

84. Ibid., pp. 87–88.

85. Salt and dragonflies were often linked in folk songs throughout Japan, though the reasons for the association are not clear; see NKBZ 25:315.

86. Toba refers to the Toba Palace built by Emperor Shirakawa to the south of the Heian capital, now known as Fushimi-ku in Kyoto. Jōnanji Shrine was located next to the palace, and its festival was famous for the horse races that took place at the same time. Tsukurimichi Road is a thoroughfare that connected the Rajōmon Gate in Yotsuzuka in the capital's southern sector with the area near the Toba Palace. See Shida, *Ryōjin hishō hyōkai*, pp. 200–201.

CONCLUSION

1. The Naikyōbō was established at court as a counterpart to the Gagakuryō (Bureau of Music), which consisted of males only. The earliest reference to performances by members of the Naikyōbō was 759. See Geinōshi Kenkyūkai, ed., *Nihon geinōshi* 1:250.

2. Ibid., p. 251.

Bibliography

Works in Japanese are published in Tokyo unless otherwise noted.

Agō Toranoshin. *Chūsei kayō no kenkyū*. Kazama Shobō, 1971.

Akagi Shizuko. *Goshirakawa tennō*. Akita Shoten, 1974.

Akima Toshio. "Shisha no uta: Saimei tennō no kayō to asobi-be." In *Kodai kayō*, ed. Nihon Bungaku Kenkyūshiryō Kankōkai, pp. 198–213. Yūseidō, 1985.

———. "The Songs of the Dead: Poetry, Drama, and Ancient Death Rituals of Japan." *Journal of Asian Studies* 41 (1982): 485–509.

Andrews, Allan A. *The Teachings Essential for Rebirth: A Study of Genshin's Ōjōyōshū*. Tokyo: Sophia University Press, 1973.

Anesaki, Masaharu. *History of Japanese Religion*. Rutland, Vt.: Charles E. Tuttle, 1963.

Anzu Motohiko. *Shintō jiten*. Osaka: Hori Shoten, 1968.

Asano Kenji. *Nihon kayō geinō no shūhen*. Benseisha, 1983.

———. *Nihon kayō no hassei to hatten*. Meiji Shoin, 1972.

Aston, W. G., trans. *Nihongi: Chronicles of Japan from the Earliest Times to A.D. 679*. Rutland, Vt.: Charles E. Tuttle, 1972.

Baba Mitsuko. *Imayō no kokoro to kotoba: "Ryōjin hishō" no sekai*. Miyai Shoten, 1987.

———. "*Ryōjin hishō* mikouta." *Nihon kayō kenkyū* 17, no. 4 (1978): 16–21.

———. "*Ryōjin hishō* 'oi' kō—sono ichi." *Chūsei bungaku ronsō* 1 (1976): 68–75.

Blacker, Carmen. *The Catalpa Bow: A Study of Shamanistic Practices in Japan*. London: George Allen & Unwin, 1975.

Bowring, Richard. *Murasaki Shikibu: Her Diary and Poetic Memoirs*. Princeton: Princeton University Press, 1982.

Brazell, Karen. "'Blossoms': A Medieval Song." *Journal of Japanese Studies* 6 (1980): 243–66.

Bresler, Laurence. "The Origins of Popular Travel and Travel Literature in Japan." Ph.D. diss., Columbia University, 1975.

Brower, Robert H., and Earl Miner. *Japanese Court Poetry*. Stanford: Stanford University Press, 1961.

Brown, Delmer M., and Ichirō Ishida. *The Future and the Past: A Translation and Study of the "Gukanshō," an Interpretative History of Japan Written in 1219.* Berkeley and Los Angeles: University of California Press, 1979.

"Buddhist Pilgrimage in South and Southeast Asia." In *The Encyclopedia of Religion,* ed. Mircea Eliade, 11:347–49. New York: Macmillan, 1987.

Conze, Edward. *Buddhism: Its Essence and Development.* New York: Harper & Row, 1959.

Cowell, E. B., ed. *Buddhist Mahāyāna Texts.* Oxford: Clarendon Press, 1984; reprint New York: Dover, 1969.

Dunn, Charles James. *The Early Japanese Puppet Drama.* London: Luzac & Co., 1966.

Earhart, H. Byron. *A Religious Study of the Mount Haguro Sect of Sugendō: An Example of Japanese Mountain Religion.* Tokyo: Sophia University Press, 1970.

Ebersole, Gary L. *Ritual Poetry and the Politics of Death in Early Japan.* Princeton: Princeton University Press, 1989.

Eliade, Mircea. *The Sacred and the Profane.* New York: Harcourt Brace Jovanovich, 1959.

———. *Shamanism: Archaic Techniques of Ecstasy.* Princeton: Princeton University Press, 1972.

Ellwood, Robert S. *The Feast of Kingship: Accession Ceremonies in Ancient Japan.* Tokyo: Sophia University Press, 1973.

Enoki Katsurō. "Hōmon uta." *Kokugo kokubun* 18 (1949): 83–98.

———. "Kamiuta." *Kokugo kokubun* 18 (1949): 225–42.

———, ed. *Ryōjin hishō.* Shinchō Nihon Koten Shūsei, vol. 31. Shinchōsha, 1979.

Falk, Nancy. "To Gaze on the Sacred Traces." *History of Religions* 16 (1977): 281–93.

Falk, Nancy Auer, and Rita M. Gross, eds. *Unspoken Worlds: Women's Religious Lives in Non-Western Cultures.* San Francisco: Harper & Row, 1980.

Foard, James H. "The Boundaries of Compassion: Buddhism and National Tradition in Japanese Pilgrimage." *Journal of Asian Studies* 41 (1982): 231–51.

Foley, John Miles. *Oral Tradition in Literature: Interpretation in Context.* Columbia: University of Missouri Press, 1986.

Fujiwara Akihira. *Shinsarugakuki.* Annotated by Kawaguchi Hisao. Heibonsha, 1983.

Fūzoku jiten. Tōkyōdō Shuppan, 1957.

Geinōshi Kenkyūkai, ed. *Nihon geinōshi.* 7 vols. Hōsei Daigaku Shuppankyoku, 1981–90.

Goddard, Dwight, ed. *A Buddhist Bible.* Boston: Beacon Press, 1970.

Gorai Shigeru. "Asobi-be kō." *Bukkyō bungaku kenkyū* 1 (1963): 33–50.

Grapard, Allan G. "Flying Mountains and Walkers of Emptiness: Toward a Definition of Sacred Space in Japanese Religions." *History of Religions* 21 (1982): 195–221.

———. "Institution, Ritual, and Ideology: The Twenty-two Shrine-Temple Multiplexes in Heian Japan." *History of Religions* 27 (1987): 246–69.

Hagiwara Tatsuo. *Miko to bukkyōshi.* Yoshikawa Kōbunkan, 1983.

Hakeda, Yoshito S. *Kūkai: Major Works*. New York: Columbia University Press, 1972.

Harich-Schneider, Eta. *A History of Japanese Music*. London: Oxford Univerrsity Press, 1973.

———. *Rōei: The Medieval Court Songs of Japan*. Tokyo: Sophia University Press, 1965.

Hashigawa Tadashi. *Nihon bukkyō bunkashi no kenkyū*. Chūgai Shuppan Kabushikikaisha, 1924.

Hata Kōhei. *Ryōjin hishō: shinkō to aiyoku no kayō*. Nihon Hōsō Shuppankyōkai, 1981.

Hayashi Masahiko. "Nyonin to edo jōdo (2): *Ryōjin hishō* ni okeru nyonin no iki gata o megutte." *Kokugo kokubun ronshū* 5, no. 2 (1976): 33–54.

Heianchō fukushoku hyakka jiten. Kōdansha, 1975.

Hirota Tetsu. "Imayō ni miru bushi: *Ryōjin hishō* ni okeru yottsu no kayō o megutte." *Koten hyōron* 6 (December 1969): 15–22.

Hoff, Frank. *Song, Dance, Storytelling: Aspects of the Performing Arts in Japan*. East Asia Papers, no. 15. Ithaca, N.Y.: China-Japan Program, Cornell University, 1978.

Holtom, D. C. *The Japanese Enthronement Ceremonies*. Tokyo: Sophia University Press, 1972.

Hori, Ichiro. *Folk Religion in Japan: Continuity and Change*. Chicago: University of Chicago Press, 1968.

———. "On the Concept of *Hijiri* (Holy-Man)." *Numen* 5 (1958): 128–60, 199–232.

Hurst, G. Cameron. *Insei: Abdicated Sovereigns in the Politics of Late Heian Japan, 1086–1185*. New York: Columbia University Press, 1976.

Hurvitz, Leon. *Chih-i (538–597): An Introduction to the Life and Ideas of a Chinese Buddhist Monk*. Mélanges chinois et bouddhiques, vol. 12. Brussels: L'Institut Belge des Hautes Études Chinoises, 1962.

———. *Scripture of the Lotus Blossom of the Fine Dharma*. New York: Columbia University Press, 1976.

Ichiko Teiji, ed. *Heike monogatari*. 2 vols. Nihon Koten Bungaku Zenshū, vols. 29–30. Shōgakkan, 1973–75.

———, ed. *Nihon bungaku zenshi*. 6 vols. Gakutōsha, 1978.

Iida Yukiko. *Hōgen, Heiji no ran*. Kyōikusha, 1979.

Ikeda Kikan, Kishigami Shinji, and Akiyama Ken, eds. *Makura no sōshi, Murasaki Shikibu nikki*. Nihon Koten Bungaku Taikei, vol. 19. Iwanami Shoten, 1958.

Ikeda Tomizō. *Minamoto Toshiyori no kenkyū*. Ōfūsha, 1973.

Inoue Tatsuo. *Kodai ōken to kataribe*. Kyōikusha, 1979.

Ishihara Kiyoshi. *Shakkyōka no kenkyū: hachidaishū o chūshin to shite*. Kyoto: Dōhōsha Shuppan, 1980.

Itō Shintetsu. *Heian jōdōkyō shinkōshi no kenkyū*. Kyoto: Heirakuji Shoten, 1974.

Iwahashi Koyata. *Geinōshi sōsetsu*. Yoshikawa Kōbunkan, 1975.

Jayawickrama, N. A., trans. *The Inception of Discipline and the Vinaya Nadāna: Bāhiranidāna of Buddhaghosa's "Samantapāsādikā."* Sacred Books of the Buddhists, vol. 21. London: Luzac & Co., 1962.

Joseishi Sōgō Kenkyūkai, ed. *Nihon joseishi*. 5 vols. Tōkyō Daigaku Shuppankai, 1982.

Kageyama Haruki. *Hiezan to Kōyasan*. Kyōikusha, 1980.

Kajihara Masaaki, ed. *Gikeiki*. Nihon Koten Bungaku Zenshū, vol. 31. Shōgakkan, 1971.

Kanaoka Shūyū. *Koji meisatsu jiten*. Tōkyōdō Shuppan, 1970.

Kasahara Kazuo. *Nyonin ōjō shisō no keifu*. Yoshikawa Kōbunkan, 1975.

Kawaguchi Hisao and Shida Nobuyoshi, eds. *Wakan rōeishū, Ryōjin hishō*. Nihon Koten Bungaku Taikei, vol. 73. Iwanami Shoten, 1965.

Kageyama, Haruki. *Shinto Arts: Nature, Gods, and Man in Japan*. Trans. Christine Guth Kanda. New York: Japan Society, 1976.

Keene, Donald. *Essays in Idleness*. New York: Columbia University Press, 1967.

———. *Twenty Plays of the Nō Theatre*. New York: Columbia University Press, 1970.

Kikuchi Ryōichi. "Bungei daiichigitei o enzu: kyōgen kigyo sokubutsudō." *Bukkyō bungaku kenkyū* 11 (1972): 9–48.

Kitagawa, Joseph M. *On Understanding Japanese Religion*. Princeton: Princeton University Press, 1987.

———. *Religion in Japanese History*. New York: Columbia University Press, 1966.

Kogo jiten. Iwanami Shoten, 1974.

Kojima Noriyuki, Konoshita Masatoshi, and Satake Akihiro, eds. *Man'yōshū*. 4 vols. Nihon Koten Bungaku Zenshū, vols. 2–5. Shōgakkan, 1971–75.

Kokugo daijiten. Shōgakkan, 1981.

Komatsu Shigemi. "*Nenjū gyōji emaki* tanjō." In *Nenjū gyōji emaki*, ed. Komatsu Shigemi, pp. 106–28. Nihon Emaki Taisei, vol. 8. Chūō Kōronsha, 1977.

———. "Ōchō emaki to Goshirakawa-in." In *Genji monogatari emaki, Nezame monogatari emaki*, ed. Komatsu Shigemi, pp. 114–33. Nihon Emaki Taisei, vol. 1. Chūō Kōronsha, 1977.

Komatsu Shigemi and Kanzaki Mitsuharu, eds. *Hōnen Shōnin eden*. 3 vols. Zoku Nihon Emaki Taisei, vols. 1–3. Chūō Kōronsha, 1981.

Konishi, Jin'ichi. "Michi and Medieval Writing." In *Principles of Classical Japanese Literature*, ed. Earl Miner, pp. 181–208. Princeton: Princeton University Press, 1985.

———. *Ryōjin hishō kō*. Sanseidō, 1941.

Kubota Jun and Matsuno Yōichi, eds. *Senzaiwakashū*. Kasama Shoin, 1970.

Kudō Takashi. *Nihon geinō no shigenteki kenkyū*. San'ichi Shobō, 1981.

Kuramatsu Akiko. *Fujo no bunka*. Heibonsha, 1979.

Kure Fumiaki. *Imayō kō*. Risōsha, 1965.

Kwon, Yung-Hee. "Voices from the Periphery: Love Songs in *Ryōjin hishō*." *Monumenta Nipponica* 41 (1986): 1–20.

———. "The Emperor's Songs: Go-Shirakawa and *Ryōjin hishō Kudenshū* Book 10." *Monumenta Nipponica* 41 (1986): 261–98.

———. "The Female Entertainment Tradition in Medieval Japan: The Case of Asobi." In *Performing Feminisms: Feminist Critical Theory and Theatre*, ed. Sue-Ellen Case, pp. 316–27. Baltimore: Johns Hopkins University Press, 1990.

LaFleur, William R. *The Karma of Words: Buddhism and the Literary Arts in*

Medieval Japan. Berkeley and Los Angeles: University of California Press, 1983.

McCullough, Helen Craig. *The Tale of the Heike*. Stanford: Stanford University Press, 1988.

———. *Yoshitsune: A Fifteenth-Century Japanese Chronicle*. Stanford: Stanford University Press, 1966.

McCullough, William. "Japanese Marriage Institutions in the Heian Period." *Harvard Journal of Asiatic Studies* 27 (1967): 103–67.

McCullough, William, and Helen Craig. *A Tale of Flowering Fortunes: Annals of Japanese Aristocratic Life in the Heian Period*. Stanford: Stanford University Press, 1980.

Malm, William P. *Japanese Music and Musical Instruments*. Rutland, Vt.: Charles E. Tuttle, 1959.

Matsumae Takeshi. "The Heavenly Rock-Grotto Myth and the *Chinkon* Ceremony." *Asian Folklore Studies* 39, no. 2 (1980): 9–22.

Matsunaga, Alicia. *The Buddhist Philosophy of Assimilation: The Historical Development of the 'Honji-Suijaku' Theory*. Tokyo: Sophia University Press, 1969.

Matsunaga, Daigan, and Alicia Matsunaga. *Foundation of Japanese Buddhism*. 2 vols. Los Angeles: Buddhist Books International, 1976.

Matsuno Yōichi. "Goshirakawa-in to *Senzaishū*." *Chūsei bungaku* 13 (May 1968): 17–21.

Miller, Roy Andrew. *"The Footprints of the Buddha": An Eighth-Century Old Japanese Poetic Sequence*. New Haven: American Oriental Society, 1975.

Minemura Fumito, ed. *Shinkokinwakashū*. Nihon Koten Bungaku Zenshū, vol. 26. Shōgakkan, 1974.

Miner, Earl, ed. *Principles of Classical Japanese Literature*. Princeton University Press, 1985.

Miner, Earl, Hiroko Odagiri, and Robert E. Morrell. *The Princeton Companion to Classical Japanese Literature*. Princeton: Princeton University Press, 1985.

Misumi Haruo. *Geinōshi no minzokuteki kenkyū*. Tōkyōdō Shuppan, 1976.

Mitani Eiichi and Sekine Yoshiko, eds. *Sagoromo monogatari*. Nihon Koten Bungaku Taikei, vol. 79. Iwanami Shoten, 1965.

Miyaji Naokazu. *Kumano sanzan no shiteki kenkyū*. Kokumin Shinkō Kenkyūkai, 1954.

Miyake Hitoshi. *Shugendō: yamabushi no rekishi to shisō*. Kyōikusha, 1978.

———. *Yamabushi: sono kōdō to soshiki*. Hyōronsha, 1973.

Mochizuki Shinkō. *Bukkyō daijiten*. 7th ed. 10 vols. Sekai Seiten Kankō Kyōkai, 1972.

Moriguchi, Yasuhiko, and David Jenkins, trans. *The Dance of the Dust on the Rafters: Selections from "Ryojin-hisho."* Seattle: Broken Moon Press, 1990.

Morrel, Robert E. "The Buddhist Poetry in the *Goshūishū*." *Monumenta Nipponica* 28 (1973): 87–100.

Morris, Ivan, trans. *As I Crossed a Bridge of Dreams: Recollections of a Woman in Eleventh-Century Japan*. New York: Dial Press, 1971.

———. *The Pillow Book of Sei Shōnagon*. 2 vols. New York: Columbia University Press, 1967.

————. *The World of the Shining Prince: Court Life in Ancient Japan*. New York: Penguin Books, 1979.

Morris, Mark. "Sei Shōnagon's Poetic Catalogues." *Harvard Journal of Asiatic Studies* 40 (1980): 5–54.

Murakami Toshio. *Shugendō no hattatsu*. Unebō Shobō, 1943.

————. *Yamabushi no rekishi*. Hanawa Shobō, 1970.

Murayama Shūichi. *Honji suijaku*. Yoshikawa Kōbunkan, 1974.

————. *Shinbutsu shūgō shichō*. Kyoto: Heirakuji Shoten, 1957.

————. *Yamabushi no rekishi*. Hanawa Shobō. 1970.

Nagazumi Yasuaki and Shimada Isao, eds. *Hōgen monogatari, Heiji monogatari*. Nihon Koten Bungaku Taikei, vol. 31. Iwanami Shoten, 1986.

Nakamura, Kyoko Motomochi, trans. *Miraculous Stories from the Japanese Buddhist Tradition: The 'Nihon ryōiki' of the Monk Kyōkai*. Cambridge, Mass.: Harvard University Press, 1973.

Nakao Takashi. *Koji junrei jiten*. Tōkyōdō Shuppan, 1979.

Nakao Takashi and Imai Masaharu. *Nihon meisō jiten*. Tōkyōdō Shuppan, 1976.

Nakayama Tarō. *Nihon mikoshi*. Ōokayama Shoten, 1930.

Nihon Bukkyō Gakkai, ed. *Bukkyō ni okeru jōdo shisō*. Kyoto: Heirakuji Shoten, 1977.

Nihon chimei daijiten. 7 vols. Asakura Shoten, 1967.

Nihon Fūzokushi Gakkai. *Nihon fūzokushi jiten*. Kōbundō, 1979.

Nihon koten bungaku daijiten. 6 vols. Iwanami Shoten, 1983–85.

Nihon rekishi daijiten. 2d rev. ed. Vol. 9. Kawade Shobō, 1969.

Nishiguchi Junko. *Onna no chikara*. Heibonsha, 1987.

Nishio Kunio. *Nihon no bungaku to yūjo*. Aiiku Shuppan, 1972.

Nishio Minoru, ed. *Hōjōki, Tsurezuregusa*. Nihon Koten Bungaku Taikei, vol. 30. Iwanami Shoten, 1964.

Nishitsunoi Masayoshi, Shinma Shin'ichi, and Shida Nobuyoshi, eds. *Nihon no kayō*. Nihon Koten Kanshō Kōza, vol. 14. Kadokawa Shoten, 1959.

Nose Asaji. "Shirabyōshi ni tsuite." *Kokugo kokubun* 1, no. 3 (1931): 1–35.

Ōbayashi Taryō, ed. *Ensha to kankyaku: seikatsu no naka no asobi*. Nihon Minzoku Bunka Taikei, vol. 7. Shōgakkan, 1984.

Oda Tokunō. *Bukkyō daijiten*. Daizō Shuppan, 1981.

Ogasawara Kyōko. *Geinō no shiza: Nihon geinō no hassō*. Ōfūsha, 1984.

Ogawa Hisako. "Goshirakawa-in no 'imayō netsu' to Taikenmon-in Shōshi: nyoin inshi to imayō." *Nihon kayō kenkyū* 19 (April 1980): 12–17.

Ogihara Asao and Kōnosu Hayao, eds. *Kojiki, jōdaikayō*. Nihon Koten Bungaku Zenshū, vol. 1. Shōgakkan, 1973.

Ogihata Tadao. "Yūgyōnyofu to otome gun." In *Man'yōshū taisei* 10:309–327. Heibonsha, 1954.

Oguri Junko. *Nyonin ōjō*. Jinbun Shoin, 1987.

Okada Yoneo. *Jinja*. Nihonshi Kōhyakka, vol. 1. Kindō Shuppansha, 1977.

Okami Masao and Akamatsu Toshihide, eds. *Gukanshō*. Nihon Koten Bungaku Taikei, vol. 86. Iwanami Shoten, 1967.

Okazaki Tomoko. "Shakkyōka kō—hachidaishū o chūshin ni." *Bukkyō bungaku kenkyū* 1 (1963): 79–118.

Origuchi Shinobu. *Origuchi Shinobu zenshū: nōto hen*. 19 vols. Chūō Kōronsha, 1970–74.

Ōsumi Kazuo and Nishiguchi Junko, eds. *Josei to bukkyō*. 4 vols. Heibonsha, 1989.

Ong, Walter J. *Orality and Literacy: The Technologizing of the Word*. London: Methuen, 1982.

Paul, Diana Y. *Women in Buddhism: Images of the Feminine in the Mahāyāna Tradition*. 2d ed. Berkeley and Los Angeles: University of California Press, 1985.

Philippi, Donald L., trans. *Kojiki*. Tokyo: University of Tokyo Press, 1968.

———. *This Wine of Peace, This Wine of Laughter: A Complete Anthology of Japan's Earliest Songs*. New York: Grossman, 1968.

Plutschow, H. E. *Chaos and Cosmos: Ritual in Early and Medieval Japanese Literature*. Leiden and New York: E. J. Brill, 1990.

Rhys Davids, C. A. F. *Buddhist Birth-Stories (Jataka Tales)*. Trans. T. W. Rhys Davids. Rev. ed. London: George Routledge & Sons, n.d.; reprint New York: E. P. Dutton, n.d.

Rhys Davids, T. W., trans. *Buddhist Suttas*. The Sacred Books of the East, vol. 11. Oxford: Clarendon Press, 1881; reprint New York: Dover, 1969.

Rockhill, W. Woodville. *The Life of the Buddha and the Early History of His Order*. London: Kegan Paul, Trench, Trubner, 1907.

Sagara Nanako. "*Ryōjin hishō* nōto—sono ichi: hokkekyō nijūhachihon uta hyakugojū shu." *Musashino joshidai kiyō* 8, no. 3 (1973): 41–51.

Saigō Nobutsuna. *Ryōjin hishō*. Nihon Shijinsen, vol. 22. Chikuma Shobō, 1976.

Sasaki Nobutsuna, ed. *Ryōjin hishō*. Rev. ed. Meiji Shoin, 1932.

———. *Ryōjin hishō*. Iwanami Bunko, 1933.

Sato, Hiroaki, and Burton Watson, eds. and trans. *From the Country of Eight Islands: An Anthology of Japanese Poetry*. New York: Anchor Books, 1981.

Seidensticker, Edward G., trans. *The Tale of Genji*. New York: Alfred A. Knopf, 1978.

Sekiguchi Shizuo. "Wakō dōjin: *Ryōjin hishō* to honji suijaku shisō." *Nihon kayō kenkyō* 17 (April 1978): 10–15.

Sekine Kenji. "Aohaka no bungaku geinō." *Kokubungaku: kaishaku to kanshō* 45, no. 12 (1980): 176–82.

Shida Nobuyoshi. *Kayōkenshi*. 4 vols. Shibundō, 1982.

———. *Ryōjin hishō hyōkai*. Rev. ed. Yūseidō, 1977.

Shinma Shin'ichi. "Goshirakawa-in to bukkyō." *Chūsei bungaku ronsō* 3, no. 1 (1980): 1–12.

———. "Goshirakawa-in to kayōken." *Kokugo to kokubungaku* 54, no. 5 (1977): 1–12.

———. "Imayō ni miru bukkyō." *Bukkyō bungaku kenkyū* 2, no. 2 (1964): 63–86.

———. *Kayōshi no kenkyū: sono ichi—imayō kō*. Shibundō, 1947.

———. "*Ryōjin hishō*: imayō no sakusha to jidai." *Kokubungaku* 20, no. 10 (1975): 116–19.

Shinma Shin'ichi and Shida Nobuyoshi, eds. *Kayō II: Ryōjin hishō, Kanginshū*. Kanshō Nihon Koten Bungaku, vol. 15. Kadokawa Shoten, 1979.

Shinpen kokka taikan. 5 vols. Kadokawa Shoten, 1983–87.

Shintō daijiten. 3 vols. Heibonsha, 1941.

Shirai Eiji and Toki Masanori, eds. *Jinja jiten*. Tōkyōdō Shuppan, 1979.

Sonoda Midori. "Ryōjin hishō: shiku no kamiuta zō no bungakuteki tokushitsu ni tsuite." Kaneshiro kokubun 54, no. 2 (1978): 31–41.

Soothill, W. Edward. A Dictionary of Chinese Buddhist Terms. London: Kegan Paul, Trench, Trubner, 1937.

Suzuki Hideo and Fujii Sadakazu, eds. Nihon bungeishi. Vols. 1–. Kawade Shobōshinsha, 1985–.

Suzuki Tomotarō et al., eds. Tosa nikki, Kagerō nikki, Izumi Shikibu nikki, Sarashina nikki. Nihon Koten Bungaku Taikei, vol. 20. Iwanami Shoten, 1965.

Takagi Yutaka. Heian jidai hokke bukkyōshi kenkyū. Kyoto: Heirakuji Shoten, 1978.

Takano Tatsuyuki. Nihon kayōshi. Shunjūsha, 1926.

———, ed. Nihon kayō shūsei. 12 vols. Rev. ed. Tōkyōdō Shuppan, 1960.

Takeishi Akio. Bukkyō kayō. Hanawa Shobō. 1973.

———. Bukkyō kayō no kenkyū. Ōfūsha, 1969.

Takigawa Masajirō. Miko no rekishi. Shibundō, 1981.

———. Yūgyōnyofu, yūjo, kugutsume. Shibundō, 1965.

Tanaka, Hiroshi. "Pilgrim Places: A Study of the Eighty-eight Sacred Precincts of the Shikoku Pilgrimage, Japan." Ph.D. diss., Simon Fraser University, 1975.

Taniyama Shigeru. Senzaiwakashū to sono shūhen. Taniyama Shigeru Chosakushū, vol. 3. Kadokawa Shoten, 1982.

Taya Raishun. Wasanshi gaisetsu. Kyoto: Hōzōkan, 1933.

Thomas, Edward J. The Life of Buddha as Legend and History. London: Kegan Paul, Trench, Trubner, n.d.; reprint New York: Alfred A. Knopf, 1927.

Tsuchihashi Yutaka. Kodai kayō to girei no kenkyū. Iwanami Shobō, 1965.

Tsuchihashi Yutaka and Ikeda Yasaburō, eds. Kayō I: kikikayō, kagurauta, saibara. Kanshō Nihon Koten Bungaku, vol. 4. Kadokawa Shoten, 1975.

Tsuchihashi Yutaka and Konishi Jin'ichi, eds. Kodai kayōshū. Nihon Koten Bungaku Taikei, vol. 3. Iwanami Shoten, 1957.

Tsunoda Bun'ei. Shōtei hishō: Taikenmon-in Shōshi no shōgai. Asahi Shinbunsha, 1975.

Tsunoda Ichirō. Ningyōgeki no seiritsu ni kansuru kenkyū. Osaka: Asahiya Shoten, 1963.

Turner, Victor W. "The Center Out There: Pilgrim's Goal." History of Religions 12 (1973): 191–230.

Usuda Jingorō and Shinma Shin'ichi, eds. Kagurauta, Saibara, Ryōjin hishō, Kanginshū. Nihon Koten Bungaku Zenshū, vol. 25. Shōgakkan, 1976.

Wada Hidematsu. "Ryōjin hishō ni tsuite." In Ryōjin hishō, ed. Sasaki Nobutsuna, pp. 1–23. Rev. ed. Meiji Shoin, 1932.

Wakamori Tarō. Shugendōshi no kenkyū. Wakamori Tarō Chosakushū, vol. 2. Kōbundō, 1980.

Wakita Haruko et al., eds. Nihon joseishi. Yoshikawa Kōbunkan, 1987.

Waley, Arthur. "Some Poems from the Manyoshu and Ryojin Hissho." Journal of the Royal Asiatic Society, 1921, pp. 193–203.

Watanabe Shōgo. Ryōjin hishō no fūzoku to bungei. Miyai Shoten, 1981.

Wilson, William R., trans. Hōgen Monogatari: The Tale of the Disorder in Hōgen. Tokyo: Sophia University Press, 1971.

Yamada Shōzen. "Goshirakawa-in wa naze teihen no uta imayō ni tandekishita ka." Kokubungaku: kaishaku to kyōzai no kenkyū 26, no. 8 (1981): 32–37.

Yamagami Izumo. *Miko no rekishi*. Yūzankaku Shuppan, 1981.

———. *Nihon geinō no kigen*. Yamato Shobō, 1977.

Yamagishi Tokuhei et al., eds. *Kodai seiji shakai shisō*. Nihon Shisō Taikei, vol. 8. Iwanami Shoten, 1981.

Yanagita Kunio. "Miko kō." In *Teihon Yanagita Kunio shū* 9:223–301. Chikuma Shobō, 1977.

———. *Josei to minkan denshō*. Okashoin, 1932.

———. "Kugutsu." In *Teihon Yanagita Kunio shū* 4:473–92. Chikuma Shobō, 1968.

Yokomichi Mario and Omote Akira, eds. *Yōkyokushū*. 2 vols. Nihon Koten Bungaku Taikei, vols. 40–41. Iwanami Shoten, 1964.

Index of First Lines

Index of Subjects

Acrobats (*jushi*), 143
Age, old, 133–37
Akomaro, 161n. 19
Akutagawa Ryūnosuke, xv
Amaterasu (Sun Goddess), 6, 102, 103, 141, 144–45
Amatsu hikone no Mikoto, 145
Amatsuyuwake, 55, 175n. 39
Ame no futotama no Mikoto, 144–45
Ame no tachikara o no Mikoto, 103
Ameno uzume no Mikoto, 6
Amida, 61, 69–73, 74, 178n. 30, 179n. 31; Shinto-Buddhist syncretism and, 91, 92, 94, 96, 97
Amidism, 61, 69–73, 96, 157, 178n. 30
Ānanda, 65, 66, 67, 177nn. 15, 16, 177n. 20, 178n. 22
Antoku, Emperor, 24, 160n. 4
Aratama, xv
Arhats, 67, 178n. 23
Aristocracy, xviii, 156–57; artistic dialogue with lower classes, 5, 13, 17, 19, 22, 30; and *asobi*, 9, 10–13, 163n. 49; and Buddhist fivefold practices, 85–86; colors of clothes, 143; and *imayō*, 3–4, 5, 16, 38, 114, 161n. 16; *jinja uta* and, 109–10, 114; and Lotus Sutra, 85–86, 88; orality/literacy of, 38; pilgrimages, 9–11; Shinto-Buddhist syncretic cults and, 100; and *waka*, 27, 156
Arjaka trees, 87, 181n. 58

Arukimiko (walking *miko*), 7, 14
Asceticism, 169n. 45; *shugendō*, 100–109. See also *Yamabushi* (mountain ascetics)
Asita, 79, 180n. 42
Asobi (courtesans), 5, 7–13, 14, 16, 82, 116, 156, 162–64; gifts to, 11; Go-Shirakawa performances, 17; Koko, 12–13; Miyagi, 12; and old age, 134; pilgrimages and, 9–11, 99; and quasi-children's songs, 152–54; *Ryōjin hishō* songs, 10, 117–18, 121, 126, 132–33, 139, 153–54; Tae, 12; Tonekuro, 41, 171n. 18
Asobi-be (court morticians), 7–8
Aśoka, King of India, 95
Ato (trace), 64
Atsuta Shrine, 145
Awa Shrine, 144–45
Aya no Kōji family archives, xv

Ban Dainagon ekotoba (Picture-Narrative Scroll of Ban Dainagon), 29, 31, 168n. 25
Bifukumon-in, 160n. 1
Biwa music, 4, 162n. 21, 171n. 11
Bonsan (hymns written in Sanskrit), 48
Buddhahood: for all, 75–82; attainment of, 64–65, 75–82, 92, 180n. 48; for women, 80–82, 180n. 44
Buddhas, 60–61, 175–83; Four Great Disciples, 66, 76, 151, 179n. 37;

Compositor: Terry Robinson & Co.
Text: 10/13 Aldus
Display: Aldus
Printer: Braun-Brumfield, Inc.
Binder: Braun-Brumfield, Inc.